ents started complaining, you know, 'cause.... myself is keep busy
Nathan: He was always walking around campus when we and make things right
were there, and he'd have like a briefcase handcuffed to his
hand, walking around with this wig on and like a three-
piece suit that's like four sizes too small for him.
Luis: Good and Smelly." — — Kim Deal and the Amps talk
about everyday life in Dayton, Ohio, Ray Gun #33,
February '96

"Drugs were about opening people's minds. Technology
can achieve that without actually doing the drugs. Virtua
is like cooking. Giving your kid a Sony Playstation or Sega
is like giving them a hit of E. Or giving them a trip. 'There from hell. Well, when I
you go. There's a nice tab of acid for you, son.' And it's a rock the jam session,
lot safer." Goldie, Ray Gun #33, February '96 that's how it is to

"Maybe the moment/Whatever it means/Is under a pile/Of whup a horse's ass.
old magazines/That I can re-read/Whenever I choose/To And each time I rock
find myself lost/In used to be news." Ken Nordine, Ray it good, I rock it to the
Gun #33, February '96 brink of dawn. I love
to have fun. I love to

"It's hard for anybody to believe in anything anymore. In be proud of myself
history, people used to believe in things, but now believing and I'm going to be a
is out of fashion. I believe in my own thing, but even then rich man one day. I'm
there's nothing much to help me believe in that anymore not going to be poor
either." Ethan Buckler of King Kong, Ray Gun #34, March like I used to be poor.
'96 At least I work to get
things right for

"My particular little agonies are really quite precious to myself. At least I work
me and they're things I prefer to keep and examine rather hard to get things
than get rid of — besides, I've never found that writing done right for myself.
about something got rid of it. The more I recognize it, the At least I'm proud of
more powerful it is. It's a little antidote for life, my way of myself for being a
elevating myself beyond or above the hum-drum, musician. At least I'm
mediocre existence." Nick Cave, Ray Gun #34, March '96 doing something to
stay out of trouble. It's

"It's stupid and small and yet so important. Like a T-shirt better than going out-
it's so insignificant, and it has this tremendous street side robbing gas sta-
power." Mike Mills, Ray Gun #34, March '96 tions, shooting people
with guns, raping

"Anger is so easily faked. My focus is usually more positive women and killing
than negative. I don't go around angry at anybody. I'm not women, molesting lit-
one of those 'angry women.' But I think outrage is OK, and tle kids and breaking
so is righteous indignation." Exene Cervenka, Ray Gun out windows. And
#34, March '96 breaking in houses
and shooting police-

"Between 1973 and 1980 we didn't have a Saturday off. If men and killing secu-
you're a Mexican-American and got married between 1973 rity guards, etcetera."
and 1980, we were there." Louie Perez of Los Lobos, Ray Wesley Willis, huH
Gun #35, April '96 #20, April '96

Woodstock. I hated that shit. Still hate it. I hate it. The 'n' roll background,
worst. Crosby, Stills and Nash. Just so loathsome. Just not you always hope in
music. And that's what everybody would say (about me), the back of your mind
'It's not music.' That's what I always got. I don't know what that one day this will
it was about it. I don't even know if it was the sound of it. be redeemed as some-
be grounded also. But it's repressive here in America, too, though it's more think they just didn't like us. And the words. For whatever thing more than just
an 'cute' Japanese girls to our benefit. We'll use hip-hop language or say some- reason, we got nailed 'cause it wasn't the blues." Iggy Pop pop music. 'Cause
Orleans language. We can do all these things by looking like none of them." — Yukwith Perry Farrell, Ray Gun #35, April '96 when you were a kid,
ary '96 it was so powerful and

"When you see Beat The Devil, you see Humphrey Bogart shaped your whole
people are gonna say what they're going to say. It's really gonna come down to the you see that he has, uh, bad teeth. And in all the other life." John Sinclair
or myself. You've got to put thought into what you say, into what you do. Malcolm movies, you don't know that Humphrey Bogart has bad with Wayne Kramer,
objective criticism of my work." — Ben Harper, Ray Gun #33, February '96 teeth. And it's not like they made his teeth up, it's just that Ray Gun #42, Dec/Jan
for once they didn't shoot it in a way that you don't see '97
how bad his teeth are. And so, something's going on there

all their music. 'E Music' and 'U Music.' If it's 'E Music,' then it's serious, and if it that is sort of direct. Humphrey Bogart is in this movie "I had this conversa-
a lot of rock 'n' roll is E. It masquerades as U, but I think that's the whole point. And he's letting his teeth be shown and it has a direct tion with John Cage,
's why I wish I wasn't so much of a fucking frontiersman. People say, 'Why are you munication with me. And that's direct." Palace's Will when he discovered
I think I'm being really clear here." — Julian Cope, Ray Gun #33, February '96 Oldham on direct communication in media, Ray Gun #35 this horrifying fact:
April '96 that there are more
living people on earth

int everything white, and then the tornado's won't come. So he paints his whole now than there are
his engine white. And he had to keep cats in his backyard in cages so the torna-
the local grocery store and bring a wheelbarrow, which is also painted white. "I'm 'a say one thing, I play music because I love to enjoy people who have ever
dummy, Charlie McCarthy size, saying, 'This is Jerry Dan Jenkins.' myself. I play music I love to do it. I play music because I lived on this planet.
love to have fun. I play my music so I can have fun and be on't that a frightening
on the right track and be proud of myself. I play music thing? It's a lot of peo-
40 frozen turkeys one day. And he threw them in the wheelbarrow and took them because I want to be proud of myself in Jesus' name. I'm ple with plans. It's a
says tornadoes don't hit white houses. And he puts his cats in cages so the torna doing well for myself, that's one thing I have to do for lot of dreams. It's a lot
of desire walking
night on a bicycle with two dogs pulling him. And he had those like little shocker around. It's over-
atever. Anyway, he was making the dogs pull him. whelming, sometimes.
You just look around
had one of those Indiana Jones-looking jackets on. And they said he had a stock- on the streets. All
Jer!' and he goes, 'Good and smelly!' And they're like, 'What?,' and then they go, these people wanting
he goes, 'Dog shit,' and they said he had his leather jacket covered with dog shit. things. It's exhaust-
he dogs pull him on his bicycle. ing." Laurie Anderson,
nd he puts like this grandma wig on. For what purpose, I mean, it's just nuts. huH #3, November '94
the time.

all know who Jason is, a friend of mine. And Jason wrestles with him and stuff.
you smell like dog shit.'
ays, like, 'Children should be felt and not heard.'
Dairy, and he had those puppets so kids would come around him. And all the par-

out

out o

88

Cont

6/11/96 7:03 pm   Page 1 (2,2)

f   con -

Ray Gun

Ray Gun
Out of Control

Published by Booth–Clibborn Editions

First published in 1997 by
BOOTH-CLIBBORN EDITIONS,
12 Percy Street,
London W1P 9FB

Design:
Chris Ashworth & Neil Fletcher (Substance, London)

Copyright © 1997, Booth–Clibborn Editions
Copyright © 1997, Text and Artwork Ray Gun Publishing,
except for original contributions, copyright for which
rests with the writer, artist, designer or photographer
Copyright © 1997, How the Art Was Done Mark Blackwell & Marvin Scott Jarrett
Copyright © 1997, The Closing Down David Bowie
Copyright © 1997, Foreword William Gibson
Copyright © 1997, Are You the Bomb? Dean Kuipers
Copyright © 1997, Alternative by Design? Rick Poynor
Copyright © 1997, Marvin's Room Marvin Scott Jarrett

Published and distributed in the United Kingdom

All rights reserved. No part of this publication may be reproduced,
stored in a retrieval system or transmitted in any form or by
any means, electronic or mechanical, including photocopying,
recording, or any information storage and retrieval system, without
permission in writing from the copyright owners.

ISBN 1 86154 040 X

Printed and bound in Hong Kong

While every effort has been made to ensure the
accuracy of captions and credits in this book, Booth-Clibborn Editions
does not under any circumstances accept any
responsibility for errors or omissions.

Contents

639

12-36

14-120

111

W-

TIME

ILLEGIBILITY

AXED AND REPAID INTO

......THE DESIGNERS OF THIS BOOK ARE NATA

:CAY OF L

HORIZON OF FUTURITY, CLOSE AS A

IN PROGRESS TOWARD S

NOTEBOOKS OF WIL

OK

001310

THE
SCREE...

OF CA...

A REALITY VIRTUAL AS ANY...

THE PRINTED PAGE WAS OUR...
NOW THE WORD, THE PRINTED W...
BEFORE AN OPERATOR CAN ACCESS...
PRESSES.)WE ARE TOLD THAT TYPOGRA...
SCIOUS OF ...
TO ACCEPT THIS TOO LITERALLY IS TO RE...

THE MOST RADICAL TYPOGRAPHICAL...

...EED, WORD WITHOUT END.

...RFACE OF QUITE ASTONISHING DEPTH AND COMPLEXITY -- SO COMPLEX THAT WHOLE YEARS O...
...ANY WRITTEN LANGUAGE. (SKILLED READERS, ACCESSING TEXT, ALTER THEIR INNER STATES A...
...INTIMATE DESIGN, ITS "LOOK AND FEEL" HAS TENDED, FOR THE PAST TWO CENTURIES, TO EVO...
...OUR AWARENESS OF THE INTERFACE TO CONSTITUTE A MAJOR AND ONGOING ASPECT OF TEXTUAL...
...ED THE STRATEGIES OF RAY GUN, BIKINI & CO. ARE SOME OF THESE) R...

...MOUSLY VITAL MODES OF INTERFACE DESIGN ...CREATORS OF THE...
AND SPIRITUAL ENERGY IN A SKATER'S TAG THAN
A CONTEMPORARY BIBLE.)

THE VANITY PRESS OF WILLIAM BLAKE, THE TRA...
DADA, THE NOTEBOOKS OF WILLIAM S. BUR...
DRAWN, IN PROGRESS TOWARD SOME EVER...

THE EVent-HORIZON OF FUTURITY, CLOSE AS ANY WINDSHIELD, ITS TEXTU...
SEQUENTIAL DECAY OF IMAGES FA...
ILLEGIBILITY ....THE DESIGNERS OF THIS BOOK ARE NAVIGATORS, RETURNING TO THE FIRST s...

R...

THIS IS DESIGN PUSHING BA...

FIRST

ER

The vanity press of William Blake, the transgressive typographies of Dada, the notebooks of William S. Burroughs (over-written, over-drawn, in progress toward some ever more gestural state) ....

Foreword

The walls of caves were our first screens, a reality virtual as any we've derived.

The printed page was our first automated medium, replication guaranteed, word without end.

Now the word, the printed word, is an interface of quite astonishing depth and complexity — so complex that whole years of training are required before an operator can access anything like the full bandwidth of any written language. (Skilled readers, accessing text, alter their inner states at will. This is why dictators still seek to control presses.)

We are told that typography, this potent interface's most intimate design, its "look and feel," has tended, for the past two centuries, to evolve toward transparency, the optimal interface being viewed as one which the reader is least conscious of ....

To accept this too literally is to rule out designs which allow our awareness of the interface to constitute a major and ongoing aspect of textual pleasure.

The event-horizon of futurity, close as any windshield, its textures mapped in channel-zap and the sequential decay of images faxed and refaxed into illegibility ....

The designers of this book are navigators, returning to the first screen with strategies drawn from newer screens. Thoroughly roughed up: brave new worlds abraded on the concrete of the now.

This is design pushing back against the onslaught of an unthinkable present.

The most radical typographical strategies of our century (and the strategies of Ray Gun, Bikini & co. are some of these) return to older but still enormously vital modes of interface design. (The creators of the Book of Kells might well find more beauty and spiritual energy in a skater's tag than in a contemporary Bible.)

William Gibson, Vancouver
11/01/96

Marvin's Room by Marvin Scott Jarrett

14/15

could get my hands on — Rolling Stone, Crawdaddy, Circus and Creem. Creem really spoke to me at that time. It influenced me to buy music like David Bowie, Mott the Hoople and New York Dolls. This was the birth of the glam era and I wanted to be a part of it — the theatrical nature of it was really exciting. It influenced me to buy my first electric guitar. I would practice four hours a day, go to concerts, and follow the bands. Music became my life.

As I was growing up, playing in garage bands and listening to music, magazines continued to be my passion. I read all sorts — car magazines, motorcycle magazines, surfing magazines, skateboard magazines,

Marvin's Room

Photography by Doug Aitken

I remember reading music magazines when I was thirteen, growing up in a small town in Florida. I used to buy most of my magazines at Lakewood Pharmacy, but on special occasions I'd get to go to Jake's Newsstand downtown, and he carried everything. I used to buy whatever I

and of course music magazines.

I dreamed of doing one of my own. When I was 14, my friend Marshall Spevak and I bought a used printer at a junk store, with the idea of starting a magazine called Retrospective. I remember writing a review of the new Deep Purple album. We were going to sell copies

at school for 25 cents. Back

Issue 01. Ray Gun. September 1992.
Cover.
Art Direction & Design by David Carson.
Photography by Steve Sherman.
Art by Larry Carroll.

Marvin's Room
Page Nos

16 / 17

then, magazines were

our only source of information about music. and I craved getting those new issues

when

then, mag

our only

informa

music. a

getting

1.
Issue 01. Creem. August 1990.
Cover.
Art Direction by Gary Koepke.
Photography by Greg Gorman.

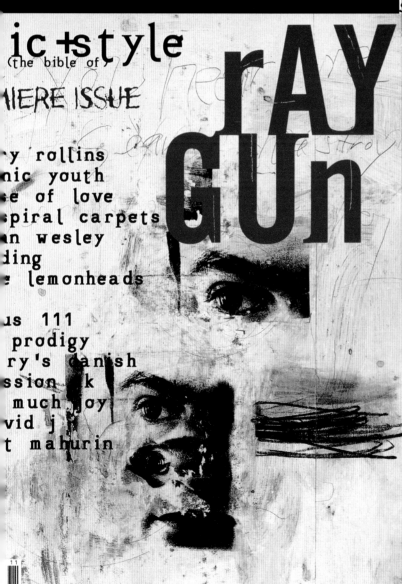

ic +style
(the bible of)

MIERE ISSUE

y rollins
nic youth
e of love
piral carpets
n wesley
ding
lemonheads

us 111
prodigy
ry's danish
ssion k
much joy
vid j
t mahurin

RAY GUN

if

MOSES

had
a
GUN

7-24-96

This is an actual figment
of material from Moses'
Robe. The Robe he wore
when he ascended Mt.
Sinai to speak to JAHWEH,
the master of the universe.
I found it in a clay pot
in a Palestinian carpenter's
home during a trip to the
Middle East on April 21,
1984.
thank you and
goodbye.

Marvin's Room
Page Nos

18/19

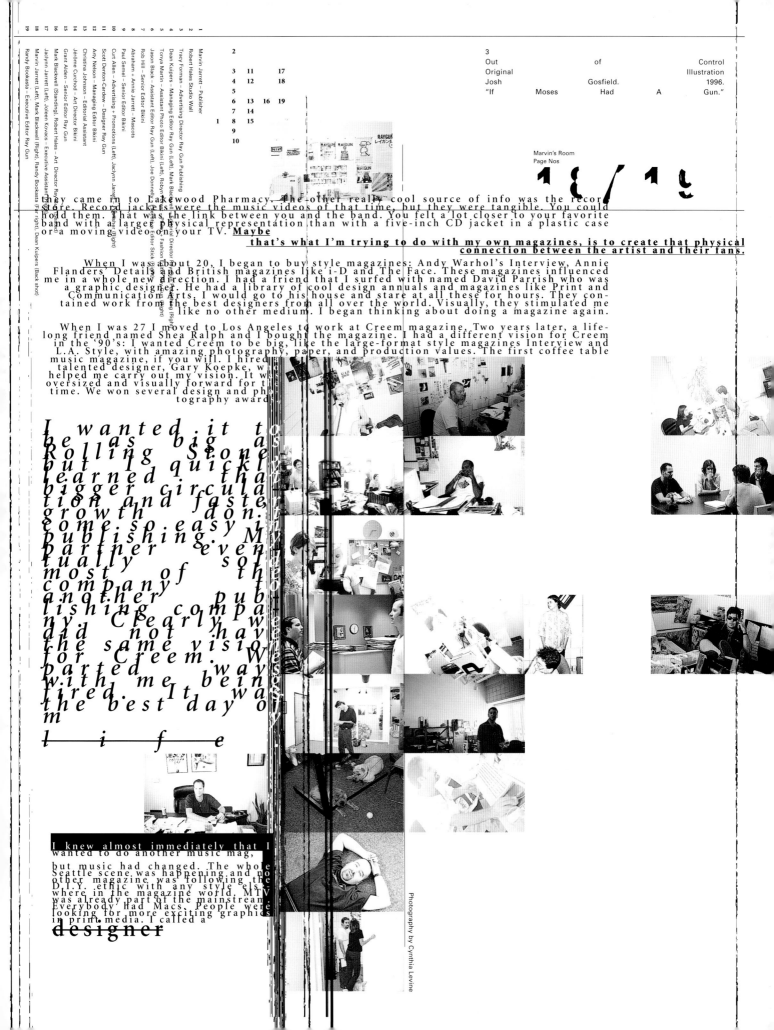

they came in to Lakewood Pharmacy. The other really cool source of info was the record store. Record jackets were the music videos of that time, but they were tangible. You could hold them. That was the link between you and the band. You felt a lot closer to your favorite band with a large physical representation than with a five-inch CD jacket in a plastic case or a moving video on your TV. **Maybe that's what I'm trying to do with my own magazines, is to create that physical connection between the artist and their fans.**

When I was about 20, I began to buy style magazines: Andy Warhol's Interview, Annie Flanders' Details and British magazines like i-D and The Face. These magazines influenced me in a whole new direction. I had a friend that I surfed with named David Parrish who was a graphic designer. He had a library of cool design annuals and magazines like Print and Communication Arts, I would go to his house and stare at all these for hours. They contained work from the best designers from all over the world. Visually, they stimulated me like no other medium. I began thinking about doing a magazine again.

When I was 27 I moved to Los Angeles to work at Creem magazine. Two years later, a life-long friend named Shea Ralph and I bought the magazine. I had a different vision for Creem in the '90's: I wanted Creem to be big, like the large-format style magazines Interview and L.A. Style, with amazing photography, paper, and production values. The first coffee table music magazine, if you will. I hired talented designer, Gary Koepke, w[ho] helped me carry out my vision. It w[as] oversized and visually forward for t[he] time. We won several design and ph[o]tography award[s]

I wanted it to be as big as Rolling Stone but I learned quickly that bigger circulation and faster growth don't come so easy in publishing. My partner eventually sold most of company to another publishing company. Clearly they did not have the same vision for Creem. We parted ways with me being fired. It was the best day of my life

I knew almost immediately that I wanted to do another music mag, but music had changed. The whole Seattle scene was happening and no other magazine was following the D.I.Y. ethic with any style elsewhere in the magazine world. MTV was already part of the mainstream. Everybody Had Macs. People were looking for more exciting graphics in print media. I called a designer

Photography by Cynthia Levine

named David Carson, who was working at Surfer magazine at the time. I asked him if he would be interested in designing a music magazine that I was putting together. I knew David's work from the magazine Beach Culture. The thing that I loved about Beach Culture was that, even if all the

individual elements on a page

"put the ray gun to your head and freak out in a moonage day dream all your own" — and I knew that was it! Ray Gun. That name was so different for a music magazine, and the magazine I was creating was going to be different. Six months later I launched Ray Gun with my partner and wife, Jaclynn.

Initially, Jaclynn and I worked out of our dining room. David designed the first issue at Surfer at night and on the weekends. David's studio was in San Juan Capistrano, which is about 50 miles south of LA and over two hours away in traffic, so David was pretty much on his own. In the early days he turned in simply amazing stuff.

I just let him run with the ball. That's my style. I like to hire great people and let them do what they do best.

I remember going to Ehrlanger Kentucky, with Jaclynn to watch the first issue come off the press. It was the coolest fucking thing I'd ever seen in my life.

After the second issue we brought in another person to expand our expertise in new music. Randy Bookasta and I met initially in Glasgow, seeing a band that was fronted by Shirley Manson (later the lead singer in Garbage). I was doing Creem at that time and Randy had an alternative fanzine called Contrast. Randy had literally grown up in the Los Angeles music scene. His father founded KROQ, one of the original alternative rock stations and still the biggest in the US, and every band was a household name or face for him. Randy was the missing link that we needed. He was a 24-year-old authority on all types of music, particularly the alternative and indie music scene, and I trusted his judgment.

Randy came aboard literally carrying his own desk and chair into our dining room. We had three phones and a fax in a 12 X 14 foot room. We were all selling ads. Randy sold the indie label ads, sold the major labels, and Jaclynn and I both called on the bigger consumer advertisers. The record companies were immediately supportive of our first issue, and that made me more confident after the whole Creem downer. Jim Wagner and Howie Klein at Warner Bros., Brian Cohen at Elektra, Jim Guerniot at A&M, Caroline Debunet at MCA, and Raju Pathukarian at Warner Music Enterprises all took out full-page ads to help finance the debut.

A year later, Ray Gun was going strong and I decided to put another idea in motion. I felt like all the men's magazines had grown older with their audience and that there was room for a magazine that was for men in their 20s. I wanted it to be about everything young guys were into — cars, action sports, rock 'n' roll, film, and girls. I thought of the name Bikini. It was a really cool word and worked well when juxtaposed with being a magazine for guys. The Ray Gun experience had already made me a graphics junkie, so I wanted Bikini to be graphically edgy. I hired Scott Clum, who was doing all the graphics for Morrow Snowboards at the time. I had seen a catalog that he did and it was one of the coolest things I'd ever seen. He is also part of the action sports scene, which was going to be a substantial part of the magazine, and I felt he brought knowledge and credibility from (and to) that industry.

In 1994, Raju Pathukarian from Warner Music Enterprises, a division of Time-Warner, Inc., approached me to create a new music magazine for an existing project called Rock Video Monthly. I agreed, as long as I could do it on my own terms. I needed total creative control, to choose the size and paper for the magazine, and of course come up with the name. I immediately started putting huH together. It was the first time I had a budget to hire a full staff, albeit small, at the start of any magazine I'd done.

The first person I went after was Mark Blackwell. He was living in NYC and just left Spin. He had already interviewed Elvis Costello for Ray Gun and I loved his writing. I convinced him to move to LA and become the editor of huH. This was also the first time I'd hired an editor before my designer.

Later I flew to London to meet with Vaughan Oliver. I was huge fan of his dark emotional work with 4AD Records. We had already talked on the phone a

couple of times and immediately clicked. Over Peking Duck and a few pints at London's Nan King one night, Vaughan greed to be the Creative Director for huH. He flew out to LA a couple weeks

later and we mutually hired Jerome Curchod as in-house Art Director. Mark's

old friend Dean Kuipers used to be the West Coast editor for Spin, and we asked him to come down from San Francisco to talk to us about joining huH. I read Dean's clips and, again, a tremendous writer. A week later he showed up with everything he could carry on his motorcycle, freshly sunburnt and with a headful of ideas. The last original member to join the huH team was Paul Semel, our Reviews editor, who had worked at New Review of Records in New York. He was a little out of place at first, because his tastes in music clashed with those of the other Raygunners (he's into the H.O.R.D.E. bands and heavy metal), but he quickly became a valued member of the Ray Gun gang.

weren't so unbelievable, the finished page David constructed somehow took on a life of its own. The magazine page became a piece of art. It was very cool though very raw. The problem with Beach Culture, in my mind, was there was no editorial focus. We met the next week at a publishing trade show and over lunch decided to work together. I thought that bringing David into a music magazine would be amazing. And it was.

I had a list of about 20 different names for the new magazine, but none of them really felt right. One night I was driving

around LA and I was listening

to Bowie's Ziggy Stardust. Moonage Daydream came on with that line —

Art Direction & Design by David Carson.
Photography by Steve Sherman.

4
Ray Gun Ratecard {Inside}.
Art Direction & Design by David Carson.
Images by Steve Sherman, Elliott Earls and John Weber.
Lettering by Carolyn Fisher.

music + style

ray
Gun

Marvin's Room
Page Nos

Under Warner Music Enterprises, huH magazine went on to gain over **300,000** subscribers in just over a year. This was unbelievable to me. I'd never seen a magazine grow like this.

Growing up as a surfer, I'd always been into skate and surf culture, immersing myself in all the magazines, and once I'd been introduced to snowboarding I knew I had to do a boarding lifestyle magazine. During the winter of '95-96, we debuted Stick, the Ray Gun take on snowboarding. That winter became increasingly busy as MTV Europe approached Ray Gun Publishing to launch and design a UK music magazine called Blah Blah Blah. This was an ironic twist, considering the influence MTV had on my early design awareness. It will be interesting to see whether the company now running that magazine can maintain our commitment to fully-realized graphic design — or if this radical approach will resonate with UK music fans the way it has in the US.

I think I have realized a lot of my original vision: to create a new graphic involvement with magazines, and use it to bring the artists one step closer to their fans. But I constantly have new ideas. There are magazines in my head just waiting for their moment, as well as websites, TV shows, and films. As long as I can make it cool, I'm interested. Magazines, however, remain my first love, because I believe magazines are magic. They took me from a small town in Florida and brought me to LA, where I live happily with my wife Jaclynn and my two dogs Annie and Abraham. Every time I look at a finished issue of Ray Gun, I think of my life back in Florida. I bet, right now, there's some kid standing in Lakewood Pharmacy who is going to pick this up and discover a whole new world — a world that looks totally Out Of Control.

{a} {a} {a} {a} {a}

Out of contro

of control

g

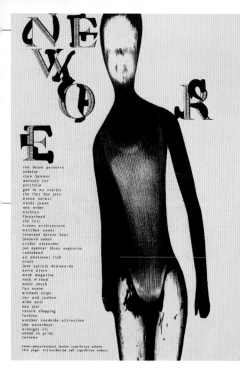

NE WO RE
E
R S

red house painters
codeine
claw hammer
mercury rev
portfolio
god is my copilot
the flat duo jets
mecca normal
wendy james
new order
anthrax
flowerhead
the fall
frozen architecture
matthew sweet
reverend horton heat
leonard cohen
arthur alexander
jon spencer blues explosion
radiohead
an emotional fish
crush
love spirals downwards
kevin ayers
monk magazine
rock n' road
sonic youth
fan scene
michael stipe
ter and jawbox
mike muir
bon jovi
record shopping
fashion
another roadside attraction
the waterboys
midnight oil
sound in print
reviews

cover: photo/michael lavine type/brian schorn
this page: art/catherine yuh type/brian schorn

1
Issue 07. Ray Gun. June/July 1993.
Contents page.
Art by Catherine Yuh.
Type by Brian Schorn.

said, 'What can I
do so that my head

doesn't explode when I
go in a airplane?' He
said,

'Well, the best thing
to do would be to put
your thumb up your
butt, and

then blow." I found that
it works for a lot of
things, like I was having

trouble getting a good
kick drum sound the

other day..."—

"I got this one off my

doctor friend. I have a
problem with my ears

when I fly, something
'bout my my...I've got

Eustachian tube trouble,
you know? I don't brag

about that to a lot of
people, but I do, and I

Trent Reznor, of Nine Inch Nails,
Ray Gun #17, June/July 1994

You're supposed to ask, you know, what was it like living in the Sharon Tate house and I just start talking, the same answer I've told everybody. And then where'd the name Nine Inch Nails come from? Are you really depressed? Boy, your record's sad!" — **Trent Reznor, of Nine Inch Nails, Ray Gun #17, June/July 1994**

have come fo
is now the mo
The lunatic fo
W
a chec
screaming p
in. Yoshik
club like v
ceiling via be
while scre
HE
B
ALL

drummers,
mers, Yo
delicate, beau
avant-garde
the set, Yo
with (obs

He
it soun
Guitarist Yo
cap. is the
most aural
tian dive
quickly poll

POP TATARI.
RECENTLY IS
GEOUS AS A
TITLES LIKE
NOW
APPROA
LISTEN
REAL H
FLIES
SPINS.
STRAIGHT
BAND MAN
PATIENCE
BASS RIF
BIZARRE
AND "COR
ACTION"
GEORGE C
GIVE WAY
(AND REQ
YOU'LL N
BOREDOM
IS MORE LIKE A
YOU LET
PORARY B
EXCITEME
BE YOUR
MAKE DO
NOTHING.
THE WAY
AND ANSW
THING, R
LY, DONE
AGER/TRA

05. huH. January 1995.

ve Direction by Vaughan Oliver. Design by Jerôme Curchod.
grahy by Kevin Westenberg.

3
Issue 13. Ray Gun. February 1994.
Boredoms Dps.
Art Direction & Design by David Carson.
Photography by Wayne Stambler.

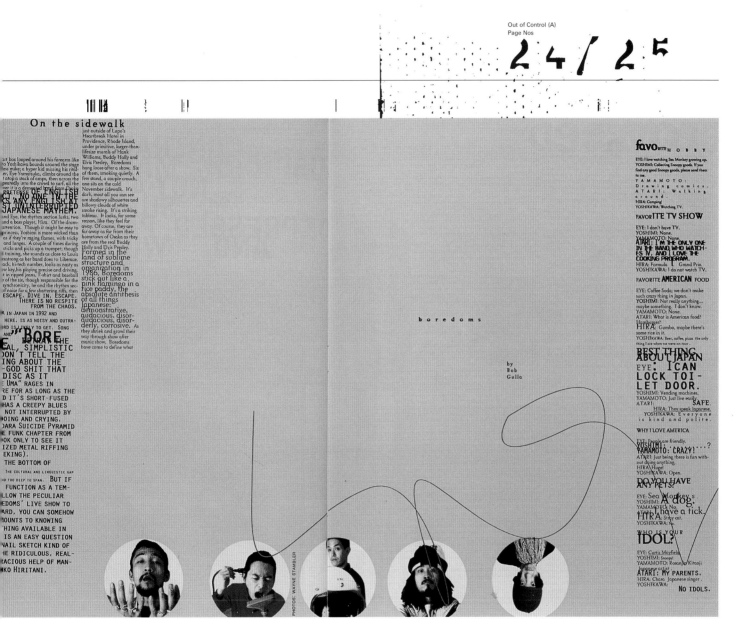

On the sidewalk

art box looped around his forearm like
o Yoshikawa bounds around the stage
ess mike; a hyper kid missing his rital-
er, Eye Yamatsuka, climbs around the
t atop a stack of amps, then across the
eatedly into the crowd to surf, all the
ver it is a demented trek from Osaka.
PRETENSE OF LENGTH
NO ONE IN THE
S ANY ENGLISH AT
S UNLEASHED UTTER
JAPANESE MAYHEM,
and Eye, the rhythm section lurks, two
and a bass player, Hira. Of the drum-
attention. Though it might be easy to
princess, Yoshimi is more wicked than
and lunges. A couple of times during
sticks and picks up a trumpet; though
l training, the sounds as close to Louis
mstrong as her band does to Liberace.
ack, hi-tech number, looks as nasty as
w key, his playing precise and driving,
t in ripped jeans, T-shirt and baseball
p of the six, though responsible for the
synchronicity, he and the rhythm sec-
of noise for a few shattering riffs, then
ESCAPE. DIVE IN. ESCAPE.
THERE IS NO RESPITE
FROM THE CHAOS.
A IN JAPAN IN 1992 and
HERE. IS AS NOISY AND OUTRA-
RD IS LIKELY TO GET. Song
AND
"BORE
BEWARE THE
AL, SIMPLISTIC
ON'T TELL THE
ING ABOUT THE
GOD SHIT THAT
DISC AS IT
UMA" RAGES IN
RE FOR AS LONG AS THE
D IT'S SHORT-FUSED
HAS A CREEPY BLUES
NOT INTERRUPTED BY
OING AND CRYING.
ARA SUICIDE PYRAMID
E FUNK CHAPTER FROM
OK ONLY TO SEE IT
IZED METAL RIFFING
EKING).
THE BOTTOM OF
THE CULTURAL AND LINGUISTIC GAP
ND TOO DEEP TO SPAN. BUT IF
FUNCTION AS A TEM-
LLOW THE PECULIAR
EDOMS' LIVE SHOW TO
ARD, YOU CAN SOMEHOW
MOUNTS TO KNOWING
HING AVAILABLE IN
IS AN EASY QUESTION
NAIL SKETCH KIND OF
E RIDICULOUS, REAL-
ACIOUS HELP OF MAN-
KO HIRITANI.

just outside of Lupo's
Heartbreak Hotel in
Providence, Rhode Island,
under primitive, larger-than-
lifesize murals of Hank
Williams, Buddy Holly and
Elvis Presley, Boredoms
hang loose after a show. Six
of them, smoking quietly. A
few stand, a couple crouch,
one sits on the cold
November sidewalk. It's
dark, most all you can see
are shadowy silhouettes and
billowy clouds of white
smoke rising. It's a striking
tableau. It looks, for some
reason, like they feel far
away. Of course, they are
far away as far from their
hometown of Osaka as they
are from the real Buddy
Holly and Elvis Presley.
Formed in the
land of sublime
structure and
organization in
1986, Boredoms
stick out like a
pink flamingo in a
rice paddy, the
absolute antithesis
of all things
Japanese:
demonstrative,
audacious, disor-
qudacious, disor-
derly, corrosive. As
they shriek and growl their
way through show after
manic show, Boredoms
have come to define what

boredoms

by
Bob
Gulla

PHOTOS: WAYNE STAMBLER

favoRITE HOBBY

EYE: I love watching Sea Monkey growing up.
YOSHIMI: Collecting Snoopy goods. If you
find any good Snoopy goods, please send them
to me.
YAMAMOTO: Drawing comics.
ATARI: Walking around.
HIRA: Camping!
YOSHIKAWA: Watching TV.

FAVORITE TV SHOW

EYE: I don't have TV.
YOSHIMI: None.
YAMAMOTO: None.
ATARI: I'M THE ONLY ONE
IN THE BAND WHO WATCH-
ES TV, AND I LOVE THE
COOKING PROGRAM.
HIRA: Formula L Grand Prix.
YOSHIKAWA: I do not watch TV.

FAVORITE AMERICAN FOOD

EYE: Coffee Soda; we don't make
such crazy thing in Japan.
YOSHIMI: Not really anything,
maybe something. I don't know.
YAMAMOTO: None.
ATARI: What is American food?
Hamburger?
HIRA: Gumbo, maybe there's
some rice in it.
YOSHIKAWA: Beer, coffee, pizza the only
thing I ate when we were on tour.

**BEST THING
ABOUT JAPAN**
EYE: I CAN
LOCK TOI-
LET DOOR.
YOSHIMI: Vending machines.
YAMAMOTO: Just live easily.
ATARI: SAFE.
HIRA: They speak Japanese.
YOSHIKAWA: Everyone
is kind and polite.

WHY I LOVE AMERICA

EYE: People are friendly.
YOSHIMI:
YAMAMOTO: CRAZY!...?
ATARI: Just being there is fun with-
out doing anything.
HIRA: Huge!
YOSHIKAWA: Open.

**DO YOU HAVE
ANY PETS?**

EYE: Sea Monkeys.
YOSHIMI: A dog.
YAMAMOTO: No.
ATARI: I have a tick.
HIRA: Stray cat.
YOSHIKAWA: No.

**WHO IS YOUR
IDOL?**

EYE: Curtis Mayfield.
YOSHIMI: Snoopy
YAMAMOTO: Rosanna Kitaoji
ATARI: MY PARENTS.
HIRA: Charo. Japanese singer
YOSHIKAWA: NO IDOLS.

RAYGUN

beck

ORBITAL

MANIC STREET PREACHERS

UNDERWORLD

CHARLIE WATTS

SEBADOH

MO'WAX

MUSIC + STYLE
ISSUE 39
SEPTEMBER 1996
$3.50 USA
$4.50 CAN

09 >

0 71486 03510 7
PRINTED IN USA

"So I was hung up in a hotel room in Toronto

recently

"Maybe our *thoughts* are nonsense, y'know; but they're still our thoughts. It's the way we're taking something in. I might be talking now, but in my brain I'm thinking, 'There's that polka dot fish in the tank over there, and then here's a cooked fish over here.'"
– Beck, Ray Gun #39, September 1996

4
Issue 39. Ray Gun. September 1996.
Cover.
Art Direction & Design by Robert Hales.
Photography by Dewey Nicks.

5
Issue 39. Ray Gun. September 1996.
Manic Street Preachers Dps.
Art Direction & Design by Robert Hales.

You 26 / 27 can't

with a lot of **time on my hands, and the**

Live at Red Rocks.' So I watched it with some

stop watching it.

FREED FROM THE MEMORY
ESCAPE FROM OUR HISTORY
AND IF YOU NEED AN EXPLANATION
THEN EVERYTHING MUST GO
FREED FROM THE MEMORY
ESCAPE FROM OUR HISTORY
AND IF YOU NEED AN EXPLANATION
THEN EVERYTHING MUST GO
FREED FROM THE MEMORY
ESCAPE FROM OUR HISTORY
AND IF YOU NEED AN EXPLANATION
THEN EVERYTHING MUST GO
FREED FROM THE MEMORY
ESCAPE FROM OUR HISTORY
AND IF YOU NEED AN EXPLANATION
THEN EVERYTHING MUST GO
MANIC STREET PREACHERS
MANIC STREET PREACHERS
MANIC STREET PREACHERS

grave architecture.

By Michael Hodgman
Photography by Colin Bell

only thing on TV was 'John Tesh

friends, and after a couple minutes we couldn't stop watching it. We were, like, hyp-mo-tized. That shit starts to take on a power all its own, a **strange, undeniable ritual fervor or something.**

It won't let

go of you."

– Beck, Ray Gun #39, September 1996

6
Issue 03. huH. November 1994.
Cover.
Creative Direction by Vaughan Oliver. Design by Jerôme Curchod.
Cover logo photo by Jason Love.
Photograhy by Melodie McDaniel.

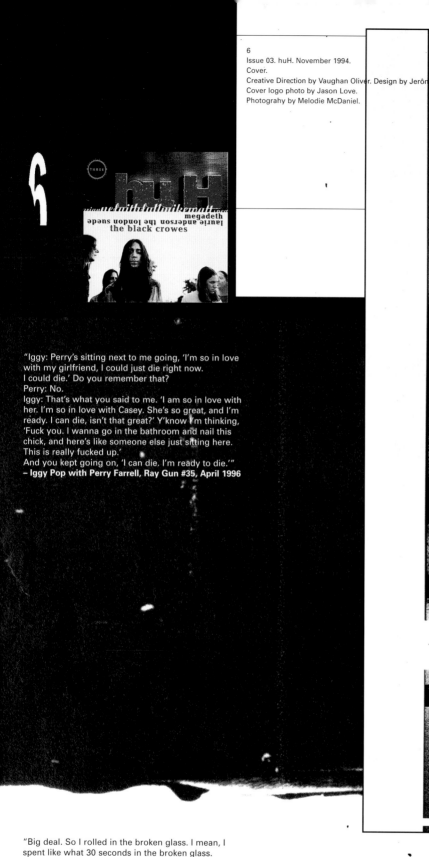

"Iggy: Perry's sitting next to me going, 'I'm so in love with my girlfriend, I could just die right now.
I could die.' Do you remember that?
Perry: No.
Iggy: That's what you said to me. 'I am so in love with her. I'm so in love with Casey. She's so great, and I'm ready. I can die, isn't that great?' Y'know I'm thinking, 'Fuck you. I wanna go in the bathroom and nail this chick, and here's like someone else just sitting here. This is really fucked up.'
And you kept going on, 'I can die. I'm ready to die.'"
– Iggy Pop with Perry Farrell, Ray Gun #35, April 1996

: some call him the River

so mark. we call him...

MR. BLAH B

BLAH

"Violent peace

Blah Blah Blah
Buy it right now,
Blah Blah Blah.
We Are The World.

We are so huge,
Blah Blah Blah

"Big deal. So I rolled in the broken glass. I mean, I spent like what 30 seconds in the broken glass.
I didn't even feel the broken glass. I scored a cool chick after. I was too stoned to fuck her.
And other people, what do they do, they sit around really uptight for like 40 years waiting for the chance to say, 'So Iggy, are you gonna roll in the broken glass again?' Now broken glass is a major corporate advertisement. It's fucking Converse.
There's a little Iggy shoe with the broken glass."
– Iggy Pop with Perry Farrell, Ray Gun #35, April 1996

7
Issue 01. Blah Blah Blah. April 1996.
Iggy Pop Dps.
Art Direction & Design by Chris Ashworth @ Substance.
Photography by Alison Dyer.

Out of Control (A)
Page Nos

some call him the godfather of grunge. others call him a no use junkie

AH

WORDS. ALASTAIR McKAY   PICTURES. ALISON DYER

8 & 9
Issue 13. Ray Gun. February 1994.
Contents page Dps.
Art Direction & Design by David Carson.
Illustration by Heidi Heims.

10
Issue 17. Ray Gun. June/July 1994.
Cover.
Art Direction & Design by David Carson.
Photograhy by Melodie McDaniel.

Out of Control {A}
Page Nos

h I did drivewa
pave my y once.
dad's

— Al Jourgensen of Ministry, huH #19, March 1996

"We're not industri al. I've never worked on a construc tion crew in my fucking life. I don't know anythin g about forklifts, althoug

3

THE JESUS LIZARD AL JOURGENSEN ound in
ULTRA MARINE
FASHION BOREDOMS CROWDED
ROBERT WILLIAMS
reviews COVER: PHOTO: MICHAEL GRECCO, KE
TON/SYGMAN. STYLIST: AROLYN SMI
THIS PAGE: HEIDI NELMS, "CONNIE"
WATER

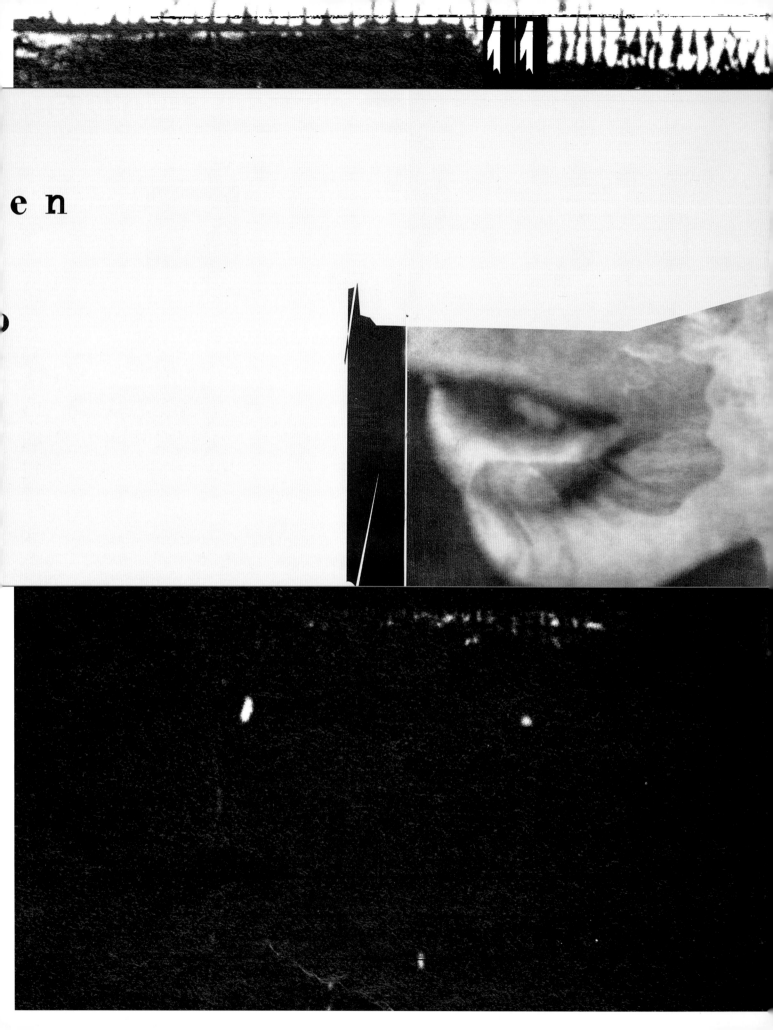

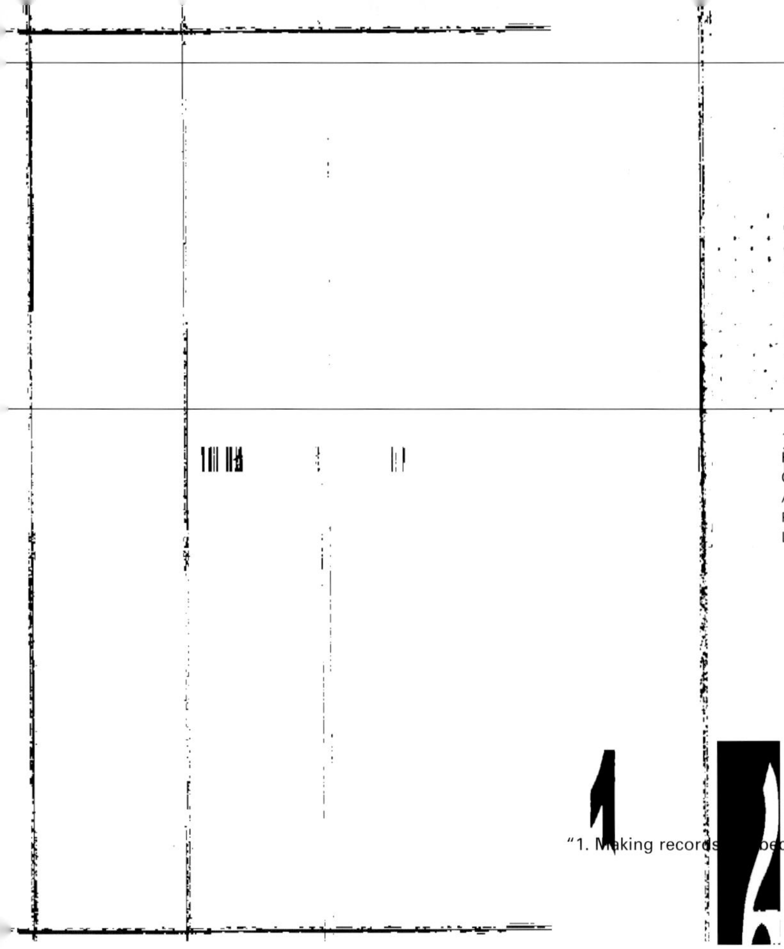

11.
Issue 11. Ray Gun. November. 1993.
Brian Eno Dps.
Art Direction & Design by David Carson.
Image by Ophelia Chong.

(because it involves months sitting in a box looking at computers).

2. The idea of a record release as an event has become boring. The records as a thing, as a cultural space, is no longer as exciting as it used to be.

3. I would like to be involved in making things that are bigger, vaguer and less 'ownable' than records have become — that cover a broader cultural territory. I want to make things that don't reside easily in normal categories, but straddle lots of them.

4. Also, I want to have a good time, which means doing the sharpest, most extended work I can imagine. It means constructing working situations that are in themselves original. It's designing new games, then playing them.

2/2/2

12
Issue 06. Ray Gun. May 1993.
Cover.
Art Direction & Design by David Carson.
Photography by Colin Bell.
Logo by Marcus Burlile.

1

"1. Making records has become terminally boring

music + style (the bible of)

raygun

6

PJ HARVEY

$3.50 USA
$3.95 CANADA
MAY 1993

– Brian Eno, four notes to David Bowie before they recorded Outside, Ray Gun #30, October 1995

"I always write in a bed or a toilet because those are the only two places I really feel like the things are real life going on." — Iggy Pop,

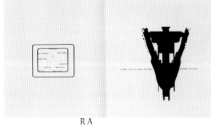

RA GUN

Y

#8,

—A ugust 1993

14
Issue 22. Ray Gun. December/January 1995.
Iggy Pop/Big Chief Dps.
Art Direction & Design by David Carson.
Iggy Pop photo by Steve Stickler.
Big Chief photo by Terry Richardson.

13
Issue 13. Ray Gun. February 1994.
Culture Story Dps.
Art Direction & Design by David Carson.

15
Issue 03. Ray Gun. February 1993.
Cover.
Art Direction & Design by David Carson.
Photography by Thomas Sherlitz.
Typeface by Industry Sans.

Out of Control (A)
Page Nos

2 4 / 2 5

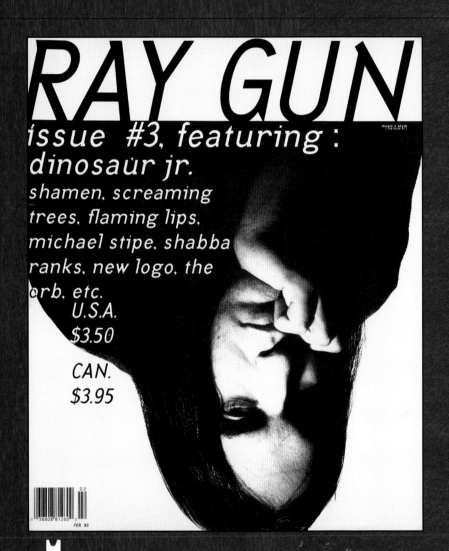

RAY GUN

music + style
[the state of]

issue #3, featuring :
dinosaur jr.
shamen, screaming
trees, flaming lips,
michael stipe, shabba
ranks, new logo, the
orb, etc.
U.S.A.
$3.50

CAN.
$3.95

FEB '93

1 5

TrEES

> `screaming` <

Really all the Screaming Trees needed was Love and Lee Hazelwood. Together
ties Los Angeles band of psychedelic pioneers. Lee Hazelwood wrote "These Bo
eases. In Ellensburg, Washington, the small college/rodeo town on the east s
ner, Mark Lanegan and Mark Pickerel grew up, well, in Ellensburg. Lee Hazelw
yed up one after another.
Since there really wasn't anything else for four such disheveled misfits to do,
t to join, studied Hazelwood's vocals (as did Beat Happening's Calvin Johnson).
Sweet Oblivion, their sixth long-player (plus assorted EPs, singles and solo p
widely purchased *Singles* soundtrack. The Trees' stew of loud guitars and dar
uced obscurity. They finally signed to Epic a disc back, losing long-time drum
emporium). Now it's up to Barrett Martin, late of Skin Yard, to keep order behind
Phoning home from San Juan Capistrano, Van tries to sort out what his mom
jacket with pie filling means. Letterman, by the way, was not amused, but maybe
"We pulled the bus over to the side of the road and watched ourselves play
weird watching it.
Word around Seattle is that their antics caused Letterman to cancel an appeara
were never booked. Van cackles anyway.
"It's a good rumor," he agrees. "But I didn't want to burn anybody else's bridge
Blame him anyway. For the first time, Lee and Mark invited him to take a m
Trees just because they were pretty cheesy," he says without rancor. "But this tim
them so they weren't quite as helpless.
Now, with the onset of fame comes unaccustomed duties, including fashion c
Seattle scene's fashion sense. "I looked down at my clothes. I was wearing Conve
anybody who dresses like this really thinks about it. You wouldn't, because it's no
Without a shred of irony, he seems genuinely puzzled by the prospect of bei
else," he says. "I don't know what

16
Issue 03. Ray Gun. February 1993.
Screaming Trees Dps.
Art Direction & Design by David Carson.
Shoe Illustration by Doug Aitken.
Landscape photo by Anne Brit Aase.
Portrait by David Hawkes.

2 7

photo: anne brit aase   portrait: david hawkes

by Grant Alden

e was Arthur Lee's storied
e Made for Walking, and lent his deep, rich vocals to a string of vaguely country
f the Cascade Mountains (a long bus ride from Seattle) where Van and Gary Le
Love, Black Flag and Kiss and whatever else turned up at garage sales made sens
tarted a band. Lee (no one calls him Gary) stole Arthur Lee's riffs. Lanegan, th
de later, they are on the verge of making a decent living.
) is in danger of becoming a hit, in part because the first single also appeared o
ls has also appeared on the usual litany of indie labels since 1986, enjoying slowly
ark Pickerel (who now runs a record store in the back of the Conner family vide
nner brothers' spontaneous enthusiasms.
their video on MTV or watching Lanegan inadvertently nail David Letterman's sui
teach him not to make fat jokes.
t aired," says Van. "I don't know it if was a good thing or what, but I felt really
y Mudhoney. Although a spokeswoman responds brusquely that "The Mud Honey
itches, maybe."
ole in the songwriting process. "My songs have always been turned down for th
some reason Mark was really into getting my songs in there. Plus they changed
ations. "The other day in Texas, an interviewer asked me what I thought of th
nnis shoes, shorts, a flannel shirt and a T-shirt and went, "Oh, shit. I don't thin
host attractive attire. It's supposed to be comfortable."
ashion statement. I'm trading in my shorts, flannel and Converse for something

y

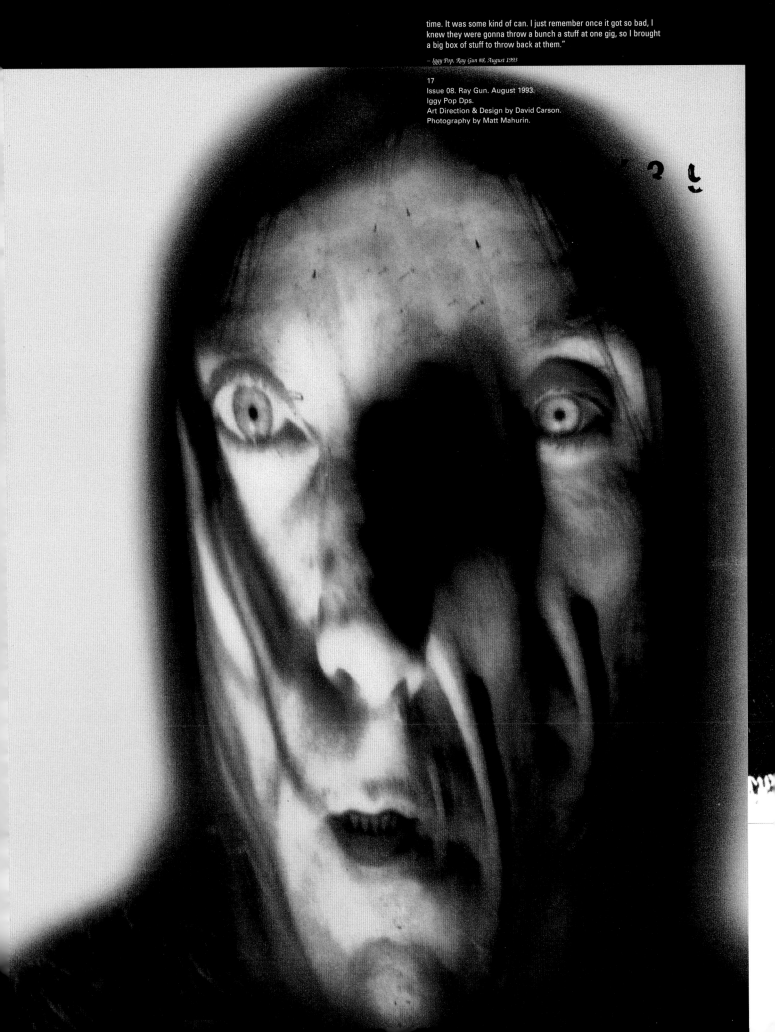

time. It was some kind of can. I just remember once it got so bad, I
knew they were gonna throw a bunch a stuff at one gig, so I brought
a big box of stuff to throw back at them."

– Iggy Pop, Ray Gun #8, August 1993

17
Issue 08. Ray Gun. August 1993.
Iggy Pop Dps.
Art Direction & Design by David Carson.
Photography by Matt Mahurin.

18
Issue 01. Blah Blah Blah. April 1996.
Cover.
Art Direction by Chris Ashworth & Neil Fletcher @ Substance.
Photograhy by Phil Poynter.

19
Issue 09. Ray Gun. September 1993.
Cover.
Art Direction & Design by David Carson.
Photography by Lisa Spindler.

"Dumb is great. We love dumb. If you're a real rock purist, as we are, you can't get it dumb enough. When you need that rock fix, you're looking for the dumbest rock you can find, Motorhead or Misfits or Devo, or something that's really fucking dumb as shit that makes you feel really intelligent. Rock can't be wrong enough. The lower, the better. That's why bands like the Stooges and MC5 who went nowhere in their time are being considered legends. There was no demand for it at the time, but now everybody realizes that was a high point for dumb rock." —Nash Kato, Urge Overkill, Ray Gun #9, September 1993

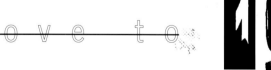

play
somewhere
like Vegas
or Paris
and fly all
the gang

kids from
our
neighborho
od into
watch
We could

give them
each a
little
stipend
and let
them go
nuts and
do
whatever
they
wanted to
do. Only,
they'd
have to
leave their
guns at
home." —NASH

KATO, URGE OVERKILL,

RAY GUN #9, SEPTEMBER 1993

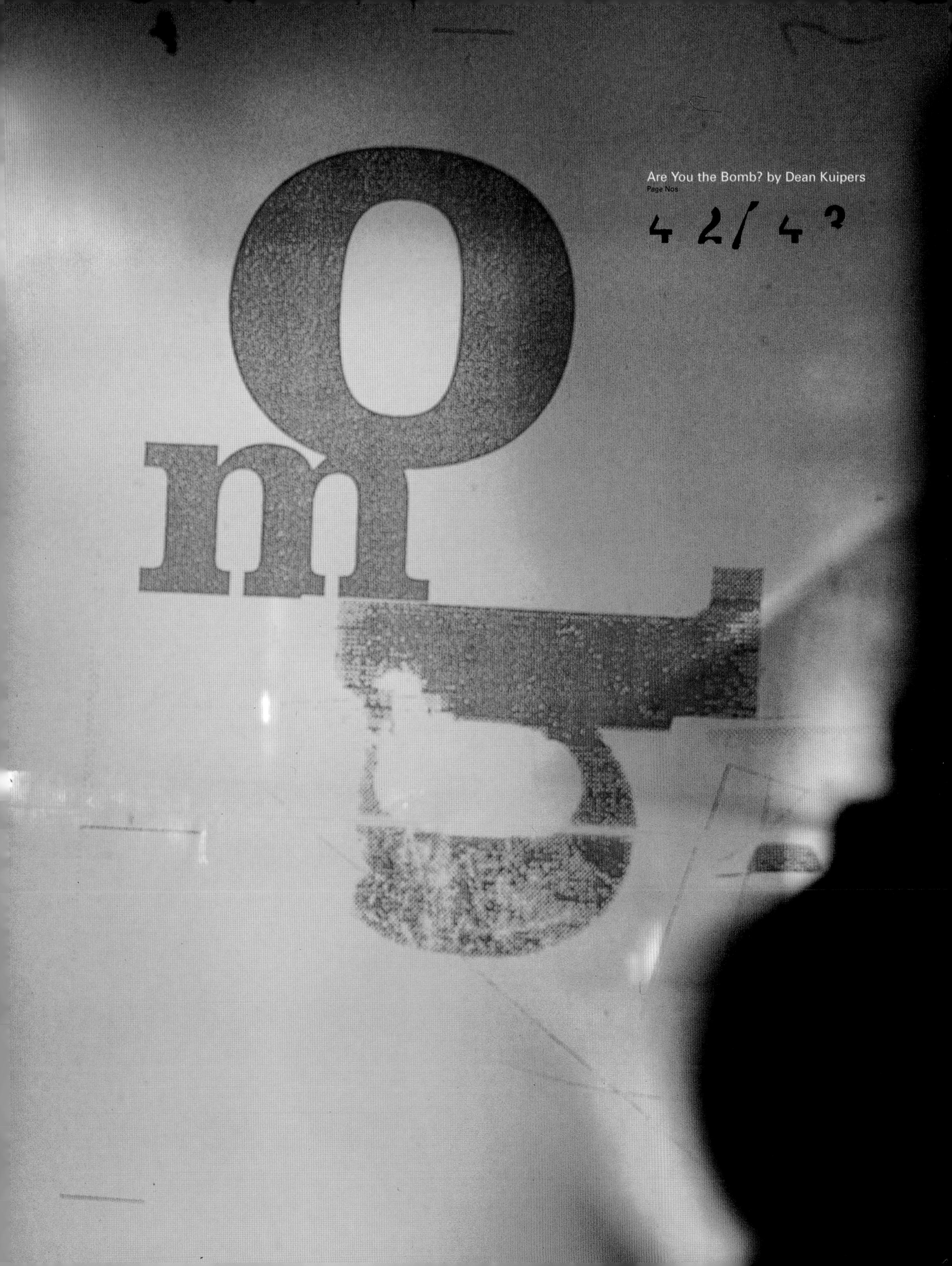

Are You the Bomb? by Dean Kuipers

Page Nos

42/43

Are You the Bomb?
Speaking Ray Gun to the New Niche Cool

have subscribed over the years are less than useless here, now, at this moment in Japan. Against the backdrop of Tokyo, any notions of purity of program begin to wobble, inspire vertigo, then look utterly ridiculous. What would the end-goals be? How could anyone want the same things anymore? Even if they did, they probably shouldn't. Where two people agree to formulate a program, a fascism is probably taking root. All these years, we've been tricked by the illusion of permanence. The idea of planned obsolescence could be the most brilliant concept of the 20th Century.

1.
What We Do Is Secret

My identity itself has dissolved in the rain. What do I belong to? Nothing. What does that get me, in terms of power? Less than nothing. How many people would it take to change that? All of them.

This is what happens on the night you finally meet the revolution. It pukes on you. Just to prove it doesn't care about being any kind of revolution. You start laughing because your romantic boyhood ideas about joining comrades at the barricades are not only dead, they are probably counter-revolutionary. And your utopia looks like everywhere else. You wake up in the back seat of a minivan belonging to some tertiary subcomponent of Toshiba/EMI, shushing through a black rain silencing mile upon labyrinthine mile of residential Tokyo, a stout can of hot vending machine coffee in your hand seeming like the only worthwhile human idea ever, and your first thought is: get small.

What does it mean to get small? It means there is no dogma. Only systems to be customized. Only manifestations of your own singular heart. Niche heroics.

Rejecting the notion of one common media and one common American experience used to be a fear response. Now it's become a survival strategy. Our footsoldier minds are being liberated by a guerilla necessity. I look out the window at the rain. I think about the millions of people around me moving in synch, but without orders, like fish with sensors on their midlines turning together as a school. It means very little that Tokyo is porous and easy to figure out, a vast smiling neon reef. You walk in through one logo and out through the next, internalizing nothing. Its meanings are spelled in rain; they disappear into the sewer. I sit in the back seat staring out at the English language billboards hawking Lark cigarettes on every corner, thinking — for whatever reason and for the first time in

Sometimes — this particular moment in the van, for instance, with a crazy laughing Japanese driver trying to connect by barking "Speak Lark!" over and over into the rear-view mirror — the only way to feel committed to the people and hearts around you is to nurture some ideal of enlightened communication itself. Get small. Smallness is pure communication. Suddenly, that is the program. I look down the wet alleys of a global culture united only by purchases and see the rise of an Artpolitik. Where the only good thing I can make with these people, this overwhelming otherness, is a new way to talk.

Tokyo's Cool Resistance Council talks this talk. They are dedicated to the idea of "Individualism," a corollary to the dimly anarchist principle at work behind my belief in the organizing power of language. The Council's take is a blunt be-yourself-ism — still a radical idea in Japan, and bound to cost one popularity or even status in the community, but one that is catching on as rigid class structures (and corporate monoculture) seem more and more like a liability. Not to mention no fun. In principle, the more people follow their passions, the more likely they are to make sane and informed (rather than programmatic) choices. The Council's principal work is publishing a music magazine called Bar-f-Out, whose motto is: "Magazine for Cool Resistants of the World / Standard of the 90's." This is their party organ. Their concerns appear mostly stylistic, but it's really a case of form following function. They hope the idea of Individualism will catch on and spread throughout Japan and Asia. Calling it a movement is paradoxical, since it is against groupthink, against trends. It is an anti-movement movement.

The van empties and we climb to the 5th floor of a non-descript concrete residence — Ray Gun Executive Editor Randy Bookasta and Art Director Robert Hales and myself — where we are greeted at the door of an apartment by Council members Toshimitsu Aono and Natsuo Kitazawa. They motion for us to take off our shoes and sit at the kitchen table in Bar-f-Out world headquarters.

I cannot accurately say why we are supposed to be meeting with the Cool Resistance Council. We've made the visit solely on a recommendation. A blind date with someone living so far on the other side of the tracks that they don't even have the same alphabet. As Cool Resistants scurry around the place making more coffee, we flip through the first copies of Bar-f-Out we've ever seen: conceptual photo layouts, brilliant typography, a fine art/design-driven interpretation of Japan's music community. You don't need to speak Japanese to get it. I suddenly feel like I'm floating. As we sit there in virtual silence, us hunched over our Bar-f-Out and they over their Ray Gun #35, I'm flooded by a strange lucidity — like I know and understand (however falsely) each person's role in the vast luminescence of Tokyo, and I'm able to allocate each one their own reservoir of peace and industry —

1
Issue 08. Ray Gun. August 1993.
Cover.
Art Direction & Design by David Carson.
Photography by Matt Mahurin.

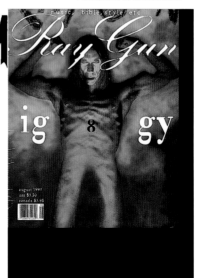

2
Issue 35. Ray Gun. April 1996.
Cover.
Art Direction & Design by Robert Hales.
Photography by Peter Morello.

3
Issue 38. Ray Gun. August 1996.
Big In Japan. Contents page.
Art Direction & Design by Robert Hales.
Photography by Alia Malley.

レイガン

Raygun 0.38

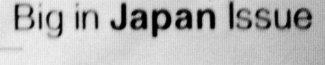

Are You the Bomb?
Pa.. Nos

august 1996

contents

(Hot Space 1996...Let's Go!)

Big in **Japan** Issue

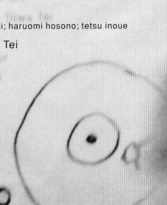

store my duck

because I'm suddenly aware of the graphic languages by which we've found one another. As though they were flags.

"I have subscribe to Ray Gun issue number one," says Kitazawa in somewhat labored English. Both editors go on to explain that they have collected and studied every issue of Ray Gun because it is the most modern outburst of a tradition that Aono calls "graphic journalism." Here, artists, designers, and writers present a subjective interpretation of their journalistic subject — in our case, pop culture. Kitazawa looks at the new copy of issue #35 we've just brought, which has Iggy Pop and Perry Farrell on the cover, then fishes around and produces a copy of issue #8, featuring Iggy alone, and holds it up to issue #35. He rattles issue #8 and says, "This one is my favorite." In it, visual artist Matt Mahurin's bat-like photo treatments of Iggy reveal something truly menacing and even evil about the man who is rock's unrepentant Id, the raw libido, the monster. There is no need to explain in words how Iggy could be such a gothic horror, or that he even is. The graphic journalism has moved the reader beyond the text, in which Iggy reveals himself to be an affable

David Bowie
3rd anniversary issue

4

Issue 30. Ray Gun. October 1995.
Cover.
Direction & Design by David Carson.
Photography by Kate Garner.

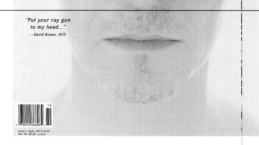

*"Put your ray gun
to my head..."*
--David Bowie, 1972

sweetheart
cruising Christopher Street to buy underwear.

The Cool   Resistance Council   know   Ray Gun's entire history.   Their

e garner
+contents)

5

Issue 30. Ray Gun. October 1995.
David Bowie. Contents page.
Art Direction & Design by David Carson.
Photography by Kate Garner.

4

6

6

Issue 30. Ray Gun. October 1995
David Bowie.
Art Direction & Design by David Carson
Photography by Kate Garner

AUTHOR

devotion is a little unsettling. They grill Robert about why David Carson left. They remember when Randy moved his offices to the Jarrett's dining room to begin editing on Issue #2. They protest the quote on the cover of the 3rd Anniversary issue, which features David Bowie and the line "Put your raygun to my head" from "Moonage Daydream." They think it's too obvious. "Arrogant," smiles Aono.

The Japanese script favors a clean typography, so the text in Bar-f-Out is very clean, but the Council wants to know why we moved Ray Gun toward legibility. They are afraid this is damaging those trying to progress toward Individualism. We tell them we believe that a text can help make the individual's understanding of music that much more precise. You have to be able to read poetry in order to receive it's tranformative power. The Cool Resistance Council are worried that this urge to control meaning is the first sign of the onset of commercialism.

The hours pass in listening and defense, and every so often I glance out the window at the dark, where the towering J-WAVE radio building and others scintillate in the shining black like backdrops from Blade Runner, thinking about the throngs of people we've seen jamming the streets here. I see what the Resistance Council really wants. They want to leave the door open to magic. I have always believed that the terms "post-modern" and "deconstructed" — two schools of literary and design theory often applied to Ray Gun — are really just intellectual rationalizations for a belief in magic. The Council wants to encourage the unpredictable in order to reduce the power of their predictable culture. Even if my perceptions of a Japanese monoculture are just part of a convenient Western myth, they seem dead serious about the impact of Individualism. Earlier in the week we had visited the home offices of Motoharu Sano, an established Japanese pop star now producing a music and poetry magazine called This, whose cover logo reads: "Multi Cultural Magazine For The Individualists." Music is their vehicle to escape Japan, Inc. The Japanese people in the room with us are young, hip, digging for identity and style, armed with the weapons of punk but aware of the dead-end at which punk eventually arrives. Leaving them hungry for content. They are using style to prop open the doors of perception. Aono himself is dressed so fine in wools and nice shoes, like an Italian movie star on summer holiday at Lago de Garda. These are the folks we'd see later at the hottest, deepest-underground clubs in Tokyo, drink in hand, sunglasses on, smiling briefly in Beat recognition of their own cool.

Our graphic languages brought us together only to emphasize that our common purpose is a sham. A break has happened all over the world. We have left the idea of "belonging" to stand and rust like so much broken-down schoolbus abandoned at the side of a country road. These people aren't looking to join any kind of "Alternative Nation." They don't trust us any more than they trust Japan, Inc. All they know is that Ray Gun, like Bar-f-Out, is a magazine whose social contract shifts the responsibility for producing and understanding pop media from the

many to the One. The revolutionary potential of the entire community of readers or contributors resides in the question: are you the bomb?

Out on the balcony, putting my shoes back on, the crazy van driver holds up a copy of Bar-f-Out to his chest and says, "What it means, 'barf out?'" I explain that it means to throw up.

"OH! Puke!" he says, smiling broadly. I laugh and he gets real excited. He spends the rest of the night driving us around, looking up in the rear view mirror every ten minutes to make eye contact with me and yell, "I barf out to you! Ha ha! I barf out to you!"

Issue 16. Huh. December 1995.
C   o   v   e   r
Creative   Director   Vaughan   Oliver.
Art   Direction   by   Jerôme   Curchod.
Photography   by   Yelena   Yemchuk.
Cover logo photo by Dominic Davies.

We Crucify the Insincere Tonight, Tonight

16

SMASHING PUMPKINS
OZZY OSBOURNE   BLUR   THE PHARCYDE

8
Issue 16. huH. December 1995.
Letters page Dps.
Art Direction by Jerôme Curchod.
Drawing by Travis Shope.

9
Issue 28. Ray Gun. August 1995.
Last page Sp.
Art Direction & Design by David Carson.
Artwork by John Langham.

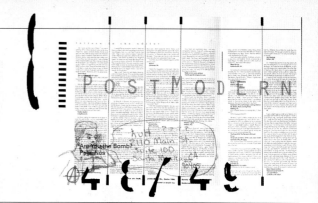

POSTMODERN

IF ANY OF ME ITS IN PART THIS SSAGE ILLEGIBLE, PLEASE FORM SENDER

America's angriest children tear at one another like starving dogs in "Post Modern," the letters column in huH magazine. Reading the scores of letters — sometimes hundreds — that come in each month is like watching a human body or an overextended empire convulse and shatter into its most elemental parts. I feel the country reshuffling itself into tiny camps composed not of a half-dozen people, but single individuals. Sometimes even smaller units than that. In this surrealistically violent forum, "correspondants" threaten one another with grievous bodily harm or death, mock each other's understanding of the media-driven society they are inheriting in terms that reveal their own lack of understanding, and defend their choices against repressions that stalk them from the dark parking lots in their own minds. They lash out at figures in their dreams. They make enemies for themselves because of the apparent lack of meaningful enemies. They lob genre grenades and shred each other with a shrapnel of split hairs so thin they pierce the skin without being felt, at war with belonging. They define themselves by what they are not.

What they are not is you. Or anyone like you. The two of you cannot even agree on what you hear in something as supremely simple and consumable as a pop song.

Ray Gun Editorial Director Mark Blackwell and I want to put together a fanzine comprised of all the unedited letters sent to huH. We'd call it Cruel And Unusual. It would probably inspire a raft of congressional reports and campaign newspeak. We'd eventually see it on TV as a show uncomfortably similar to American Gladiators. Admittedly, this represents only one of the realities inhabited by readers of Ray Gun Publishing's family of magazines. And letter-writers themselves must represent a small fraction of huH's readership, since the magazine gleaned over 300,000 subscribers in the first year following it's debut in September, 1994. But the fact that so many would take the time and energy to pour out this steady stream of vitriol is worth taking a look at. Over the last two years, Mark and I have read these letters with amazement, sometimes laughing to tears over a particularly outrageous insult or malaprop or fantastic twist to the language, sometimes writing responses. Interior dialogues have developed, with readers flailing away at each other from issue to issue. But the laughter always fades, and what floats to the top of consciousness like an oil slick is the anger, the isolation, and a deadly serious fear of being just like everyone else.

"...AND WHILE YOU'RE OFF BUM CHUMMIN' YOUR DAD, TRY TO THINK OF THIS: SOME PEOPLE IN SOME PARTS GET REALLY PISSED WHEN YOU INSULT KURT COBAIN. I'D LIKE TO SEE YOU COME UP HERE AND SAY KURT IS A 'WASTE OF HUMAN FLESH' TO MY FACE WHILE

WE'RE ON THE SUBJECT OF HURTING YOU, HAS A CHICK EVER KICKED YOUR ASS? 'CAUSE I'M ABOUT READY TO COME DOWN THERE AND BEAT YOUR BRAINS IN WITH MY LOWER EASTSIDE SHOES. I THINK THAT YOUR LETTERS ARE VERY ENTERTAINING, BUT HAS YOUR MOTHER EVER TOLD YOU, 'IF YOU DON'T HAVE ANYTHING NICE TO SAY, KEEP YOUR KURT COBAIN INSULTING, MARILYN MANSON WORST BAND EVER, SHIT TALKIN', FUCKIN MY DOG FOR A DOLLAR FIFTY —AN HOUR, DICK SUCKIN' MOUTH SHUT!?' HAVE A NICE DAY."
— FEMALE READER IN CORINNE, UTAH.

This is not to say that we don't occasionally get these same acidic letters at Ray Gun. We do. You can almost smell them right through the envelope, feel them coming on like tornado weather, products of the almost limitless, clawing rage that can visit an Outsider in desperate need of an acceptable identity. But Ray Gun's audience tends to be somewhat older and — snobby as it sounds — vastly better educated, and these would be an exception. Because Ray Gun invites a graphic interaction with its subject, a bunch of its letters come in as graphic works themselves, usually collages and sometimes quite accomplished, involving custom typefaces, etc. Design students, artists, and relatively enlightened professionals have always made up a certain percentage of Ray Gun readers, and though their cynicisms are as corrosive as any other, they do tend to be more positive. And forgiving.

huH readers, however, interest me more at present. For whatever reason, huH seems to appeal to the very core asshole "alternative" American consumer. The salt of the earth. And the more they identify their likes and dislikes in these letters, the more they reveal what poet Ed Sanders once called our nation's "Protestant mean streak."

huH letters come from every conceivable household, prison, school, barracks, and trailer park in the global village. Decatur, Georgia. Cle Elum, Washington. South Bend, Indiana. Riverview, New Brunswick, Canada. On duty in Guam and Puerto Rico. Most of them consider themselves the "freaks," which they somewhere in the late '60s, lost its true glamour at the end of wear like a badge of honor. They can't relate to the locals. So the '70s, and lost it's power as a potential social movement they reach out to each other thru huH. Like Linsy Love, from Port Charlotte, Florida: "...some dicks at Spin wouldn't print my letters in their shit box coz it had too many fucks in it. im just a girl who writes bad poetry, and i bleach my hair to white and paint my nails (and i dont know exactly why) and i like to go barefoot, i like to sing and act and watch movies (but i tend to drift a lot) buts dont bother me and i dont scream like a girl when i see a spider....so if youre considered — or labeled — a 'freak' or a 'raver' or whatever and care to write — go for it. ill

write back."·

At this moment in consumer society, the logo is supreme. Like Ray Gun, huH has tapped into a community at once threatened and transfixed by marketing and media manipulation. The coy. The refuseniks. A couple huH readers even decided they'd fallen in love through "Post Modern," so he stole a car and drove to where she was and they eloped into the night to get married. Mark put their picture in the magazine. Which is all cool, so long as you don't try to classify the kind of people who are reading and writing to the magazine, because if they suspect they're part of a trend, a number of them will fade into the deeper, colder waters like elusive trout. It doesn't matter that you can feel them wanting to talk. You feel their voices emboldened by the print medium, like people thrilled to be on a TV talk show. But they want to talk about how everyone else sucks without having to accept a label or commit to a marketing scheme or identify with any kind of "Nation." They want to hang out with one another as a loose cadre of unrelated, pissed-off outsiders.

Perhaps the unacknowledged paradigm rising through the murk of these letters is actually the sinister silence of a forced tolerance. Like the paradoxical, maddening battles raging over words and political correctness on college campuses and in the workplace, dissenting voices tend to be howled down. In that same wistful letter by Linsy Love, for example, she also raves, "i was a bit disappointed in one writer — 'bad boy.' (yeah you kick ass, dont you?) you are obviously just another redneck tobacco chewin beef eatin baby killin gun slinger mother fucken 'somewhere in idaho.' you have offended me. my friends are the 'blazed-out meth freaks' who would love to kill a fucker like you. deal with it."

We have hundreds of letters like this. These are American kids talking about songs. They are our legacy, the price of encasing all our lives in a franchise reality — the same malls with the same stores selling the same lifestyle requiring the same damaged spirit to grudgingly accept, or, conversely, the same blind punching to reject. Rock 'n' roll lost its innocence in the late '60s, lost its true glamour at the end of the '70s, and lost it's power as a potential social movement (in the West) with the end of the second wave of Anglo-American punk in the mid-'80s. Now there are thousands of acutely aware young listeners who are denying what is perhaps the essence of rock as we have known it: the desire to rock with other people. The idea of identifying with other fans is now too loaded to be cool. Maybe this is our much-lauded American "rugged individualism" come home to roost like a mutant, 60-ton rooster with steroids in its feed. As John Lydon once said when he was still on the rising road with

john langham

We Crucify the Insincere Tonight, Tonight

10
Issue 17. Ray Gun. June/July 1994.
Illustration by Ted Jouflas.
Art Direction & Design by David Carson.

11
Issue 18. Ray Gun. August 1994.
John Lydon Dps.
Art Direction & Design by David Carson.
Photography by Michael Lavine.
Are You the Bomb?
Page Nos

5 0 / 5 1

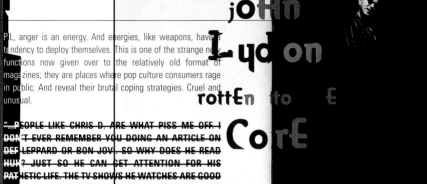

joHn **Lyd on** rottEn ito E CoIrE

PIL, anger is an energy. And energies, like weapons, have a tendency to deploy themselves. This is one of the strange new functions now given over to the relatively old format of magazines; they are places where pop culture consumers rage in public. And reveal their brutal coping strategies. Cruel and unusual.

"...PEOPLE LIKE CHRIS D. ARE WHAT PISS ME OFF. I DON'T EVER REMEMBER YOU DOING AN ARTICLE ON DEF LEPPARD OR BON JOVI. SO WHY DOES HE READ HUH? JUST SO HE CAN GET ATTENTION FOR HIS PATHETIC LIFE. THE TV SHOWS HE WATCHES ARE GOOD EXAMPLES. I'D BE WILLING TO BET THAT WHEN HE GETS TO COLLEGE, WHEN ALL THE 'ALTERNATIVE' PEOPLE ARE OUT AT RAVES AND GETTING LAID, HE'LL BE IN HIS DORM, JACKING OFF TO FRIENDS AND THE WOMAN ON X FILES (IF NOT THE FUCKING ALIENS! WE DON'T KNOW THIS GUY!). HOW LOW CAN A PERSON GO TO TALK ABOUT WHERE A PERSON LIVES? I DOUBT JASON COLE OR CAL OSTOMY CAN HELP WHERE THEY LIVE. OR THE WAY CAL FEELS ABOUT CHRIS D. I DON'T THINK CHRIS D. HAS THE FUCKIN' BALLS TO REALLY DO WHAT HE SAID HE DID TO CAL. AND I'M WILLING TO BET HE WOULD GET HIS TEETH BROKEN. DON'T FUCK WITH US PUNKS. ESPECIALLY THE YOUNGER ONES. OUR COUNTRY IS GETTING WORSE AND WORSE AND ONE DAY, SOMEONE WHO READS HUH IS GOING TO RUN INTO YOU, AND THE NEXT TIME WE'LL SEE YOUR NAME ON UNSOLVED MYSTERIES. THIS SHIT IS REAL CHRIS. IF YOU CAN'T HANDLE IT, STAY OLD, STAY DEF LEPPARD AND QUIT FLAPPIN' YOUR FUCKIN' GUMS AND WATCH YOUR LITTLE TV SHOWS."

———READER IN PRISON, DECATUR, GA.

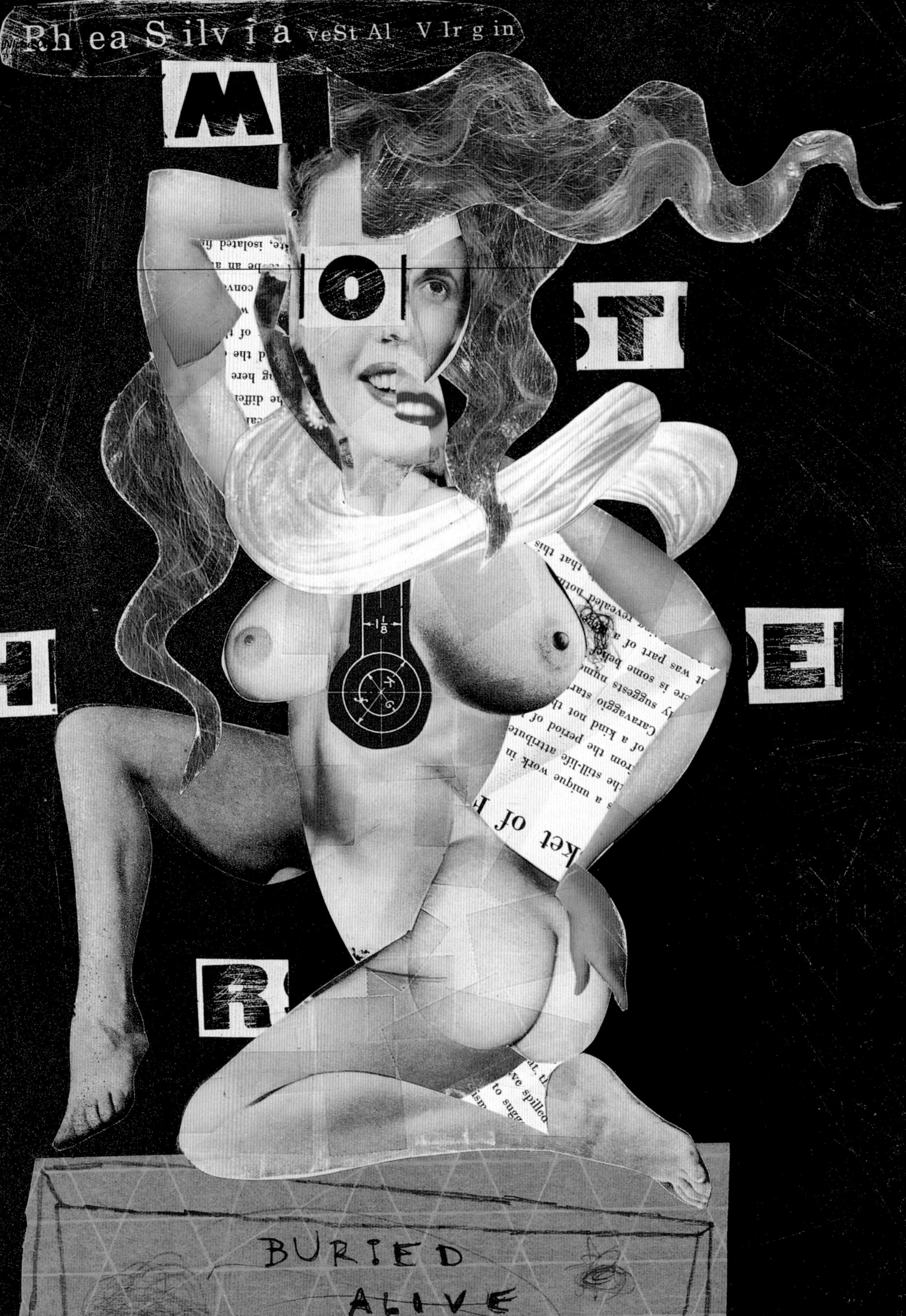

Rhea Silvia veStAl VIrgin

3.
Hardcore Porn!

BURIED ALIVE FOR BREAKING VOWS

PLUNKERT

puked up fractals and graphs and computerese. This revealed a truth I'd never known before: people can really get down to explicit pornography. Even Japanese people, who, from what I'd seen in clubs, generally don't get down much to anything.

I've seen Butter 08, too, the currently smokin'-hot rock band wherein graphic designer Mike Mills dons a blond Warhol wig (the Warhol connection is a comment in itself; he thought VU was so cool because it was his discovery, his invention) and plays bass in a most overt rock star gesture, and they are really popular, too, but that doesn't change my opinion a lot. It seemed to matter a hell of a lot, however, to the young movie-and-music types out in LA's woodsy Silverlake district. Butter 08 played there last spring, at a dark, mirrored, ex-strip club type joint called Spaceland, and I would guess the most design-conscious rockers in town were there, given Mills' rep as a graphic force. Butter 08 is an art-damage supergroup comprised of Yuka Honda and Miho Hatori of Cibo Matto, the current darlings of the ultrasweet Japan-pop underground (a sort of unofficial Church of Burt Bacharach), drummer Russell Simins of the apocalypse blues group Jon Spencer Blues Explosion, guitarist Rick Lee of Skeleton Key, and then Mills. We had just run a four-page piece on his work in the "Music By Design" section of Ray Gun, featuring his designs for Kim Gordon's X-Girl clothing line and the imagemaking album artwork and posters he's done for Sonic Youth, the Beastie Boys, Blues Explosion, Pizzicato 5, and others. His videos for Marc Jacobs, Frank Black, and Ornette Coleman are superb. This is a man creating the graphic language that weirdly unified everyone in the house that night — including King Buzzo of the Melvins, Vivian Trimble from Luscious Jackson and Kostars, every recording industry exec who could stay awake that late, and every superfan available. The show was not publicized, so of course it was jammed. We stood there cheek-to-jowl with the young monied hipsters who were most likely to have recently purchased their first architectural property. Even though I was standing on the dance floor six feet from the band, I couldn't see them half the time because Sean Lennon was pogoing up and down in front of me with his wild long hair

In the course of a great many conversations I've had concerning Ray Gun, someone has almost always thrown out the line, "Well, designers are the rock stars of the '90s." Well, no they're not. They dress the rock stars of the '90s. Whether we are talking about graphic design, couture, architecture, interiors, whatever, the fact that designers are so conspicuously creating superstars by affixing their clothes and logos to someone else's heavenly body points out exactly why they are not rock stars: design does not engage the body. Rock is about an emotion so dumb and primal only your spine can express it. You can stare at the most effective graphic design job on the planet and it won't make you dance. Logos don't get anybody off. Not even when they're done by designers who also happen to rock, like Tomato designer Karl Hyde's great band, Underworld. Style's star is ascendant at the moment, and clothing designers' catwalk shows are considered more radical chic and draw more celebrities (and sometimes make more money) than a lot of transcendent rock, but let's not make the mistake that cool visuals can guarantee a really worthwhile rock 'n' roll experience any more than pure celebrity can (no need to go into the scores of trash actor bands — Dogstar, anyone? Pee? John Tesh? I just got a whole album of the John Travolta singles from the '70s! Terrible!). Art supergroups like Destroy All Monsters, which has been around for quite a while and includes Art's Great Hip Hope Mike Kelley and emerging Detroit painter Niagara, rarely transcend the idea of themselves to actually rock out — in the sense that, say, Husker Du would rock out.

The closest thing I've seen to live graphic performance, per se, was Pizzicato 5's DJ Konishi and Towa Tei, formerly of Deee-Lite, performing at the Shinjuku Liquid Room in Tokyo. Towa Tei has a crew of graphic designers, image terrorists, and projectionists called Graphickers who provide the visual backdrop to the otherwise undynamic stage presentation that plagues all DJs. In performance, Towa Tei basically just stands there getting a kink in his neck and slapping records on the turntable. So he made sure nobody watched him. He had two gorgeous Japanese models in shiny white vinyl one-piece swimsuits parading back and forth in front of the stage like ring girls at a boxing match, holding up album covers and signs that said, "Design Or Die!" and "No More Bad Design!" Then the Graphickers started pumping hardcore porn films onto the video screens, mixed with landscapes, pieces of the movie Cannonball Run, advertisements, logos, and just plain bizarre digitally

a Guitar maKes a band

3.
Hardcore Porn!

streaming across my face, bouncing over every once in a while to shout something probably very working-class-hero-like to his mom, Yoko Ono. My girlfriend Liza and I were standing between one of the Beastie Boys and the Coppola kids, Roman and Sophia. I started to flash on some descriptions I'd read of the scene at
Max's Kansas City around 1975 (when I was about 11, just to give some perspective). This had all the trappings of a

(((sorry)))
no graphix

generation-defining performance.

Which is weird, considering that Butter 08 sounded like someone playing Jon Spencer outtakes on a speed-damaged Close N' Play. In Japanese. Okay, there were musical moments, too, but maybe only one or two. Oh well. Reminded me of that classic Lester Bangs story called "My Night of Ecstacy with the J. Geils Band," where Lester goes on stage with his typewriter and types to the beat. Stupid. I am sure, however, having met Mike Mills and respected his work, that he and his acolytes have already discerned that what he is making is more Art than Rock. Maybe I should take the initiative right now and dub it "designer rock."

Which shouldn't make a good-humored dude like Mills feel bad at all, considering it places him in some really illustrious company. What about super-painter Julian Schnabel? He's the toast of New York City after his Basquiat movie, but does anyone remember his 1995 pop record? Me, neither! Cartoon genius and Pee-Wee Playhouse set designer Gary Panter put out a single or two that people tend to hang on the walls as objets d'art. Psychotic cancer-painter and blows-himself-up-with-dynamite performance artist Joe Coleman also had a vicious art-damage (literally) band in the '70s called Steel Tips. David Byrne, Chris Franz, and Tina Weymouth all went to the Rhode Island School of Design before they were Talking Heads, which is probably why they sometimes commit designer rock.

Kim Gordon went to art school before she became a Sonic Youth, but they overcome their obscuro tendencies and rock out in a big loud way. Which is to say that some rockers who also paint or draw or fashion fatuous displays of public art do not commit designer rock: Perry Farrell did fantastic, large-scale sculptures for the covers of both *Ritual de lo Habitual* and *Nothings Shocking*; Daniel Johnston is a great folk artist; genius Seattle illustrator Ed Fotheringham also has a pretty cool on-again/off-again band called the Thrown Ups; Mellencamp paints!; weirdo comic artist Steve Cerio was once the drummer in Railroad Jerk; Pearl Jam's Jeff Ament does all their graphic design; every time I eat at Hal's in Venice I have to look at Joni Mitchell paintings; Billy Childish paints; and what about Yoko, who is a great fluxus happener, and Devo's Mark Mothersbaugh, who is excellent at just about everything? And Big Chief's Mark Dancey, who is a fantastic comic artist and designer of the high-concept fanzine Motor Booty? And R.L. Burnside, who is recognized as both a blues master and celebrated folk artist? The overachiever among them all, though, is David Bowie — contender for the throne of the King of All Media — who now puts some of his seemingly-limitless energy into painting and theorizing about conceptual art, managing recently to score the only known interview with French surrealist painter Balthus (at age 90!), after already proving himself to be a strangely cracked actor, not to mention one of the greatest rock musicians and space aliens of all time.

None of these people would say design is the new rock 'n' roll. And let's not forget the indisputable truth that some of the best rock music was and is made by people who would be considered the enemy of style and art. Like Motorhead. Or Michael Jackson.

15
Issue 38. Ray Gun. August 1996.
Urusei Yatsura Sp.
Art Direction & Design by Robert Hales.

16
Issue 34. Ray Gun. March 1996.
x–girl Dps.
Art Direction & Design by Robert Hales.
Are You the Bomb?
Artwork by Mike Mills.
Page Nos

music the rest of us were just too insensitive to grasp. Maybe
he's just liberated enough to rock out in a room full of critics. Or

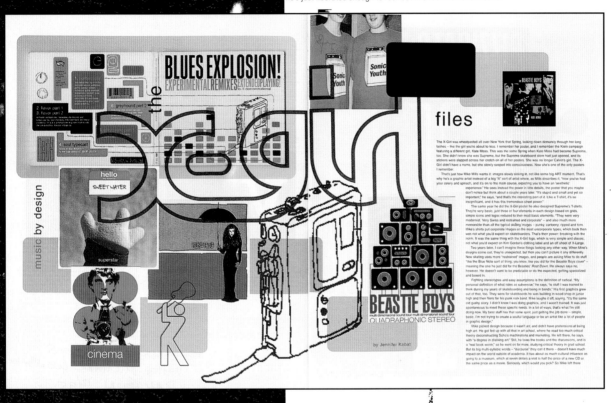

by Jennifer Kabat

But I digress. All I'm trying to say is that Style is not Rock. Being
a "rock star" signifies leading a ritual of liberation that is old
and intractable in the body's memory, as old as cave man days,

maybe someday real soon he'll be the best-dressed man in
rock 'n' roll.

maybe, and one that empty style simply cannot conjure. Maybe
I like Mike Mills even more because his band can't. Everyone
else in the house seemed to like Butter 08 just fine. I obviously
hadn't had enough drinks. The only person who was genuinely
losing his mind over it, though, was Sean Lennon. Which made
me like him a lot more, too, just for the weirdness of it. Maybe
he saw the future in this performance, some unrealized new

ᴀ dense flow of wet, 90-degree air moved across my shoulders to slowly spin the blades of a fan in the firedoor at the end of the cellblock, air heavy with the weight of all the men staring down the tier at us "free world people." Corporal P. Galloway, a woman, walked three of us up and down the tier rattling the cages in an unnecessary show of bravado at Cold Creek Correctional Facility in West Tennessee. This is an old medium-security prison, built during the Depression, and the cinderblock tiers there are narrow and claustrophobic, six of them holding about 100 men each. Ninety percent of those men are black. Which is about average for prisons in the USA. We walked between open cells facing each other across maybe six feet of floor — floor choked with "offenders" (as they're called in Tennessee) lounging under the phones, hanging on the doors to gape, jeering at Galloway. Through the circular fan you could see flickers of green, rolling green cotton fields and gorgeous hardwood forests hung with honeysuckle running the mile to the banks of the Mississippi and straight on to heaven. Just to remind you you were in hell.

17
Out of Control.
Original Illustration.
Jeff Tady. 1996.

back of the gym, squeezed in with about a dozen prisoners in their blue jeans with the racing stripe down each leg that reads "Property of Tennessee Department of Corrections" and a gaggle of Warner Bros. and MTV execs, most of them women wearing sunglasses. Ray Gun, at its inception, was inspired in part as a print response to the visual excitement of MTV, the computer/video graphics revolution. In pseudo-McCluhanesque terms, MTV is white-hot media. There is very little distance between your delicate little retinas and that manipulated slab of color hocus-pocus. It's invasive. Subsequently, MTV tends to feel very personal. And local. Like they made it in your backyard. For you. Which is a quantum shift from network television. When you were 16 and watching "Don Kirshner's Rock Concert" on midnight TV, that big-time glamour was a million miles away. Those guys were stars. Which meant they were in the sky, inaccessible. Now, when you're sitting in your apartment watching MTV with a camcorder next to your bed, it's easy to see how you could just step down to your local jukejoint and make that stuff yourself. Lots of people do. Ray Gun works that way, too. Anybody with a Mac can slap crazy illegible type over scanned pictures of their girlfriend's band and call it a magazine. It's an illusion, of course, but an illusion that inspires some kind of loyalty. Loyalty to a dream of interactivity.

in the Cold Creek prison gymnasium to tape a special called "Steve Earle: To Hell And Back." Earle, an outlaw Nashville rocker who'd just released a pair of excellent albums of pure Americana, had been busted for heroin possession two years earlier and was doing a show here as part of his probation. MTV had two huge production trucks parked outside in the exercise yard and a crew of about 20 men and women rigging hanging camera platforms from the rafters and setting up 24-track remote recording equipment. I was the only print media there.

"That's against my rights, man!," yelled another con. "You didn't get my permission to take me on video in here!"

"No, wait, yo yo yo, man," said the first, shouting the other man down. "Yo, my man, can I say something on camera? Will they let me do that?"

Galloway leaned into a cell and talked directly to a reticent, soft-spoken young black man. "You comin' tomorrow?"

"Fuck MTV," he said, smiling. "Fuck the motherfucker. Why I care about that? Come in here to make their special program on my back? No MTV gonna play the music I like."

Men began to echo his attitude down the tier. "Yeah, fuck that, bitch!"

"Hey, Galloway, bitch!"
"Yeah, why they don't bring no rap music to jail?!"
"Yo, my man, don't let me down! I got to get on the TV for an important message! Don't let me down!"

The next day, when the stage lights came up at sundown, there were plenty of men there. Maybe 400 for the second show. But you couldn't miss the odor of So What? spritzing through the sweltering gym. They might as well have been filming an oboe concerto in the jungles of Sarawak. Or Mars. Although Steve Earle played with passion, played a few radio hits the men knew, like "I Feel Alright" and "Copperhead Road," and brought to their prison comraderie with enough charisma to get them dancing and hooting by the end, these men had no idea what a Steve Earle was supposed to be. A white guard assured me that 95% of the men in Cold Creek listened to rap and, up until a week earlier, had never even heard of Steve Earle. By the night's end, Steve's performance proved two things: great music transcends its audience; great media does not.

"This ain't no Beach Party," Steve joked, and the men laughed. He was right in a way that he didn't intend. The MTV "Beach Party" segment is full of kids who fully understand the image power, scope, and even irony of MTV, and they perform accordingly on camera. These men had no use whatsoever for MTV, and (probably because of that) they lacked the sophistication to meet it. I sat there on a set of aluminum risers in the

The guys in Cold Creek Correctional Facility also dream a variation of this dream. I realized as I was sitting there with the boom camera swinging low over my head, that they expected this event to be about them. They'd bought into the false promise of interactivity that permeates MTV. They expected that this entity, super-friendly MTV, of all media, had honestly moved away from being canned entertainment to being a personal hotline to the electronic world. I watched infinite subtle shades of awakening around me as they discovered it had not. Oh, the let-down. Let-down is not a good thing to put on frustrated prisoners. They weren't going to get their personal moment with this media. They were being used. Some of the men who'd shunned the event had evidently already figured that out.

Which is the point. Ray Gun offers a very similar promise. The graphic treatment promises

"Hey, y'all here with that MTV?" cried an anxious man crouched in the front corner of his cell with his head against the bars, one of the few under lockdown. "You gonna be filming it all tomorrow for MTV?"

We were. This was June, 1996, and spaceship MTV had landed

4.
Don't Let the Stars Get in Your Eyes

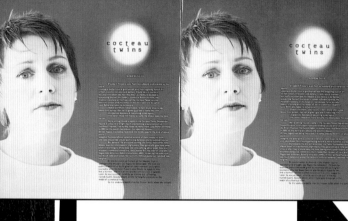

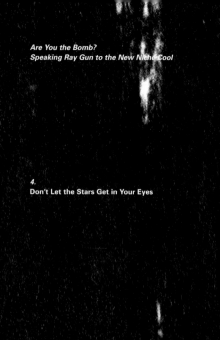

BY ANITA SARKO

Summer in the city ain't pretty, even on the best of days. And this has certainly not been one of those. Rather than glide effortlessly to the Grammercy Park Hotel, headquarters of choice for world-class, post-Chelsea generation demi-monde royalty such as David J., I battle Manhattan rush-hour gridlock to get uptown, due to a last-minute change in locations. Fan though I am of this man's past work (bassist/singer/writer of Love and Rockets and, before that, Bauhau), I'm not into sweating to any oldies, no matter how dense the pedigree. After a cab ride, a subway trick and a six-block run, let's just say I'm pissed off by the time I get to the elegant, leather-and-wood-till-you-vomit conference room at M.C.A. Records.

As I drown my sorrows in the chill of a canned soda, I hear a mid-range, sexy, Brit-inflected growl of a greeting from the doorway, where a slender man plays with a light dimmer switch. Adjusting, glancing at the lights above the conference table, re-adjusting, glancing and dimming the room to a nightclub's murky warmth.

He sits down, appraising his atmospheric engineering, and I'm awestruck at how much he looks like the stick figure drawn by my friend Craig at Bleeker Bob's Record Shop.

"He looks like this," Craig had said, producing a small round head, round glasses draping a roundish nose, all topped by a thatch of hair. "You'll like his looks. He's a redhead."

"Red hair is a bad setting for a penis," I answered, repeating a line I had heard on t.v.

That horribly sexist flippancy, along with my rotten mood, chokes me with guilt over the next couple of hours because Daniel J is lovely, calm, bright and absolutely unaffected, as well as being a mesmerizing storyteller.

It was in the town of his birth, Northampton, in the midlands of England, at 15, in youth clubs that only played rare reggae tracks, that he first felt the need to master the instrument that drove the soundtrack of this recently discovered netherworld.

"It was slightly dangerous and threatening, and there was a thrill in that, and there was this music and the clubs were dark, and there were these heavy-looking characters, this skinheads, hangin' around, and that was really the first musical form that had an effect on me," he says.

He bought a six-string guitar and removed two of them and played along to his four Reggae Chartbuster albums, which along with a Roy Orbison record and The Kinks' "Sunny Afternoon" comprised his entire record collection.

opening act

A real bass led to The Submerged Truth, a punk band that was banned from playing Northampton by the local "traditional musical bores" after three gigs. The guitarist left, and was replaced by Daniel Ash. A couple of years later, Bauhaus, which lasted four "intense" years, was born.

Internal friction, "the same thing that made the group work," also ended the band.

Did it just dissolve then, I ask.

No, he laughs. "It exploded."

Ten years later, David could hear Peter Murphy on a song he wrote for his own solo album, *Urbane, Urbane*. Murphy, also recording an album, had the same idea about David being on his record. Although that didn't happen, Murphy guested on "Candy on the Cross."

"There was something in the air that night," says David of it. "It was really charged. Something happened."

The album, based mainly on his travels through the U.S. documents David J.'s idea of fun. "I like to spontaneously put myself in a situation which surprises me. I'll be in my hotel and think I could be in a different part of town in a half hour, experiencing what it has to offer. So 'Go Now.'"

The Walk on the Wild Side? "Someplace that has the potential to be interesting," he admits. "Usually a seedy part of town. It's a compulsion. I sometimes frighten my friends," he says.

The darker side of human nature gets explored as well. "The Smashed Princess" was sparked by Princess Stephanie's "damaged" appearance on t.v. Then there are the streetwalkers, the hoods, the druggies, the serial killer, the actor worth more dead than alive, people with dreams and good intentions who just weren't the "chosen ones."

If that's not enough to make you slit your wrists, there's my favorite, "Ten Little Beauty Queens." "It's a true story about a guy, Jeffrey Jones. He used to live with his mother and wouldn't go out with or talk to people and got his kicks persuading young girls to go into this basement and dress, for money, in black satin, which was his fetish. He'd put a noose around their necks and photograph them and let them go free. He'd never harm them; that wasn't his scene."

"Then, one time, a girl accidentally got hung." Whoops. "When Jones went to court, all he said was 'Black satin rules my life, and what turns you on will eventually control you.'

"The same kind of obsessive, dark impulse is within myself and everyone else. It just differs in degree of latency and expression. I had to touch on that in myself to put it across the song. I put off recording it for ten years."

In spite of the subject matter, there's something incredibly gleeful about this album. He's planning to tour, this time, with new influences such as the rave, ambient and rap scenes.

And what does he make of the new generation of Goths? "It's funny that 17-year-old kids are getting into Bauhaus.

We laugh. But what if they had barely been born in the band's heyday. Guess ol' Bela Lugosi was just playing possum.

"It's just schtick."

"It's time for a new name."

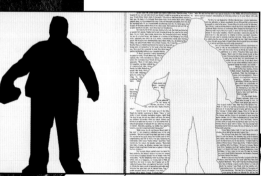

DAVID J

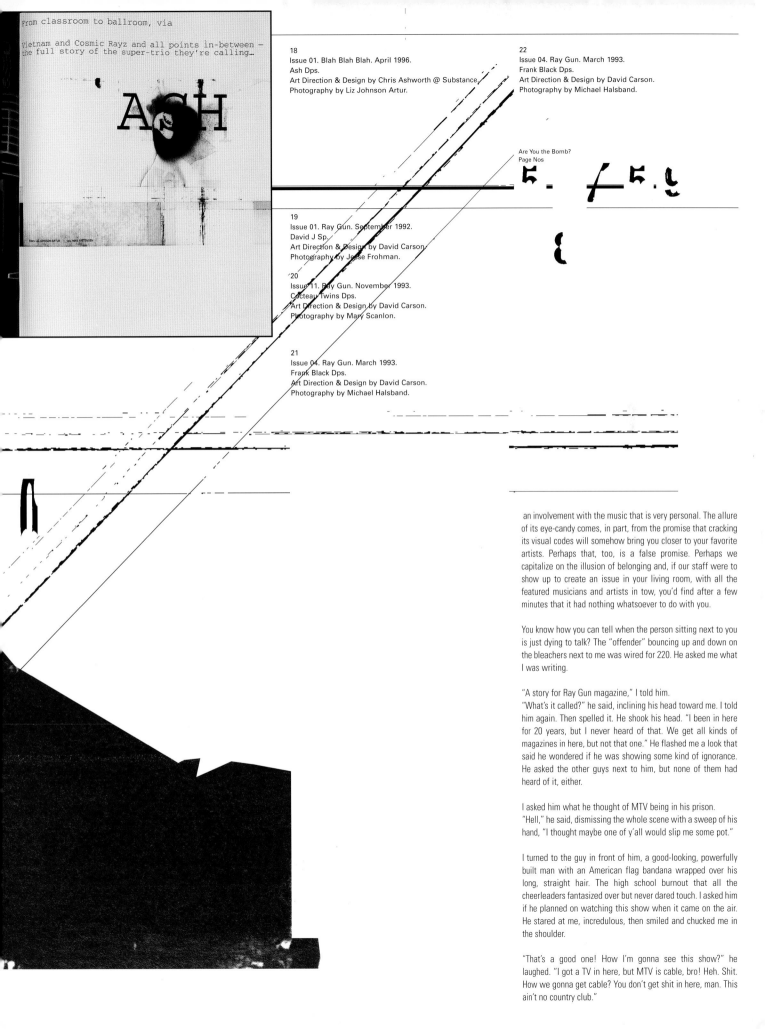

From classroom to ballroom, via
Vietnam and Cosmic Rayz and all points in-between —
the full story of the super-trio they're calling…

ASH

Are You the Bomb?
Page Nos

an involvement with the music that is very personal. The allure of its eye-candy comes, in part, from the promise that cracking its visual codes will somehow bring you closer to your favorite artists. Perhaps that, too, is a false promise. Perhaps we capitalize on the illusion of belonging and, if our staff were to show up to create an issue in your living room, with all the featured musicians and artists in tow, you'd find after a few minutes that it had nothing whatsoever to do with you.

You know how you can tell when the person sitting next to you is just dying to talk? The "offender" bouncing up and down on the bleachers next to me was wired for 220. He asked me what I was writing.

"A story for Ray Gun magazine," I told him.
"What's it called?" he said, inclining his head toward me. I told him again. Then spelled it. He shook his head. "I been in here for 20 years, but I never heard of that. We get all kinds of magazines in here, but not that one." He flashed me a look that said he wondered if he was showing some kind of ignorance. He asked the other guys next to him, but none of them had heard of it, either.

I asked him what he thought of MTV being in his prison.
"Hell," he said, dismissing the whole scene with a sweep of his hand, "I thought maybe one of y'all would slip me some pot."

I turned to the guy in front of him, a good-looking, powerfully built man with an American flag bandana wrapped over his long, straight hair. The high school burnout that all the cheerleaders fantasized over but never dared touch. I asked him if he planned on watching this show when it came on the air. He stared at me, incredulous, then smiled and chucked me in the shoulder.

"That's a good one! How I'm gonna see this show?" he laughed. "I got a TV in here, but MTV is cable, bro! Heh. Shit. How we gonna get cable? You don't get shit in here, man. This ain't no country club."

5.
Peaches En Regalia

The Monday after Frank Zappa died, Randy Bookasta received a phone call from Frank's daughter, Moon Unit, a frequent contributor and interviewer for Ray Gun. He hadn't expected to hear from her, keeping a respectful distance to afford her some escape from the knot of ambulance chasers plucking at one of America's greatest and funniest musicians. She and the family were on their way to Hawaii to regroup, but she called to say that if Ray Gun were going to print anything about her dad, she wanted to do it. Randy agreed, and heard nothing for over a month. Then a fairly sunny fax arrived, saying, "After much contemplation I've decided that what I'd like to see in the magazine is a photograph...." The Zappa family office sent over the photo, which was then published on page one of issue #14: a very straightforward black-and-white of Frank peering into the camera, his face thin, hair long and wild mustache gray and defiant, his trademark wry cynicism dulled enough by cancer and mortality to wring love for him out of any heart, his eye gone almost imperceptibly soft. As if Frank were saying, "The bastard's beating me. Who's going to step up to hold him off?" This was all Moon needed to say. Anybody who didn't know the story by now would just have to go listen to the work: 57 known albums, weeks of unreleased recordings, scores, and unfinished works; books, movies, and videos; plus the intangible impact of his many classes, travels as an unofficial political emissary to Eastern Europe, and scalding appearances in the press. Despite the fact that most of Frank's work and teaching had to do with what you would call classical compositions, rock had claimed him as its own, and Moon grabbed him back. She had enclosed a caption: "Frank Zappa. American Composer. 1940-1993."

Ray Gun was designed to be an open forum for this kind of comment by the artists who define youth (or music) culture. In many ways, the magazine has more in common with the "inside out" approach of fine art magazines, where artists print statements and reveal their working processes, than with rock fanzines catering to the outsider looking in. The barrier between "star" and "fan" that so characterized rock music's high mythology period in the '70s simply disintegrated in the proto-intellectual punk and hometown indie label chaos of the '80s and early '90s, and the first Ray Guns struck a nerve exactly because they put the artist and the consumer on the same page. In it, they hunkered down together. For the previous ten years, bands had been crashing on fans' floors all over North America. Tastes have become more eclectic and forgiving, as well. A lot of people I know threw out their Led Zeppelin records when punk hit in the '70s, as vestiges of what Rage Against the Machine's Tom Morello identified as "7-11 parking lot rock," but in the last ten years they've gone out and bought them all again 'cause nobody has to be that purist anymore. The journalistic filter between artist and fan has become impossibly bogus to the ever-more-eclectic music listener, who is taking in more and more music every day as the history of rock burgeons with age, and Ray Gun acknowledges a closing of ranks by assuming the reader can stay afloat in the raw surf where the artists themselves are thrashing. It reflects

a working truth that David Bowie expressed in an interview

that the most stimulating thing about other arti not what

with Moon Unit in the October '95 Ray Gun: "I've always found

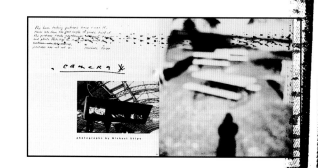

23
Issue 14. Ray Gun. March 1994.
Frank Zappa Sp.
Art Direction & Design by David Carson.
Photography by Fritz Brinckmann.

24
Issue 01. Ray Gun. September 1992.
Sound in Print Sp.
Art Direction & Design by David Carson.
Illustration by Lane Smith.

25
Issue 20. huH. April 1996.
Camera Dps.
Creative Direction by Vaughan Oliver.
Art Direction by Jérôme Curchod.
Photography by Michael Stipe.

26
Issue 30. Ray Gun. October 1995.
David Bowie Sp.
Art Direction & Design by David Carson.
Computer Images/Concept by David Bowie/Denovo.
Photography by John Scarisbrick.

Are You the Bomb?
Page Nos

here."

Looking at "how they get there" means looking at the whole trip, including the detours and incursions into arts other than music. Ray Gun assumes you need to know about, for instance, David Bowie's painting and computer graphic compositions, so he provided several full-page images and captions for that story in Ray Gun #30, originals he'd created for his collaboration with Brian Eno called Outside. These are not, however, "celebrity art." Visual clues to a musician's mindset are essential to founding designer David Carson's graphic expansions, especially apparent in the regularly-occuring Sound In Print pages, where graphic artists offer visual interpretations of individual songs. Musician's contributions — graphic or otherwise — have been solicited since the debut issue in September '92.

Country bright spark Joe Ely published a series of brilliant paintings and mixed-media works in Ray Gun #8, a "Jail Series" rendering some of his experiences in prison, and his Lubbock-area homeboy Butch Hancock provided some fine black-and-white photography to illustrate an article about his own music. Robyn Hitchcock's paintings appeared in Ray Gun #10. Publisher Marvin Jarrett has always been particularly proud to claim that R.E.M.'s Michael Stipe "shoots for Ray Gun." Besides appearing on numerous R.E.M. CD booklets, Stipe's ghostly, motion-bent photos have been featured three times in Ray Gun, and a full feature on his photo work appeared in issue #20 of huH magazine, another Ray Gun publication. Allen Ginsberg's photos of William S. Burroughs and hand-written captions illustrated a story about the gray magician in Ray Gun #32.

In some cases, like Moon Unit's statement about her father, visual comment is just more appropriate than verbal clutter. When asked to provide a tour diary of his 1996 journey across the US for Ray Gun #39, Underworld's Karl Hyde turned in a fantastic four-page snapshot collage with the words "I loved your kittens, O.K.?" typeset on it. Arizona redneck punks the Meat Puppets contributed their calculatedly-naive line drawings to Ray Gun #14. Belly's Chris Gorman has shot photos of bands Scarce and Warrant for huH, and some of his more abstract photography was used in Ray Gun #37. Leonard Cohen provided computer-generated drawings of his own design for an article on his album The Future in Ray Gun #7. In that same issue, Ray Gun's first "on the road" issue, Kim Gordon and Thurston Moore of Sonic Youth turned in a pile of captioned photos to illustrate a tour story written by the band (well, Lee Renaldo really wrote the whole thing, but nobody knows that).

There's more, and literally scores of top illustrators that could and probably should be named here, but you get the

point. The corollary to these muso visual contributions, of

their things mean, which is always sort of boring 'cause I'm

quite happy with my own interpretation, but how they get

2   7
Issue   22.   huH.   June   1996
C   o   v   e   r   .
Creative   Direction   by   Vaughan   Oliver
Art   Direction   by   Jerôme   Curchod
Photography   by   Jana   Leon
Logo treatment by Timothy O'Donnell

STONE TEMPLE PILOTS: Weiland Talks • DE LA SOUL   **22**

27

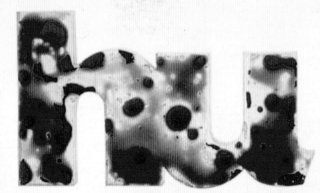

hu H

MAGNAPOP • SPACEHOG VS. SPACE GHOST • TYPE O NEGATIVE

THIS IS A MAGAZINE ABOUT MUSIC. IF WE WERE YOU WE'D BUY IT.

june 1996

butthole **surfers'** head man
gibby haynes
talks to director of *"dead man"*
jim jarmusch

*about music, movies,
shotguns, and cars.*

07 >

0 71486 03512 1

$2.95 usa
$3.50 can

course, is the Ray Gun habit of having the artists themselves   work as journalists. While Ray Gun certainly didn't invent the

28
Issue 33. Ray Gun. February 1996.
Brian Wilson & Matthew Sweet Dps.
Art Direction & Design by Robert Hales.
Photography by Peter Morello.

29
Issue 35. Ray Gun. April 1996.
Iggy & Perry Dps.
Art Direction & Design by Robert Hales.
Photography by Peter Morello.

30
Issue 38. Ray Gun. August 1996.
Yoko Ono & Cibo Matto Dps.
Art Direction & Design by Robert Hales.
Photography by Michael Wong.

Yoko Ono with Cibo Matto (RG38), Iggy Pop with Perry Farrell (RG34), William Gibson with Henry Rollins (huH2), Willie Nelson interviewing the Supersuckers (RG29), Gibby Haynes with Dead Man director Jim Jarmusch (huH22), Deborah Harry with L7 (RG12), Green Day with Jello Biafra (huH17), Brian Wilson with Matthew Sweet (RG33), Frank Black with the Reverend Horton Heat (RG7), and Thurston Moore with Redd Kross (RG12). David Lowery of Cracker (ex-Camper Van Beethoven) wrote a story on Pioneer Town, where they recorded the first Cracker album, in Ray Gun #7. X diva Exene Cervenka lamented the late, great Los Angeles in a piece called "Acres of Defeat" for the LA issue, Ray Gun #12. Marilyn Manson gushed over the Tom Petty box set in huH #16. Admittedly, some of these discussions teeter on the brink of mutal admiration circle jerk, but the mixes are so intriguing they're impossible to resist. Sometimes they are also the only route available. When Austinite Kathy McCarthy interviewed reclusive folk genius Daniel Johnston for Ray Gun, she was probably one of two or three people in the world who could get it. Without her work as one of Johnston's few collaborators, his admirers would have to go on regarding him as simply crazy and silent.

If this approach is so effective, then, resonating so honestly within the culture itself, why don't more magazines do it? Control. Most editors and publishers — and all critics — feel useless if they can't tell you what a cultural artifact like a Nirvana record "means." I know. Sometimes I am one. Critics have to box art into a social context. Editors have to demonstrate a vision, a consistent set of "important" values that you should care about. Publishers have to construct a grand pretense behind which you cannot see them, like the Wizard of Oz pulling levers behind his curtain and amplified voice, scrambling to simply articulate what everyone has already indicated months earlier that they will buy if it's presented to them in some glossy, celebrity-laden format. And cruising just under that glossy surface, of course, is a menace as big as Bruce the Shark and infinitely more deadly: the megalomanical need to control people, to steer culture away from the radical and toward the safe. They have to sell you a bill of goods. That's some really glamorous drudgery. Like any other magazine, Ray Gun has to sell, but its unique position in the culture affords it more latitude: Ray Gun takes the huge-money commodity that is Music and gives it all of its possibilities back. Jerks it out of the context wrappers like, "Essential listening for parents struggling to understand their kids," or "Indication of the modern moral malaise," or "Important because it has sold 13 million copies," or "Black music." Instead, Ray Gun asks: "How does this work as music? As art? What happens if we contextualize it with a painting or a dialogue? Do we really have to tell our readers why they should care about Frank Zappa? Do we need to legitimize ourselves with Moon Unit's presence, or should we just let her discover what she wants to say so we can all learn from it?" Ray Gun trusts the smart map

one of the 41 issues completed at the time of this writing have

contained a couple articles, interviews, or discussions delivered by musicians whose work Ray Gun would consider essential to its readers — not to mention the celebrity columns in the Jarretts' Bikini magazine and the regularly-appearing "Think" artist editorial columns in huH — and though listing them all would be pedantic, a few serve to illustrate the style:

practice, few magazines have used it to greater effect. Every

reader to figure out how to "get there."

6.
South of No North

Big-A Anarchy is an organizing principle, a political strategy whereby democracy is localized to place decision-making power in the hands of those most affected by those decisions. Rock 'n' roll is little-A anarchy, a bomb. An abberation. A temporary liberation. A quickie in a toilet stall that no one ever mentions again. Prolonged contact will kill you. How do we talk about it? Because of course we do talk about it. I, personally, talk about it in public every month and then make hundreds of thousands of copies to leave lying around everywhere. How do we organize the way our magazine talks in order to best deliver the bomb?

I've been asking everyone, and one morning asked my friend Doug Aitken, a visual artist, photographer, and filmmaker who's contributed to Ray Gun since issue #1. We sat over breakfast in the Malibu Inn after a session at Zuma Beach where Doug surfed the rare, tubing beachbreak and I attempted to swallow enough of the ocean to create a landbridge to Korea. He said his head was all messed up over a recently-released conceptual book on architecture by Rem Koolhaas and Bruce Mau called S,M,L,XL, and suggested I take a look at it.

That evening, I ducked into Arcana bookstore in Santa Monica just at closing time, spying the book through the window. I reached over the head of a curly-headed man and lifted down this 1344-page tome more resembling a cinder block than an art book, and felt it hot and

31
Out of Control.
Original Illustration.
Doug Aitken. 1996.

32
Issue 02. Ray Gun. October 1992.

Bikini Kill Sp.

Art Direction & Design by David Carson.
Photography by Shawn Scallen.

ticking in my hand. Doug was right; this book is the bomb. Not only is it the bomb, but it is an articulation of the organizing principles behind building the bomb, through graphic design, text, and treatment of its subject, which is architecture. But not an architecture approached as an excisable discipline. Rather, this is architecture as practiced within the inclusive, graphically-textual, textually-graphic, marginally-linear experience of human beings at play in the fields of the Lord, where history has soft boundaries and the spaces transformed by structures become personalized in our minds. This is an approach to space the way we actually live in it. This is architecture à la Ray Gun.

Lee Kaplan was just locking the doors as I began to rattle off questions to him about the book. He put a hand up in front of his face. "Why don't you ask the designer?" he said, referring to the curly-headed man. "This is Bruce Mau." This was some divine intervention, considering his firm Bruce Mau Design is located in Toronto. Bruce smiled and mentioned that questions about Ray Gun often come up during his frequent lectures. We fell right away upon the Problem

constant in all discussion about Ray Gun, but were cut short by closing time. A month later, I got Bruce on the phone.

Bruce Mau: When I give lectures, designers ask me about what the relationship is between my work and Ray Gun. Or work like Ray Gun. So it's a question.

Dean Kuipers: Can you put that in some context for me? Do you teach?

BM: Yeah, I teach at Rice University. They gave me the Cullinan Chair at Rice University at the School of Architecture. Plus I go around and give lectures on my work. In art institutions and art schools, that kind of thing, museums. You saw S,M,L,XL. We do work for museums, artists, other designers.

DK: But it's purely graphic design.

BM: No, not really. We do exhibition design; we're now moving into a new area of creating our own products and producing our own projects.

DK: I described to you that we were in the middle of this ongoing battle over at Ray Gun about —

BM: About the question of legibility.

DK: — the legibility, yeah. Are those the kinds of subjects that people ask you about?

BM: Yeah. My work, for the most part, is crystal clear. So the question is, typically, what do I think about the stuff from CalArts [the California Institute of the Arts, in Valencia, CA, just outside of Los Angeles], or what do I think about Ray Gun? I'm sure you know Ed Fella. Ed's a good friend of mine. I actually taught at CalArts during one semester. Ed, I think is brilliant. But I'm not very interested in the school of it. Because I think, in the final analysis, it doesn't add very much.

DK: When you say "school of it," how would you describe that?

BM: Well, there's a whole troupe of people who've either learned from Ed or just copied him. They've learned how to do what he does. Which is to take letter forms and typographic conventions apart and reassemble them. But he has a special way of doing it. And he originated it. And it's Ed Fella. It's his work. And all the kinda second-rate Ed Fellas are just kinda tragic figures.

But, for me, the real question is: where is the most interesting area to work, and where is there the most

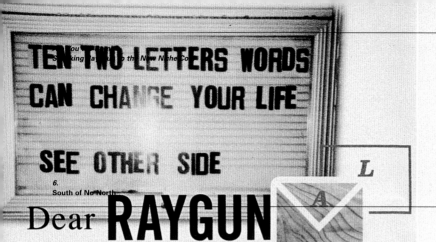

TEN TWO LETTERS WORDS CAN CHANGE YOUR LIFE

SEE OTHER SIDE

6.
South of No North

Dear **RAYGUN**

SEND ALL LOVE/HATE/WHATEVER LETTERS TO:

RAYGUN ACTUAL LETTERS 2812 Santa Monica Blvd, Suite 204, Santa Monica, CA 90404 or e-mail u**S** at raygunmag@aol.com

< s i g h >

I knew it wouldn't last...gone are the days when I used to pick up this magazine for both its content and aesthetic. I dont like what youre doing to my frontal lobes, Rob...lulling them to sleep; and I am disturbed by your forked tongue, Dean.

How can you state (**RAYGUN**) that: "This constructive anarchy is exactly what Raygun has always been about. Its what we will always be about. We want to bring you the new idea, or the new expression that changes your life.... and then turn around and replace the 'curve bending' David Carson with "this guy" Robert Hales?

You ask your readers, Dean: "Where are you going to find the inspiration, the connection, the heart meets epiphany that will lend your own art meaning....

and to answer that I must go back to the day when Rayguns premiere issue hit the stands...**I was floored that it featured** (illustrators) Lane Smith and Matt Mahurins work while exposing my budding design sense to the revolutionary typography of David Carson...while (I know I am rambling)...S I M U L T A N E O U S L Y broadening my musical horizons...and for the next 30 issues...**RAYGUN** was that "inspiration" you speak of.

I may be just some want-to-have-it-all-in-one designer/artist/musician – but I must at least reflect a good percentage of your target audience?

I cant be alone in the mindeset of what you, yourself echo, Dean. the

problem is – you seclude your belief to Rock and Roll when it needs to extend further...it needs to encompass the aesthetic of what you present as Rock and Roll. You say: "Rock and Roll continues to offer the possibility of personal transformation, precisely because its NOT organized and led...and yet...**RAYGUN** has become "organized" and follows other "leads". It has become "Mainstream" in aesthetic and design and presentation of the revolution you claim to promote. It has the effect, in my mind; (to quote you again) of having the "revolution scrubbed out of it." ("it" being **RAYGUN** in this context)

Can you rationalize this, Dean...by stating as you did to your Pal, Legs that "we're not trapped. We're just responsible"??

I very much miss David **Carson's** vision of the "constr ▼✳✳ ◗✳✲▼✝ ◗✦✳ ✳ ✩✩✦✲✳ uctive anarc hy". He inspired me...got those frontal lobes active...forced the reader to read inbetween the lines and dig deeper and question our perception of communication, not only musically...but symbolically and visually as well.

Your new commitment to "r e a d a b i l i t y" in design reeks of conformity. I read you better when I was inspired to do so visually.

The **musical content**...and features on artists are, as always...refreshing. Its not the context of content I am disturbed with. Its merely the delivery of what I "see". Its the layers I miss pulling back. As an **artist/designer/musician** I am feeling that Raygun lends me / us only a fraction of what it once did to the "Kropotkin Quotient". – ya know?

t h a n k s f o r ✳ a l l y o u r t i m e .

Ally via ✳ -mail

(all typos courtesy of Ally)

Corollary #13 to the Kropotkin Principles: The Surgeon Mental has determined that over consumption of art damaged texts and musics can lead to delusions of communication in the aesthetically-impressionable and may contribute to the onset of Cerebrus Arte Damagus.

Ally, Ally, it's got you, my dear! All these references to "frontal lobes" and these endless damned ellipses! You are teetering dangerously on the brink of being one of the "UnCommitted," the most dreaded of fringe doers and consumers. Do not be counted among the teeming millions of well-meaning but undirected and maladvised "alternative" artist/musician/hacker/graphic designer/website geek/snoboarder/ house producer/DJ/journalist/temps who confuse obfuscation and Byzantine

vagaries for intellectualism or even cool art.

Robert Hales is the germ of our mutation. Not to be trite and simplist essence of anarchy is constant flux, the willingness to let go of ossifi We're not afraid. Are you?

It's okay for us to make statements. To make judgments and have then wrong. To practice a form of dialectic where the building blocks are i cynicism, but real text and real ideas and images that hold value. The things to read in our book. Sorry if what you wanted was the kind of valuation that can only mock and never decide what it **IS.** Dean

So I'm sitting here thoroughly enjoying Raygun #32 despite the fact that the la Border's charged me the Canadian price instead of Uncle Sam's. I couldn't care Sonic Youth, but what's it matter when they and Stephane Sednaoui create the n Raygun cover to date? I used to make my friends wash their hands before they h Star Wars figures; now it's my Raygun. Big love,

Robert Winters
Fairfax, Virginia

Having read the article about Hatch Show Print, I DESPERATELY want to co learn more etc. How can I contact them!!! Please help me if you can Mr. Raygun McGonigal!

Darcy Twarog via e-mail

Contact Hatch Show Print at 316 Broadway, Nashville, TN, 37201.

Please give Corinne Day a big sloppy wet kiss for m her photography tremendously ("Goths on Acid" was send you some photographs of mine perhaps short perfection but individual expression has the privileg Great,

Paloma Medina
Corona, California

Hello. As you probably noticed from the envelope, I'm in rehab. My brain's so right now, so if this letter's fucked up in any way, it's due to "Post Acute Withdraw Swear to god, it's a real thing. It's like when your brain gets fucked-up & airhead been used to pot & psychedelics for 10 years. It's also a cool excuse for everyth I'm sending my questionnaire along w/a request that someone send me *someth* greedy for CDs or anything, I just never get any mail. Send me a letter, or *anyth* God, I'm a mail-desperate fool.

By the way, the magazine this month is cool. Got a hell of a kick out of Burro Youth, and I *always* love the reviews, as that's how I shop.

By the time the next issue comes out, I'll be out of here (hopefully). I'm from I'm bugging out in this hick town hospital.

Clean & Sober Devin!
Treehouse Apts. #115, 800 N. LBJ Dr.
San Marcos, Texas 78666

PS. w/o your magazine I wouldn't have jack-shit to read (besi over and over)!

I must give my extreme thanks to you for your story on Kim Deal (RG #33) a was just thinking of marking your reader's poll with Kim as the person I wanted cover. Well, close enough. The world needs more doses of Kim's philosophy. Th Kuipers for showing a different side of Kim, and for getting all of his questions a of. Only played on public radio here in LA, the Amps will probably stay a best ke as the masses are concerned, and that makes us feel just fine. Thanks again to having the sense to feature her. You have proved your musical integrity once ag

Los Angeles

PS. To cafe worker in Dayton, don't think you're the only pla up too drunk to play for. If only you'll play LA one mo

IF IT IS TO BE,
IT IS UP TO ME
RAYGUN

" "   " 7

Bomb?

potential? It's interesting, what you said about the authors, that the Ray Gun authors are finally saying, "Look, you know, forget it." The writers. Like, "You do that to me again and we're through." [laughs] See, in my case, all of our authors, the people that I work for, I only work with them because they have something to say. And they have something to say that I want people to know. So the last thing I want to do is put something between them and the reader. You know, that's going to make it more difficult for the reader to get it.

But I'm not producing a fanzine. And if you produce a fanzine, in a way, what you want to do is the opposite. The greater the distance and the farther you have to go, the more insane the fans become. [laughs] In fact, the distance between the Beatles and their fans was the thing that created the Beatles. But that works for any kind of performance. You know, to create fans, you put a kind of intervention between the fans and the source.

So, in the sense of Ray Gun, it makes a lot of sense to do it. Also, the fact is that most of the stuff written about bands is terrible. So it doesn't really matter too much. It's not James Baldwin's writing.

So we work in very different kinds of worlds. But there are people who are applying Ray Gun's sensibilities to things that are a lot more serious.
DK: When I attempt to take the writing more seriously at Ray Gun, and position that by announcing a shift in our readibility, it has drawn this howl from people like Emigre. I was just reading this piece that came out in Emigre, where the writer was essentially making an argument, saying, "Don't they recognize that the form-over-content formulation of David Carson was already a kind of language, and now you're going to destroy that language?"
BM: But in that case, you have to locate the design and the invention and the depth of visual form in some other place. If you put it in the cone of vision, which is where it has been in Ray Gun — in other words, if you insert screens between the reader and the text — then you're done for. But, in order to do something compelling, you have to put it somewhere else. Not just abandon it. If you abandon it, you'll look like every other magazine.
DK: Exactly. I see your point.
BM: So the problem is, if you want it to be there, where do you put it?
DK: That's what we're wrestling with. But I think there are solutions for that. I don't think it's an intractable problem.
BM: If you look at S,M,L,XL, there's almost no text in the book that is not perfectly legible. There are one or two instances where we allowed the text to basically intersect with the image, get crushed, but only in a couple of places, where it was done as a point.
DK: Do you believe that it's given people a new language with which to look at architecture? Because that's what we do at Ray Gun; that's how I posit what our process is.
BM: Yeah, I think that's a good way of putting it. Basically, we set out to change the terms on which people would consider architectural practice. Not only architectural practice, but all

kinds of creative practice. If you compare it to all the other architectural books, there's no comparison, because they've typically been sanitized to such a degree that you'd swear that people never have sex or any other kind of bodily movements in these buildings.

And the point is that this kind of work is part of life. And it just doesn't make any sense to extract it from life. I think right now it would be very difficult to make an architectural monograph in the old way, if you're serious. Now there's something on the table that stakes out a position, just the way Ray Gun did with music. And what's happening is that certain people align themselves with this new position. And other people don't. The nice thing is that they then are exposed as what they are; they are just conservative hacks.
DK: What do you think that music people are looking for, when they look at Ray Gun? Do you think that they're looking for an exclusivity, for a club that they can own, like a fanzine? Or do you think they're looking for an interpretation of the music that they don't get anywhere else?
BM: I think they're mostly looking to differentiate their identity from all those other identities out there, like Rolling Stone. Right? They don't want to be like Rolling Stone. And all those other music magazines. They want to be the new music. So the new music has to have a different language, a different visual tone, and different visual presentation. This has been happening for decades, this kind of turnover of visual style.
DK: Do you think that Rolling Stone did that when it started?
BM: Oh, yeah, when Rolling Stone happened? Look at the early Rolling Stone magazines. The '60s changed typography. The '60s were doing incredibly experimental typography in other ways. And legibility? Look at those posters for psychedelic stuff. Legibility was not really a priority. It just had to be something that, if you could identify with it, then you would have the staying power to figure out what the information was.

That's why I say, to some degree, difficulty actually works for you and not against you, in your case [Ray Gun]. Because you are differentiating yourself from the market. And you're looking for always a sort of niche market; people who define themselves against the mainstream.
DK: S,M,L,XL is positing this new language. Like you said, putting it on the table for those who choose to go that direction. Do you think that, more universally, there is a need to communicate with new forms, like new languages, across the board?
BM: Yeah, I think that is the case. Every generation has its requirements in this way. We're always in need of new methods. Because of the conditions under which those things occur.
DK: What do you think are the elements of our new needs? I know that one of them is the personal computer.
BM: Yeah, it's based on not only that, but also a kind of capacity to interact with material and content in ways that previous generations could not have imagined.

I work a lot with art museums, and they're in a kinda perpetual state of crisis now. I tell them, "Look. The problem that you have is that, even a generation ago, you basically had

34
Issue 31. Ray Gun. November 1995.
My Life With The Thrill Kill Kult Dps.
Art Direction & Design by Johnson & Wolverton.
Photography by Doug Aitken.

~~a monopoly on the image. You were the place where you could go and see images that you couldn't see anywhere else. So, in terms of dramatic engagement, the museum was one of the most impressive places that you could go. Well, today that's just not the case. Cinema has totally displaced the museum, in those terms. But more importantly, people now have the capacity to create and manipulate images themselves. So making compelling images is damn hard, relative to that."~~

~~DK: The gap has been narrowed.~~

~~BM: Yeah. And if you're working as an artist, you're now working in a context that has been virtually transformed by this new capacity to create things.~~

~~So, for instance, I was walking down the street the other day, and I saw this poster that said, "Cat Found." Somebody had found a little kitten and they did a typesetting job on their poster. Not an extensive one, but I thought, "You know, that is a late 20th century 'Cat Found' poster." [laughs] That could only be done now. Twenty years ago, or ten years ago, it would have been hand drawn and photocopied. And that's really the world in which we're moving. So the kind of interaction that people have with images and typography is just like a totally new situation.~~

~~DK: Does Ray Gun actually help people get closer to the world of their artists, the people that they really identify with in music?~~

BM: It gives them a kind of visual voice. That's, I think, what a magazine is all about. It's about a voice. If it's in Ray Gun, I assume it's a certain kind of culture. And S,M,L,XL, in a way, is a lot like Ray Gun in its cultural position.

DK: You're already going off certain assumptions about the people's sophistication within that culture.

BM: Yeah. And that's, in a way, what I rely on. I don't expect to find the same take on a band in Ray Gun that I would find on a band in Rolling Stone. I don't know if you ever saw those famous ads that they did about the Rolling Stone reader — the yuppie ads? That's as clear as it gets, right?

I'd rather be in Ray Gun than in Rolling Stone. By a long shot. Because that's where I see myself reflected. And for all the music fans it's the same thing. They see themselves reflected there. They're doing it themselves; they're producing their own little indie things, putting their own posters up around town, and all that stuff. And they're copying Ray Gun.

DK: I went to an opening last night for a show at the Los Angeles County Museum of Art featuring the works of William S. Burroughs called "Port of Entry," and we were listening to a lecture by the curator, and I saw a lot of antecedents to Ray Gun in this work. Especially in his work with Brion Gysin; he was talking about destroying language and turning it into a series of symbols and opening up language so it wasn't so restricted to alphabet and containerized languages, per se, like English and French.

And there were these great examples, where he would start off typing something on a page that would be a sentence, and then would get to the bottom of the page and it would be nonsense and then it would turn into Brion Gysin's sort of false Arabic — he used to do this calligraphy that wasn't really Arabic, but looked like it. And then it would run on there until it would just turn into colors or mush.

BM: Wow. Sounds nice. One of the things that I've come to is that images and the visual aspect of communication can do a lot, but it's really imprecise. It's much more intuitive and emotional. Whereas the text and textual communication is where the precision lies.

And, if you look back at what those two cultures represent, essentially what you have on the visual is a pagan visual culture. It's a kind of southern, Catholic, iconographic culture. And on the other, the textual, you have a northern, unemotional, Protestant culture.

DK: Indeed. Yes.

BM: So you're always navigating the space between these two cultures. Between these two regimes of communication. Music is one of those things where it also has a very similar life. In other words, the musical aspect of it is emotional, and works in a way which is very much along the lines of the pagan communication regime. And the textual component of it is what carries the other aspect of it. So one of the things about Ray Gun is that it always has to navigate those two poles; by making the text more visual, you lean toward a more pagan approach to communication and away from — and this is, I think, the critical point for me — is that you lean away from precision. Because, while those things can

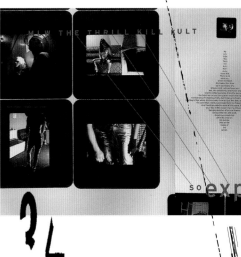

be controlled, *everyone's* interpretation is different.

35
Issue 31. Ray Gun. November 1995.
Cover.
Art Direction & Design by Johnson & Wolverton.
Photography by Doug Aitken.

Are You the Bomb?
Page Nos

71 / 69

I was standing on a surfboard the size of a castle drawbridge, the kind you can rent for $8 an hour on the beach at Waikiki, which is where I was, in fact, about a half-mile off the beach at Waikiki on this board, skimming over the reef just two and a half feet below the surface of the tepid water, all aquamarine and bone white and razor sharp. You can stand up

7.
Kill Yr. Idols

on a board this size when it is not even moving. It is fool-proof. The wave was about 18 inches tall and rolled on toward the beach, unchanging for about a half mile, under cumulus clouds as tall as God. To my right was a 13-year-old Japanese supermodel in a rubberized microkini more expensive than my hotel room and a WWII vet come back to visit the Arizona memorial at Pearl Harbor. Both cruising along just like I was. To my left was Doug Aitken, the photographer on this trip, slogging forward with one lifetime of surfing tied behind his back, as exhausted as I was after spending almost 40 straight hours trying to get a story on a band called My Life With The Thrill Kill Kult. I don't know why we had gone to such extremes to get a story about My Life With The Thrill Kill Kult, but by then we were done, and we had three hours to lay on this lovely, forgiving wave before we had to board a plane back to LA. I stared ahead at the beach in front of the Ala Moana Hotel, where a huge bunch of people were gathering in the late afternoon swelter. The air smelled like it was swollen with storms of wet plumeria, and it came tagging across the water pregnant with the sounds of Iggy Pop. Iggy Pop doing "I Wanna Be Your Dog." Except, of course, it wasn't Iggy Pop. It was the cover band doing Iggy Pop at happy hour at the beach bar at the Ala Moana. And all the tourists were fully rocking out, doing the Frug or the Fox Trot or whatever dances it is that people think they remember when they have had six too many mai tais on the beach at Waikiki. The sand was flying under their feet like one of those old comic book ads for the Charles Atlas bodybuilding program and the synth player was really laying into that one tonic piano note — tink tink tink tink tink tink tink tink tink. The singer was belting, "An' now Ah'm ready to close ma ahyes...." And the wave swept me over the brightly-colored fishes, agape, paralyzed in the grips of a hundred stinging tentacles of an anemone called time, and I thought about all those earnest young goth kids dressed in black at the show the night previous watching My Life With The Thrill Kill Kult, and I thought about growing up in Michigan listening to Iggy and knowing that nothing I could ever learn could undo the threat in his sinewy abandon, and I thought about the fact that there's always got to be somebody new to provide the threat, and that My Life With The Thrill Kill Kult seemed to be threatening, and that our job at Ray Gun was to make a picture of it, to just provide a picture so everyone could know what the threat looked like, what the promise of destruction looked like, and I looked over at Doug and I said to myself, "Just make a video of this moment,

man. This is it. This is really it."

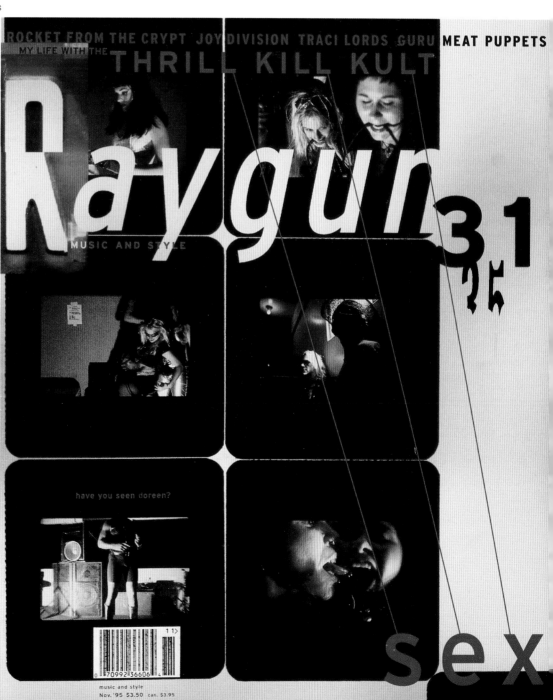

the

FIRST PAGE

AR

Black

Ray Gun. Like the best rock and roll, a magazine conceived in white heat. Raw by choice. Immediate by necessity. Alternative by design.

Why? Because we're fans. Pure and simple. We still believe that music and the people who make it can change the world. Have to, in fact. Because if we don't, no one else will.

We could, of course, give you the standard adjectival rap, and promise that Ray Gun will be penetrating, illuminating and razor-sharp. But we'd rather you find that out for yourself.

And as you do, clue us in on what you think. In the meantime, thanks to the musicians, journalists, photographers and artists, advertisers, publicists and people within the media for generously giving us support, access and belief.

Now, to paraphrase one of our inspirations, it's time to put the Ray Gun to your head and freak out in a moonage daydream all your own.

page one halfed   8/19/92 11:32 PM   Page 1 (1,1)

1

"Shaun: *Sandinista. I bought that,   I didn't steal it. And 'London Calling.'*

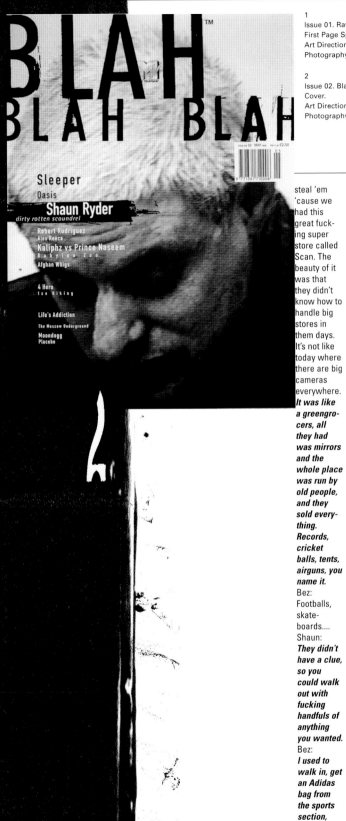

BLAH™
BLAH BLAH

Sleeper
Oasis
Shaun Ryder
dirty rotten scoundrel

Robert Rodriguez
Alex Reece
Kaliphz vs Prince Naseem
Babylon Zoo
Afghan Whigs

4 Hero
Ice Biking

Life's Addiction
The Moscow Underground
Moondogg
Placebo

MAY £2.50

1
Issue 01. Ray Gun. September 1992.
First Page Sp.
Art Direction & Design by David Carson.
Photography by Pat Blashill (top), Elliot Earls (bottom).

2
Issue 02. Blah Blah Blah. May 1996.
Cover.
Art Direction & Design by Chris Ashworth & Neil Fletcher @ Substance.
Photography by Peter Anderson.

Out Of Control (B)
Page Nos.
Issue 05. Blah Blah Blah. August 1996.
Art Direction & Design by Chris Ashworth
& Neil Fletcher @ Substance
Photography by Davies & Davies

72 / 73

booze was and get your cider and your fucking Party Seven or fucking whatev-

er, and then go in the tent and then sit eating your fucking Cakes and getting stinky fingers and partying. It was top.
Bez:
It went bankrupt." –

Joe Strummer interviews Black Grape, Ray Gun #32, December /January 1996.

steal 'em 'cause we had this great fucking super store called Scan. The beauty of it was that they didn't know how to handle big stores in them days. It's not like today where there are big cameras everywhere. *It was like a greengrocers, all they had was mirrors and the whole place was run by old people, and they sold everything. Records, cricket balls, tents, airguns, you name it.*
Bez:
Footballs, skateboards....
Shaun:
They didn't have a clue, so you could walk out with fucking handfuls of anything you wanted.
Bez:
I used to walk in, get an Adidas bag from the sports section, walk 'round, fill it up, and then skate out on a skateboard. We'd
Shaun: You had tents set

up in there so you could get your cream cakes in a box

with your bird, then go down to the aisle where the

Normally every album we had was robbed. We'd

BLAH™
BLAH
MTV MUSIC TELEVISION
Nurse, the screens...
Johnny Dean
gets some therapy
Neneh Cherry
Shampoo
Beastie Boys & Björk
Mark Morrison
Chuck D
Kate Moss
X-Large:
The Godfather of Rap
Street graffiti
Surf enda
Insane boarding
Benchmania
Computer crime
Sean Penn's
brother &
Uma Thurman's dad!!
MENSWEAR

4
Issue 39. Ray Gun. September 1996.
Beck Dps.
Art Direction & Design by Robert Hales.
Photography by Danny Nicks.

"I'VE ALWAYS FOUND THAT THE MOST STIMULATING
THING ABOUT OTHER ARTISTS IS NOT WHAT THEIR
THINGS MEAN, WHICH IS ALWAYS SORT OF BORING
'CAUSE I'M QUITE HAPPY WITH MY OWN INTERPRE-
TATION, BUT HOW THEY GET THERE." DAVID BOWIE
INTERVIEWED BY MOON UNIT ZAPPA,
RAY GUN #30,

OCTOBER 1995

"I hate the perfect take. I hate the
flawless performer because there's
nobody there. There's no picture. I
hate the flawless lyrical line. You
don't think that I could write
something that I could sell to
Whitney Houston? I could. It just
would be so bland, so universal,
everything that I would want to
say, that it would sound like a letter
from me, would turn into those

letters your mother made you
write: 'Thanks for the gift, I always

wear it.'"
— Liz Phair, Ray Gun #21,
November 1994

"IT'S REALLY HARD TO MOVE ABOVE YOUR

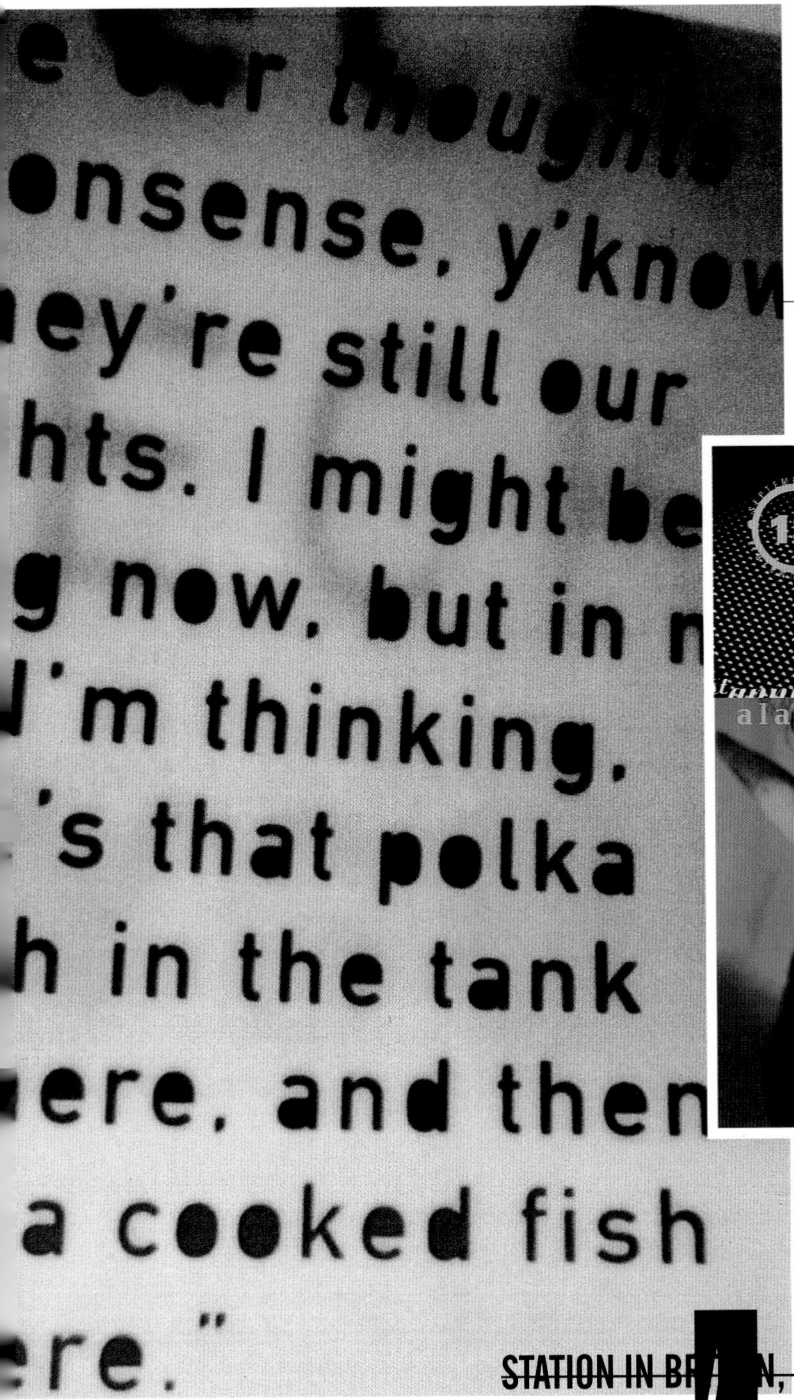

Issue 13. huH. September 1995.
Cover.
Creative Direction by Vaughan Oliver. Design by Jerôme Curchod.
Photography by Kevin Kerslake.
Cover image photo by Dennis D...

WEARING FUNNY TROUSERS." 7

Out of Control
Page Nos

DAVID BOWIE INTERVIEWED BY MOON UNIT ZAPPA.

STATION IN BRITAIN, IT'S VERY HARD TO CHANGE ROLES. AND, UH, BEING

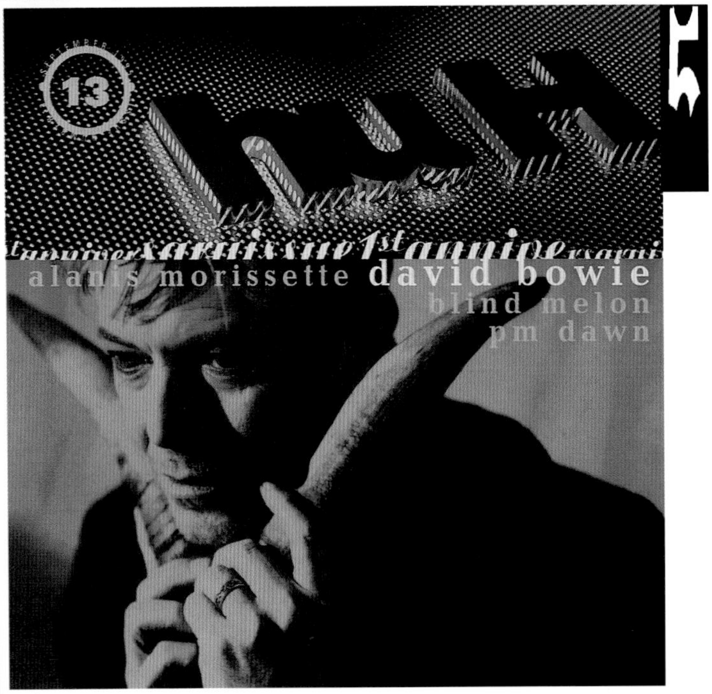

A ROCK SINGER — A ROCK GOD — IT'S QUITE

HARD TO CONVINCE PEOPLE THAT YOUR INTERESTS EXTEND OUTSIDE THE

RAY GUN #30 OCTOBER 1995

PARAMETERS OF PURELY BEING UP ON STAGE

e our thoughts
onsense, y'know
ey're still our
hts. I might be
g now, but in n
I'm thinking.
's that polka
h in the tank
ere, and then
a cooked fish
ere."

raygun #37

"Put your ray gun to my head"
— David Bowie
199

courier
helvetica
new york
palatino
symbol
times

76 / 77

2nd1stpg

Second issues are difficult. The first issue leaves you euphoric but exhausted; the second, with much self-inflicted pressure to recreate yourself all over again.

The result of this effort is now, literally, in your hands. It is, as you can see, like the music it celebrates, it is rough and raw. While polish would be nice, at this point it's a luxury. Considering our subject matter, not a particularly important one, at that.

Along the same lines, the small nature of our staff and the geographical distance separating the offices of the three principals (Marvin in Los Angeles, Neil in Laguna, David in San Diego) mean that mistakes are inevitable. We certainly made enough of them in the first issue. But bear with us. They are undeniably regretable, but matters of detail, not of spirit.

In the meantime, we'd like to thank everyone, from the writers and artists to the people in the print and record industries to the musicians and, finally, the people who bought *Ray Gun* for your support. It's a cliche but we couldn't do it without you. It's not something we plan on forgetting, either.

The Prodigy

White Heat , White Out , White Noise ,

Images: Davies & Davies
Storyboard: Lisa Verrico

"Fame's shit.

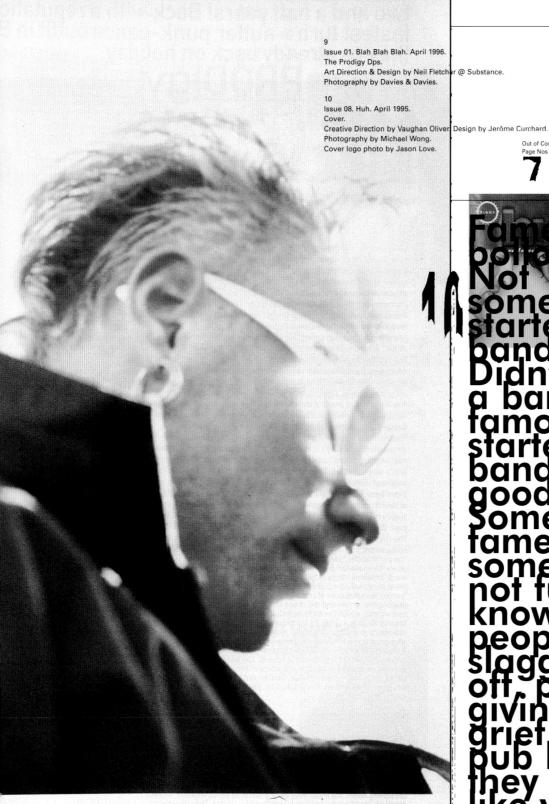

10

"Fame's bollocks. Not something I started the band for. Didn't start a band to be famous; started a band to play good music. Some of fame's fun, some of it's not fun. Ya know, people slagging you off, people giving you grief in a pub because they don't like your music. Little bits and bobs. It's 50—50." Liam Gallagher of Oasis,

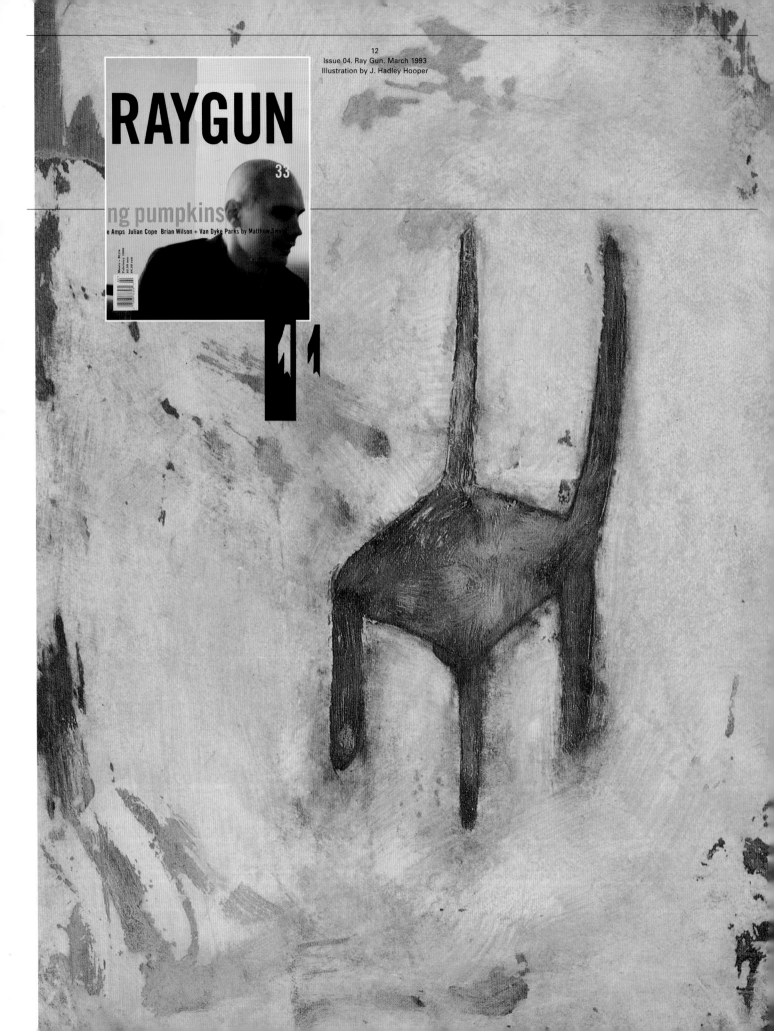

RAYGUN

ng pumpkins

e Amps Julian Cope Brian Wilson + Van Dyke Parks by Matthew Swe

"It's just music. It's like anything else. It's like wallpaper. It's not worth dying for."
James Iha of Smashing Pumpkins, RG33

"I still do think bands are important, but I don't think it's as important as it once was. I think that videos and hyper-media have all diminished that impact. In my youth, you saw the person in an idealistic way. Nowadays, rockstars are too human. So the impact of the message is not coming from up on the mount. When I was 14 and I thought about Jimmy Page, I didn't think he was, you know, unhappy and bitter. I imagined him on a jet with naked women."
Billy Corgan, RG33

"In the past, I thought, 'Okay, I'll let them see into me, the real person.'"

WELCOME TO RAY GUN 40UR. HAVE A SEAT

"I thought there was a sort of poignancy in that. I found out that that's a dead-end. Deep down, I don't think anybody wants that reality or that reflection."
Billy Corgan, RG33

11
Issue 33. Ray Gun. February 1996
Smashing Pumpkins Cover.
Art Direction & Design by Robert Hales
Photography by David Jensen

Issue 33. Ray Gun. February 1996
Smashing Pumpkins DPS.
Art Direction & Design by Robert Hales
Photography by David Jensen

Out of Control {B}
Page Nos

SURRENDER

Stealthily, sweetly, and oh so indiscreetly, Billy Corgan and his Smashing Pumpkins have resolutely stalked the un-punk-ness of megastardom. After seven years, a gold *Gish*, a triple-platinum *Siamese Dream*, and a platinum *Pisces Iscariot*, the poster-children for the dysfunctional American family finally know they're for real.

Article by Dean Kuipers
Photography by David Jensen

"So this interview is for Ray Gun. Does that mean I should speak in hard-to-read fonts?"

— Greg Graffin of Bad Religion, Ray Gun #12, December/January 1994

14

huH
the presidents of the united states of america
soundgarden's kim thayil

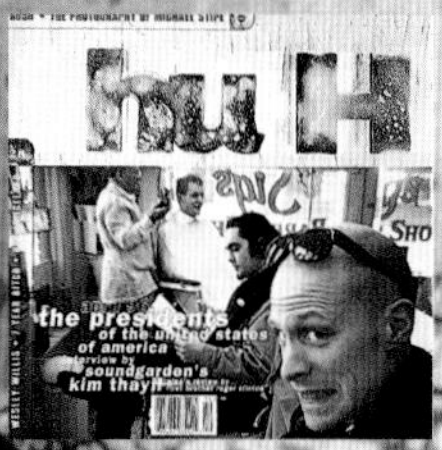

14
Issue 20. Huh. April 1996.
Cover.
Creative Direction by Vaughan Oliver. Design by Jerôme Curchod.
Photography by Alison Dyer.
Cover logo photo by Jason Love.

17
Issue 37. Ray Gun. June/July 199
The wRath of ralph.
Art Direction & Design by Rober
Illustration by Ralph Steadman.

17

The wRath of ralph
Does Ralph Steadman wield the most vicious pen in modern illustrating? Or the funniest? Kevin P. Simonson talks with him about his newest project, a 50th Anniversary issue of George Orwell's *Animal Farm*, and learns you don't get tears of laughter without tears of rage.
SUPE
DLOU
THAN
EUL
EGA(
TORF
R.SO

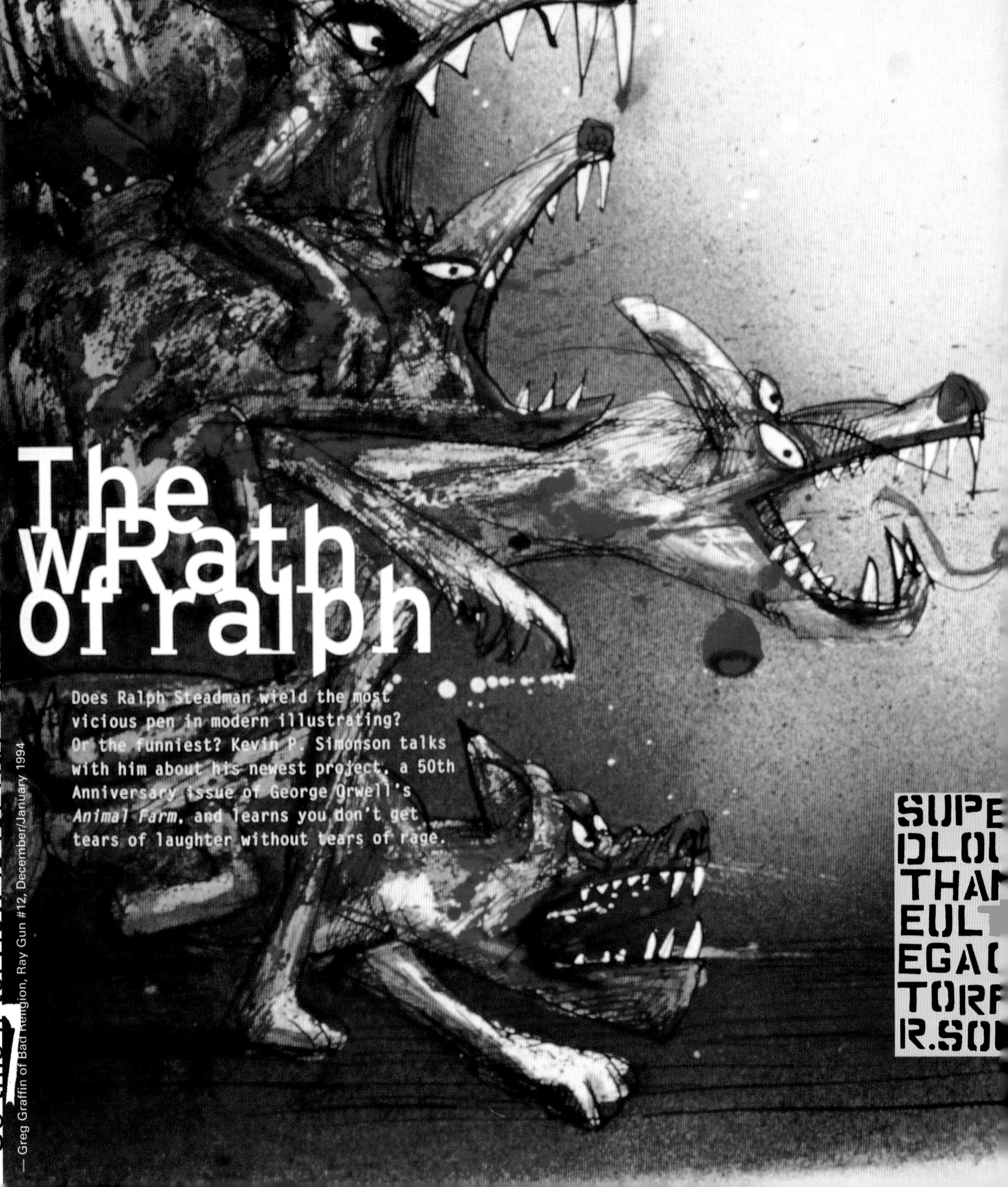

"I never got into *Apostrophe* or *Overnite Sensation*. I think it's because when I was 18 at U of Illinois, they were having a punk party and these frat types were wearing long underwear and drinking Everclear and Kool-Aid out of a garbage can; they were listening to *Apostrophe* and singing all the lyrics. That ruined my first impression, unfortunately." –

Kim Thayil of Soundgarden
remembering Frank Zappa, Ray Gun

#30, October 1995

16
Issue 37. Ray Gun. June/July 1996.
Soundgarden Dps.
Art Direction & Design by Robert Hales.
Photography by Wyatt Troll.

Out of Control {B}
Page Nos

{ 2 / { 3

Soundgarden

like falling

off a
hog

We wanted a shot of Soundgarden's Chris Cornell astride a custom sad Harley, and an interview on greasing nuts and hard helmet action. Apparently, that was "too Bon Jovi". Hey, how about some pictures back at the hotel and a 40 minute chat around at the record company offices?

across the conference table: Max Bell
suite pics: Kevin Westenberg

1 5

1 5

ЗА
IR
JV
ЛM
НO
GE
JG

15
Issue 03. Blah Blah Blah. June 1996.
Soundgarden Dps.
Photography by Kevin Westenberg.
Art Direction & Design by Chris Ashworth.

18
Issue 01. Ray Gun. November 1992.
Sound In Print Sp.
Art Direction & Design by David Carson.
Illustration by Jason Holly.

19
Issue 05. Blah Blah Blah. August 1996.
Mark Morrison Dps.
Art Direction & Design by Chris Ashworth & Neil Fletcher @ Substance.
Photography by Terry Lewis.

20
Issue 01. Ray Gun. November 1992.
Contents page.
Art Direction & Design by David Carson.
Photography by Spike Jonze.

song: two lips, two lungs, and one tongue **group:** by nomeansno **artist:** jason holly

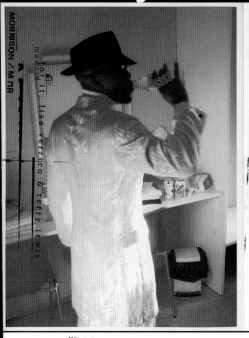

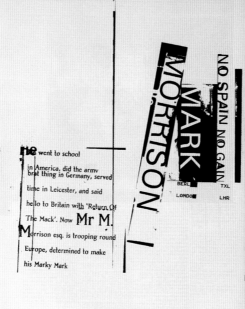

MARK MORRISON

NO SPAIN NO GAIN

He went to school in America, did the army brat thing in Germany, served time in Leicester, and said hello to Britain with 'Return Of The Mack'. Now Mr M. Morrison esq. is trooping round Europe, determined to make his Marky Mark

BERL TXL
LONDON LHR

"BACK IN THE BEGINNING, IT WAS LIKE, 'THEY'RE FROM OKLAHOMA CITY, THEY MUST SUCK.' OR THEY'D BE LIKE, 'I LIKE THEM. YEAH, THEY'RE FROM OKLAHOMA CITY, BUT ABOUT THAT PART OF IT.' WHAT'S WRONG WITH BEING FROM OKLAHOMA CITY? WHAT'S WRONG WITH BEING FROM MARS?" — WAYNE COYNE,

THE FLAMING LIPS,
RAY GUN #29,
SEPTEMBER 1995

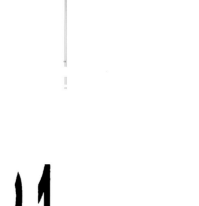

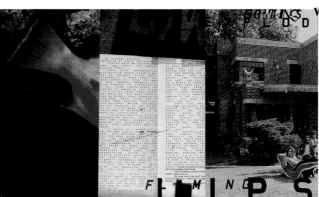

22
Issue 02. Blah Blah Blah. May 1996.
Robert Rodriguez Dps.
Art Direction & Design by Chris Ashworth & Neil Fletcher @ Substance.
Photography by John Holden.

"I THINK YOU HAVE TO BE EITHER IN A POSITION OF POWER OR BECOME A REALLY CLOSE TO

HE'S JUST FILMED A VAMPIRE MOVIE IN A STRIP BAR
CALLED THE TITTY TWISTER,
IN WHICH HE PERSUADED SEX-MEX ACTRESS SALMA
HAYEK TO GET DIRTY WITH QUENTIN TARANTINO.
ROBERT RODRIGUEZ, THE DIRECTOR WHO CAN BUDGET A
TEN DOLLAR MOVIE AND STILL HAVE CHANGE FOR THE
CAB HOME, IS TAKING A BITE OUT OF HOLLYWOOD

GARLIC PRESS: **BOB McCABE**
CRUCIFIX POSES: **JOHN HOLDEN**

24
Issue 04. Ray Gun. March 1993.
Cover.
Art Direction & Design by David Carson.
Photography by Michael Halsband.

23
Issue 18. Ray Gun. August 1994.
Lush Dps.
Art Direction & Design by David Carson.
Photography by Michael Lavine.

Out of Control (B)
Page Nos.

music + style (the bible of)
raY Gun
Goodbye pixies,
hello frank lack!
dereche mode,
the 1st interview
belly, ultra
vivid scene,
come, tommY
stinson, the
the, the sour
dragons,
John cale,
redd kross
meets
debbie
gibson,
etc.

march!
1993
number 4
$3.50 u.s.a.
$3.95 canada

25
Issue 36. Ray Gun. May 1996.
Rage Against The Machine Dps.
Art Direction & Design by Robert Hales.
Photography by Spike Jonze.

ZACK DE LA ROCHA

TOM MORELLO

BR___ WI__

T__ BO___

ABC

HIJK

OPQ

VWX

890.

I LOVED MIDWESTERN 7-ELEVEN

LOT ROCK BUT THE THING THAT I

I LOVED MIDWESTERN 7-ELEVEN PARKING
LOT ROCK BUT THE THING THAT I ALWAYS
FOUND WANTING IN THOSE SONGS WAS
LYRICAL CONTENT. IT WAS LIKE,"WELL,
THIS IS A BUNCH OF GREAT RIFFS AND I
AM BEING ROCKED BY IT, BUT IT'S ABOUT
DRAGONS AND SORCERERS"

TOM MORELLO

DEF

KLM

RST

"THERE IS NO SUCH THING AS apolitical MUSIC. ESCAPIST MUSIC IS VERY POLITICAL IN

MUSIC+STYLE 36
RAYGUN
RAGE AGAINST
THE MACHINE
PULP/CRACKER/DOGTEAL TONS/
STEREOLAB/COCKS

RAGE
AGAINST
THE
MACHINE

All the World's a Rage

At just what point does the personal become the political?
The guys in **Rage Against the Machine** may wear their revolution on their sleeves, but **Sandy Masuo** meets them in Los Angeles and halfway around the globe in Australia to find four men wrestling with the past.

Photography by **Spike Jonze**

27
Issue 36. Ray Gun. May 1996.
Cover.
Art Direction & Design by Robert Hales.
Photography by Spike Jonze.

26
Issue 36. Ray Gun. May 1996.
Rage Against The Machine Dps.
Art Direction & Design by Robert Hales.
Photography by Spike Jonze.

28
Issue 24. Ray Gun. March 1995.
Cover.
Art Direction & Design by David Carson.
Photography by Michael Lavine.

CONSTANTLY SINGING HOMOPHOBIC SONGS, IT CONTRIBUTES TO AN ATMOSPHERE IN WHICH IT'S OKAY TO DISLIKE GAY PEOPLE." – TOM MORELLO OF RAGE AGAINST THE MACHINE, RAY GUN #36, MAY 1996

ved Midwestern 7-Eleven parking lot rock. That's what I was all about as a 13-year-old, but the thing that I always found ...ing in those songs, even as a young lad, was lyrical content. It was like, 'Well, this is a bunch of great riffs and I am being ...cked by it, but it's about dragons and sorcerers!'" Tom Morello of Rage Against the Machine, Ray Gun #36, May 1996

UPHOLDING THE STATUS QUO. YOU MAY NOT HATE GAY PEOPLE, BUT IF TEN OF YOUR FAVORITE RAP ARTISTS ArE

The Closing Down by David Bowie

BOWIE DIVIDER 13/11/96 12:58 pm Page 1
Tony Oursler
Roy Lichtenstein
Yoko Ono
Oursler

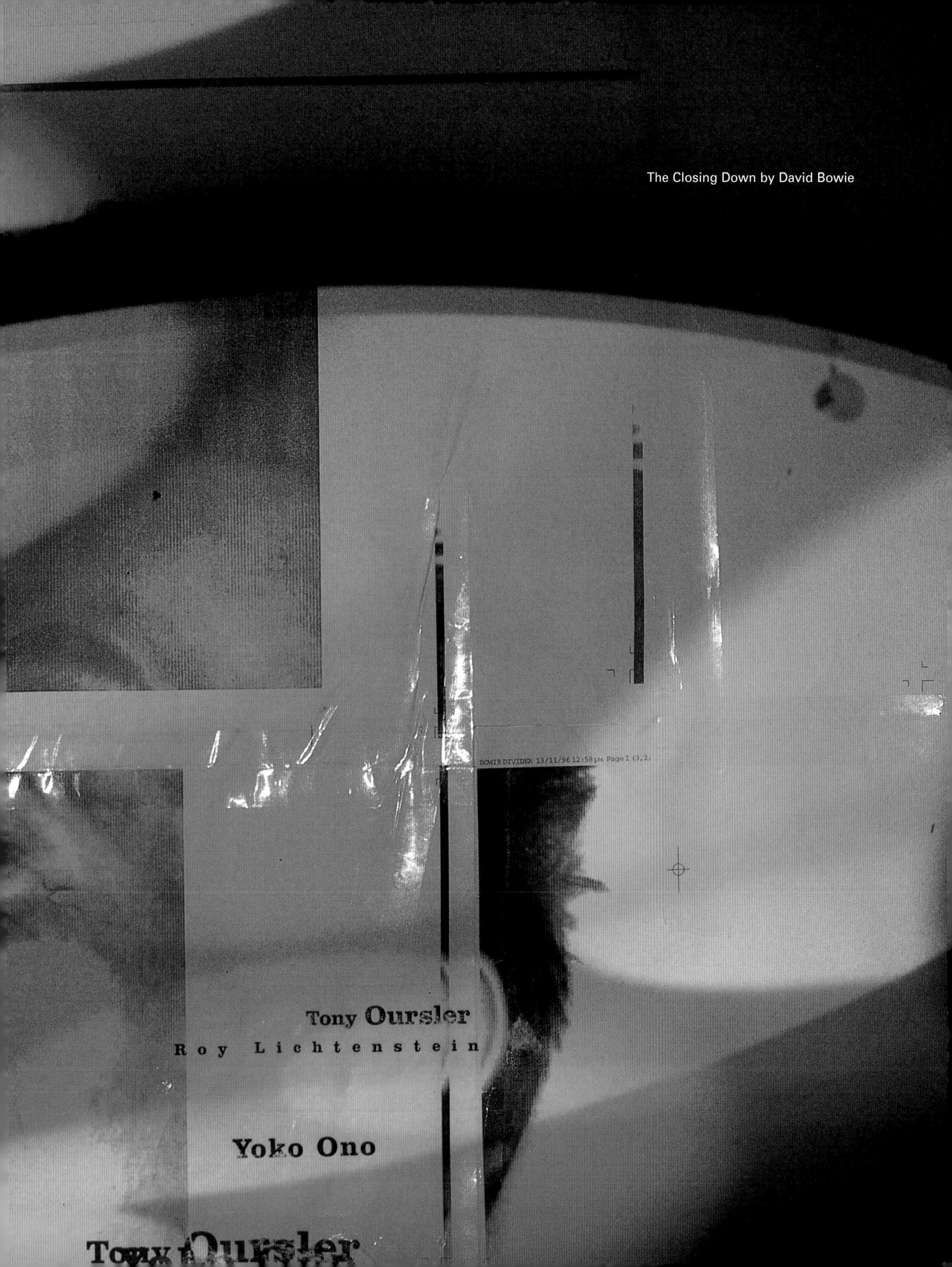

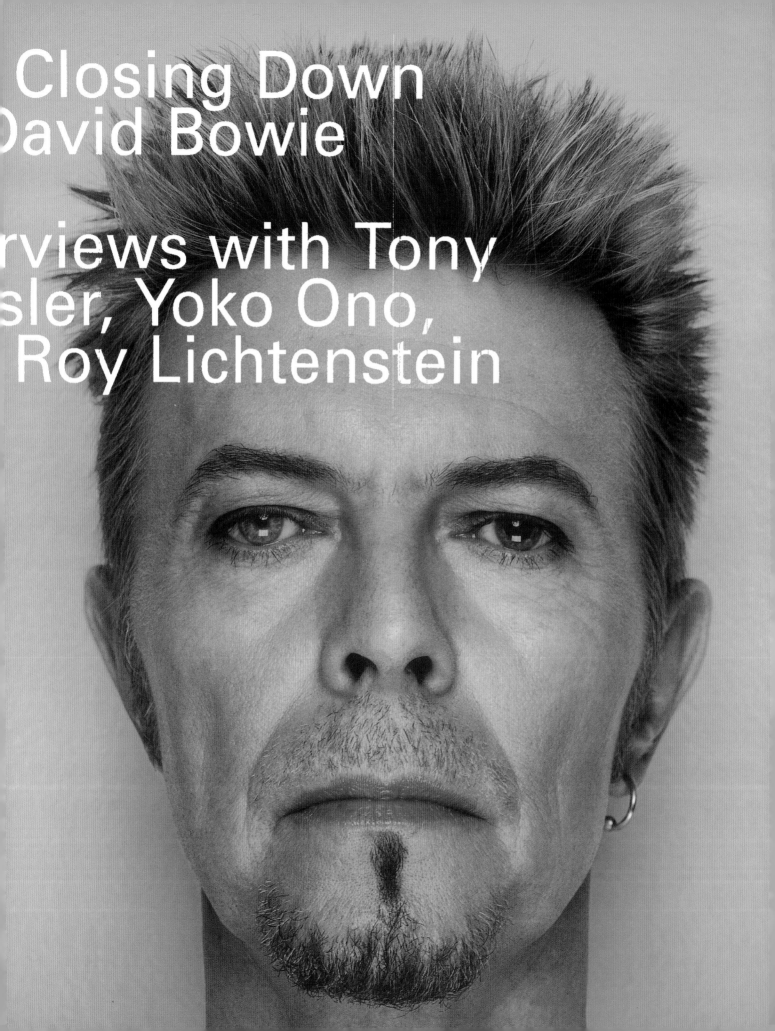

Closing Down
David Bowie

rviews with Tony
sler, Yoko Ono,
Roy Lichtenstein

The Cl...
by Da...
2/93

Intervi...
Oursle...
and R...

David Bowie photographed by
Davies & Davies

Tony Oursler

David Bowie   When do you say, "Okay, this piece is now finished?"

Tony Oursler   For me, a work is not complete until it's put into the place of the viewer — or the participant, as I like to call an audience. And I think that goes across all the arts, unless perhaps it's mathematics or something like that. But I'm always trying to make the art function as the first half of the sentence or the negative of a positive shape or any way the dialogue is going to continue in the viewer's brain, because I never really even consider the pieces finished until somebody looks at them.

DB   However, do you feel that maybe when you are creating something, are you putting yourself in the place of — or even second-guessing — the participators?

TO   Yeah, definitely. Well, I may to some degree....

DB   That you take yourself as being an everyman in terms of how you think

TO   Well, you don't want to over- or underestimate who you are. I just had this conversation with Paul McCarthy the other day. He was in town here, and he said that he really thought that artists were completely detached from society in general because, you know, in terms of politics and so many things, we

These days it's called closure. It's the resolution of something that hangs over for maybe a day, maybe a lifetime. For an artist,whether working in the musical, visual or plastic arts, attempts to embrace a closure on a piece of work can lead to both multiple-option, confusion or block. In my case, each is the result of a conflict over the status of the work.
Is it supposed to have a "meaning," or — as often happens for me —
has a certain set of dictates or creative devices
presented me with an altogether new scenario? One that I could never have forseen?

Three artists, two of whom I know and one, Roy Lichtenstein,
whom I've recently had the pleasure of meeting, allowed me to throw
questions to them that delved a little into this peculiarly art-based
situation.

First, Tony Oursler, New York media artist and installationist.
He makes these scary little creature-people imprisoned by their own video-projected faces.

P92/93 & 97–T-Shirt by Helmut Lang,
Trousers by Calvin Klein, Shoes by John Fluudg
P94–Jacket by Calvin Klein

DB

TO

DB

TO
DB

TO

DB

TO

DB

TO

DB

never know what people are into; we're always wrong (laughs). Regard the Surrealist and Communist manifestos. (Laughter) I'm not really interested in the work being a complete didactic gesture; I'm much more interested in the way that it is created. I mean, I always thought that one of the most beautiful things about music, that oftentimes gets lost in art, is that people kind of live with the music and they can drive with it or clean their house or fuck with it or whatever they want to do, and it kind of mutates into their life, you know? That's the kind of a dialogue I think is oftentimes missing from the plastic arts. But, for me, it's important from the conception of the work.

Well, that's interesting. Is it possible that you would create some thing by any means necessary to provoke a dialogue rather than having had created something assuming a dialogue would then take place?

Yeah, definitely.

So the priority for you is the dialogue rather than the piece itself?

Yeah, definitely, because I think the piece is really created in the mind of the viewer and that the key is that it wouldn't exist any other way. It actually exists in the eye of the beholder, so to speak.

When you undertake a piece, whatever it is, whether it's a more theatrical piece or whether it's a more sculptural piece, do you often find that the work contains information that you had not intended when you had started the piece?

Yeah, I think so. I mean, sometimes if a piece is really a dud, I find it doesn't have any information (laughs). I mean, oftentimes I think, looking back on the work again, it's almost a perceptual problem whether *I* change or *it's* changed. Everything changes. It's kind of hard to anchor these things.

Yes, it really is. I was going to ask you to bravely suggest why it happens that sometimes we can stand back when we finish something and say, "God, that's bigger than I intended it to be." I mean, it says much more than I thought it was going to say, and it's like, where does that third influence come from?

Yeah, you have to be able to really see what happened to learn. I guess it's 20/20 vision in hindsight, right? Super clear. Or are you suggesting a possession of sorts?

It's remarkable sometimes how the combination or materials or the choice of notes or, in your case, like

when we projected my face slightly out of position so that the eyebrows became very arched and demonic-like: it said some extraordinary thing. I couldn't put my finger on it, but it was something that I was loathe to recognize in myself. But it's certainly an aspect of myself that you had sort of created by doing that. A possession of sorts, yes.

TO I think it was the alien in you, David, that we immediately saw (chuckle). The gigantic forehead and — I don't know, yeah, that was something pretty strange, though.

DB When Iman and I first got together, there was a small story in one of the papers headlining: "African & Alien". (Laughter).

TO (laughs) That's funny.

The Clothword
Page No

Tony Oursler – "Trance" 1996
Courtesy of the artist and Metro
Pictures

Styling by Freddie Stopler & Randy Smith
at NEXT N.Y.C.
Hair & make up by Paul Starr
at Debbie Walters N.Y.C.

Yoko Ono

Yoko Ono, New York performance, musical, conceptual and visual artist. Also a sculptress. In the late '50s she was one of the much-undervalued New York group, Fluxus.

David Bowie

Yoko Ono

DB

YO

DB

YO

DB

YO

When you really started your involvement in the New York scene in the late '50s and '60s, were you particularly aware that your work was changing the nature of the dialogue between the public and the artist?

Well, I was one of those cocky people who really wanted to do something that was new, and thought that unless it was something new it didn't mean anything.

Were you more concerned to break with the conventional, or did you feel at that time that you had particular statements that you wished to put over to people?

Well, I was feeling that adding a certain action to the ordinary life was important, to add an action...without doing that, it was somehow difficult to survive, to live. That was the feeling. It was really interesting, because one uncle was a painter and one uncle was a sculptor and my mother was a very good painter, so the environment I was brought up in was like everybody was so incredibly creative, and I kind of went against it, I think...the normal route of expressing one's self in art, you know?

In terms of constructing a vocabulary, is it inevitable for the artist to be totally misinterpreted?

Sure. I think that's alright. That is to be expected. I don't think an artist is really trying to control the response as much as just wanting to express an idea. When John and I thought about bed-in, we thought it was a hilarious and interesting idea. A good idea. Then it was knocked like crazy by the journalists and the public. I really didn't think we were going to be knocked. I didn't think we were going to be praised, either. You can't presuppose the reaction to your work; it's always a gamble. It's almost like throwing the dice in the air each time.

I think the interesting thing — this is more of an observation than a question — is that when an artist is working with a new kind of vocabulary, which bed-in, for instance, was seen as at the time, that often the language is not understood until many years later. And then it's seen in its social context. So it is possible that an artist working with a contemporary vocabulary is often very out of sync during his or her own time and that, in retrospect, the language becomes clear because people will have learned the vocabulary in the intervening years.

Yeah, that's to be expected, I suppose. Sometimes they don't catch on at all, so it gets lost in the wind. It's nicer if they catch on eventually

DB

YO

(laughs). Sometimes somebody picks it up and it suddenly becomes a fad or something. But because we're trying to communicate in the moment, I feel it's nicer if they really respond at the time (laughs). Usually, I'm so out of sync I feel kind of isolated, but then I get a letter saying, "Did you know that 20 years ago, when I saw this particular piece, that that changed my life?"

Yeah that's really fulfilling when that kind of thing happens, isn't it?

Yeah, but then it's just that person. But even one person... So the thing is, what I'm doing is just expressing myself and if somebody understands it or somebody is inspired by it, you know, I have to be just thankful, that's all. I'm playing that game because, in a way, I don't know any other way of playing the game of life, I suppose.

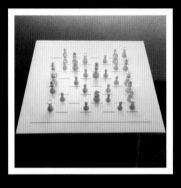

Yoko Ono – "Chess Set" 1966
Chess set of all white pieces
Instruction: For playing as long as you can remember where all your pieces

Iain Macmillan/©1996 Yoko Ono

Roy Lichtenstein

The work of Roy Lichtenstein always confused me. It took me
a long while to decide whether it was merely amusing and ironic or whether
it was cold and judgmental. Needless to say, I find it both.
Roy himself, though, proved to be an immensely generous and naturally
open man with a light but constant bemusement at the world's —
and his own — existence.

David Bowie When you begin a painting or a sculpture, do you find that the finished work often contains information that you had not intended?

Roy Lichtenstein Yeah. I think there's no doubt about it. But usually I do most things through a drawing, so a lot of things are worked out in the drawing. But because the drawing is in one medium and this is another, I allow — I even *want* to make changes.

DB Through the medium itself?

RL No, I don't think so. Well, possibly, in that the color is different, you know, from just colored pencil to colored paint are two different things. I kind of do the drawing with the painting in mind, but it's very hard to guess at a size or intensity of a color and all the colors around it and what it would really look like. It's only a guess at the beginning and I try to refine it. My things look as though once you put it down it's there forever, they seem to be very exacting, but they're really not done that way. I allow for a lot of latitude...but sometimes in order to get the color unity or contrast or whatever it is to work, I'm sacrificing something in the subject that can be very direct...and that's very interesting because that's exactly at the cusp of what I'm trying to do. I want the look very blatant and not subtle and to come on in a strong way, but you don't want to let the painting simply be unresolved in order to do this....

DB I know exactly what you mean. I find this in music as well. All the time.

RL Yeah, you like it to come on like gangbusters, but you get into passages that are very interesting and subtle and sometimes your original intent changes quite a bit. Though I want the style to appear to be mechanical. I think even now, I mean the last things I've done, the Chinese landscapes —

DB Yes, I met you when you were just working on those.

RL — they look contemplative and all of that, but they're really still made of graduated dots that are purely mechanical lines, you know?

DB Here's a really mean-spirited question: Why do you feel that a romantic or emotional situation needs to be represented mechanically?

RL Well, because I think that has a lot to do with — well, comic books for one thing, but also all kinds of things presented through the media in the modern day. I mean, even movies, where you know two people are about to kiss and in reality you've got a guy on camera with a cigar in his mouth right in your face (chuckle), and the stylist just powdered your nose and there's a hundred people watching this and it has nothing to do — I mean, you have to pretend that you're amorous in this situation (chuckle) while there are all these technical people involved. That's something that just comes to mind immediately, and then, of course, it's all transferred to film or digital or however the thing is done....

DB You still seem to ponder the symbols that are represented in the romantic or the emotional situation. You're still very much a man of irony.

RL I know this point has been gotten across (laughs), but sometimes I'm just using my kind of texture, which is only diagonals and dots and unmodulated color and black lines. They are tools I have gotten used to using, but in some cases, like the Chinese landscapes, which are really very zen, they're about something completely at odds with the style of my usual painting. I guess I'm reminded again about that. I don't think I go around continually thinking that everything is presented in mechanical ways. It's not on my mind, I don't think.

DB When you first started, you picked on Mickey Mouse and Donald Duck. Were they arbitrary choices or did you feel there was some inherent information in those two particular characters?

RL I think they were so far from serious abstract expressionism that they embodied everything; they were done mechanically, but they represent something everybody loves or is cute or something. And it's funny how a number of people have done things with Mickey Mouse — Oldenberg and Warhol, you know — they're both a symbol of America and such an anti-art symbol. I think that all this doesn't mean that anymore, probably.

DB Does the general public know when it's looking at art? (Laughter)

RL It's hard to know (laughs). I'm not sure. I'm sure some do and some don't, but you get so far away from the general public, I think, in any of these fields. You know, as you compose music or anything, you're just off in your own world. You have no idea where reality is, so to have an idea of what people think is pretty hard.

DB Are we generally smart at picking up information from art, do you think? As a society?

RL I think much smarter than we were. I think everybody knows that abstract art can be art, and the qualities of art are more abstract than representational, and I think most people know that even though they may not like it they understand that there's another purpose.... I think that most people think that painters are kind of

Roy Lichtenstein "Landscape with Bridge" 1996

Tony Oursler

Picking up on a thought that had occurred to me while talking with Roy, I went back to Tony with a question that dogs me to this day.

ridiculous, you know? (laughs). I think that they think the same of modern composers like Cage. Though I am sure the artist is reacting to something that is already there otherwise...but isn't seen by many people....

DB It is interesting how I find that myself. It's really the accumulation of these different moods that I have had throughout my life and where they've taken me, and I start looking back and I think I've actually created a life out of all of this, out of these changes of mood. They've pushed me through all these years and I seem to have a semblance of a life and if I look very carefully, I can see some thematic design to it. There's some continuity between one period and another.

RL You've created a world that even other people can see, you know what I mean?

DB It's an extraordinary thing. Yes. But to go back again to earlier days. During the '50s and '60s, what kind of effect did people like, say, Keinholtz or Beuys and Nauman and even the Fluxus/Yoko Ono movement — how did you view this? Were you affected by what they were doing in their very own emotive kind of state that kind of erupted into this work that, at the time, seemed impossible to analyze?

RL I was at Rutgers University and it was really a center for Fluxus in a way, and it wasn't what I was interested in, but I think that it had an impact — as did happenings — because I could see that art was changing from expressionism, which I was doing at the time or thought I was doing (laughs)...so it had an efect but it wasn't the direction I really wanted to go in. But....

DB Did it, in fact, even push you further into the direction you were going?

RL Maybe. It might have, actually, because mine is very anti-contemplative, I mean, apparently — though if you thought I was for these commercial products, you'd think that, well, there is no irony. The irony isn't meant to be an ironic comment on our society, exactly, I mean, I don't think I was trying to say that, either. I just felt that these kinds of images are big; it's what people really see. We're not really living in a sort of school-of-Paris world, and the things we really see in America are like this. It's McDonalds, it's not LeCorbusier. But the thing is, I've been saying the same thing over and over for 35 years.... (Laughter).

DB I mean, frankly, your latest work shows a yearning, possibly, for a more contemplative...they're quite the reverse of what you were just saying about your earlier work. There seems to be a sense of yearning towards a more serene inner thing going on with you at the moment.

RL But, in a way, I like it to appear to be serene but also to be pseudo-serene (laughs).

DB This is a stupid question so I wish you luck. Has art — I say this with a small "a," Tony — helped you define your life, or has your lifestyle defined your art and, if so, how?

TO As a kid, I remember deciding to become an artist, thinking, "I like doing these things. And you are your own boss if it works out." Well, I guess yeah, that the art has — I mean, as a path it's lead me very far, because I put myself into it at a young age. Which I guess you did, also.

DB So, like me, you possibly feel it's led you by the nose a bit?

TO Yeah. Sometimes you get used by the system and other times you can use it, zig zag....

DB And you followed all the adventures it's going to take you on.

TO Yeah, I mean, some are pretty embarrasing, but it's the energy of youth, you know. Some of the stuff I look at now, that I don't want to go back to that place or something like that, I'm happy that time exists, thank you.

DB It's interesting that because we do what we do in our way, that we're driven by something that's very emotive, that it is virtually impossible for artists — unlike some other people who can pretty much see ten years down the road — that's impossible to see from week to week what we're going to be doing or what life is going to hold in store for us. It's an incredibly exciting adventure, I think.

TO Yeah, definitely. It's a little bit frightening. I've seen a lot of people burn out along the path.

DB Yeah. That's the downside of it.

TO ...but on the other hand, yeah, I wouldn't trade it, because I feel that, in the end, it's the only way I could have gone. Did you ever imagine where you would be otherwise?

DB Okay. Coming back to these very silly questions. We are to presume, if there is a dialogue, that there's some kind of unconscious vocabulary at work — that there are ciphers and symbols that we will recognize — or, I would ask, do you think that the contemporary movement over the last 20 years or so has so thoroughly deconstructed that vocabulary that we're not quite sure what information to trust or mistrust in the dialogue that is being created? Is this a fragmented dialogue now?

TO Yeah, I definitely think it is, because the way — I mean, we have to be able to read the new language, which is always recreating itself. I noticed when were talking like the first time we met, we had a lot of stuff in common in terms of what we were looking at: pop culture. And then I suspected that maybe — like, a lot of artists whose work I like tend to just keep up on whatever is made, regardless of medium, hi lo culture...and I think that, you know not all artists really do that. Some artists are a lot more hermetic and kind of narrow, say, with color field painting and such.

DB Is a knowledge of art history a help or a hindrance? Somebody's always invented the wheel just before you. Artists in the '50s used to say they couldn't move without feeling Picasso breathing over their shoulder.

TO That's precisely why kids don't want to hear about all this stuff.

DB I know, but it's a shame, because if they were more responsive to it, they'd realize it all just becomes one's palette. That everything you hear and are influenced by merely helps you become a better artist because they become colors in what you do.

TO Well, yeah. That's well put.

DB It's not a question of slavishly imitating what's gone before; it's a question of using that knowledge, these breakthroughs, as being another way of opening the crack in the door even wider.

TO Yeah, and Nauman told me once that, you know, even if it's the same idea, that everyone is going to do it differently.

DB Tony, if something's worth doing, it's worth doing twice! That's what I always say. Nearly always. On Thursdays, anyway.

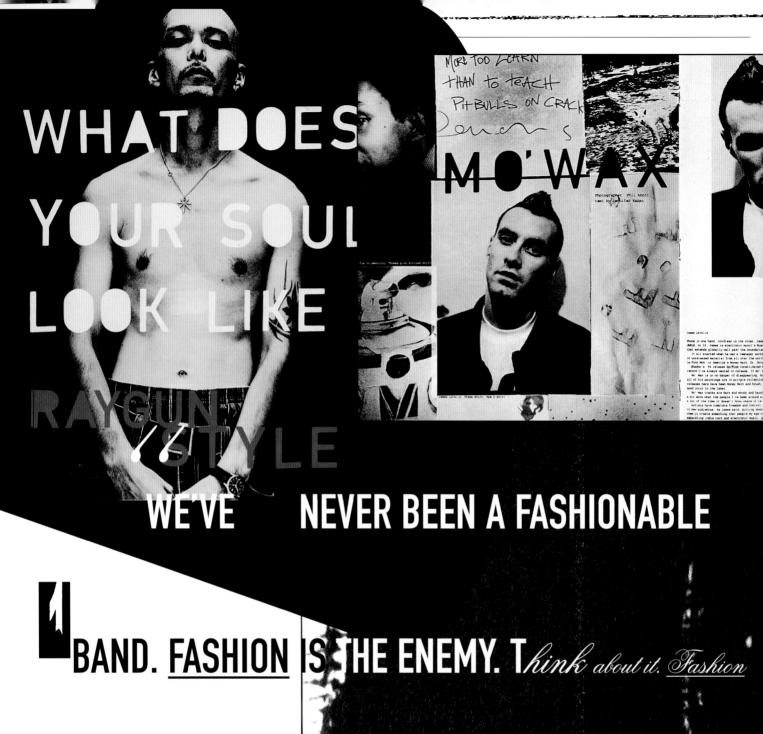

WHAT DOES
YOUR SOUL
LOOK LIKE

RAYGUN /6 STYLE

MO'WAX

MORE TOO LEARN
THAN to TEACH
PIT-BULLS ON CRACK

Photographer Phil Knott
text by Jennifer Kabat

WE'VE   NEVER BEEN A FASHIONABLE

BAND. FASHION IS THE ENEMY. T*hink about it. Fashion*

LOOKING AT ME!

Issue 39. Ray Gun. September 1996.
DJ Krush Style section opener Sp.
Art Direction & Design by Robert Hales.
Design by Anna Liebau & Karin Ludwig.
Photography by Phil Knott.

Issue 39. Ray Gun. September 1996.
Wax Dps.
Art Direction & Design by Robert Hales.
Design by Anna Liebau & Karin Ludwig.
Photography by Phil Knott.

3
Issue 39. Ray Gun. September 1996.
Cast from "Nowhere" Dps.
Art Direction & Design by Robert Hales.
Design by Anna Liebau & Karin Ludwig.
Photography by Matthew Welch.

Style
Page Nos

Katherine Hamnett
Nicole F
Helmut Lang
therine Hamnett
Sweater + Pant

is followed by people who
don't have their own sense of
style. **We've always been outside the mainstream. That's what KISS is all about. Jesus was not part of the mainstream and he didn't do so badly for a Jewish kid."**

CK dress
CK mock

— Gene Simmons of KISS, huH #12,

August 1995

4
Issue 39. Ray Gun. September 1996
Cast from "Nowhere" Dps.
Art Direction & Design by Robert Hales
Design by Anna Liebau & Karin Ludwig
Photography by Matthew Welch

home 'cause I can't have
fans seeing me carrying a
grocery bag home 'cause,
uh, it doesn't look good.'
She says, 'You're nuts with
this shit, you know?!' And
I still do it. I mean, I've
always been very careful in
what the fans are gonna
expect from me and try not
to dissapoint them." —
Johnny Ramone of the
Ramones, Ray Gun #14,
March 1994

"WHAT IF WE COULD MAKE ALL THIS MORE ENTERTAINING?" MIKE MILLS, RAY GUN #34, MARCH 1996

"When I go
out, I always
make sure
I'm

dressed in
my regular
Ramones
clothes, you
know? I
mean, I'd go
out shopping
with my girlfriend and
say, 'Uh, you gotta
carry the grocery bag

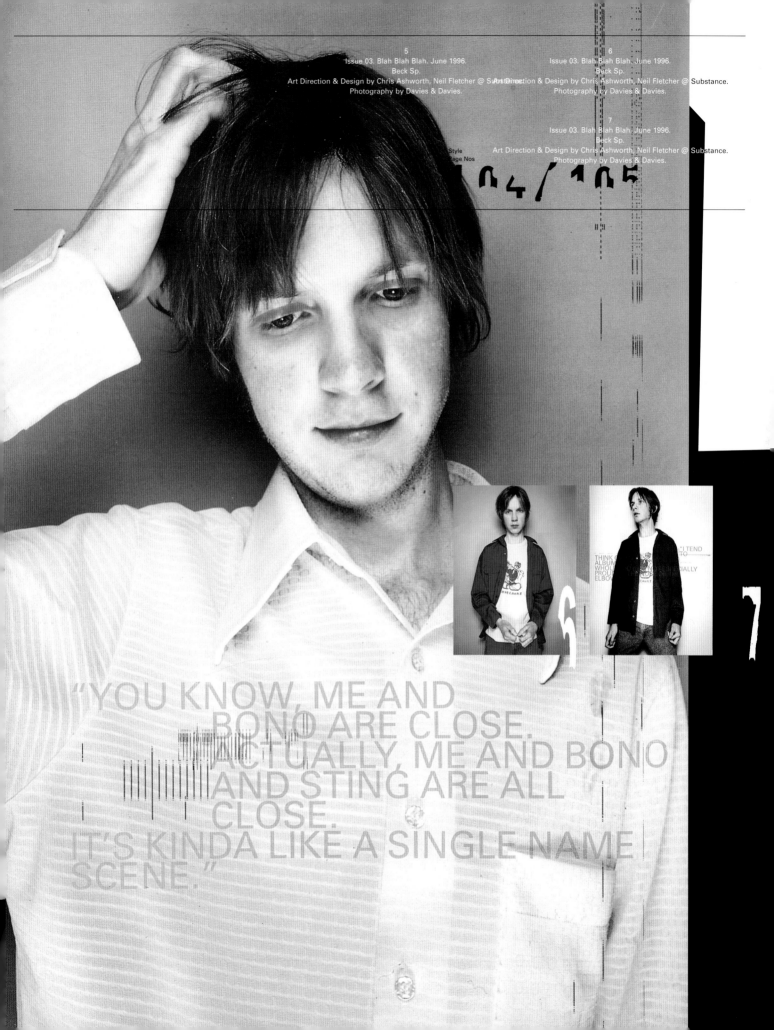

5
Issue 03. Blah Blah Blah. June 1996.
Beck Sp.
Art Direction & Design by Chris Ashworth, Neil Fletcher @ Substance.
Photography by Davies & Davies.

6
Issue 03. Blah Blah Blah. June 1996.
Beck Sp.
Art Direction & Design by Chris Ashworth, Neil Fletcher @ Substance.
Photography by Davies & Davies.

7
Issue 03. Blah Blah Blah. June 1996.
Beck Sp.
Art Direction & Design by Chris Ashworth, Neil Fletcher @ Substance.
Photography by Davies & Davies.

Style
Page Nos

"YOU KNOW, ME AND
BONO ARE CLOSE.
ACTUALLY, ME AND BONO
AND STING ARE ALL
CLOSE.
IT'S KINDA LIKE A SINGLE NAME
SCENE."

"Oh, brother, draw the line in the sand here and now! Seize the code and oust the boot-licking servants of the two dimensions! Multimedia will never go anywhere until the amteurs take over, until the primitives rule and the designers are driven back into their holes."

– David Thomas of Pere Ubu,
Ray Gun #36,
May 1996

02. Ray Gun. October 1992.
owboxing Dps.
irection by David Carson.
n by Jill Pflieger.
ography by Art Brewer.

9
Issue 01. Ray Gun. Septe 2.
Menswear/Neckwear Dps
Art Direction & Design b arson.
Photography by Matt Ma

10
Issue 01. Ray Gun. September 1992.
Footwear Sp.
Art Direction & Design by David Carson.
Photography by Ma in.

11
Issue 19. huH. Marc
Style Dps.
Creative Direction b n Oliver.
Art Direction by Jer chod.
Photography by Da vies.
Styling by Harriet C

Style
Page Nos
106/107

s h a d o w boxing

63

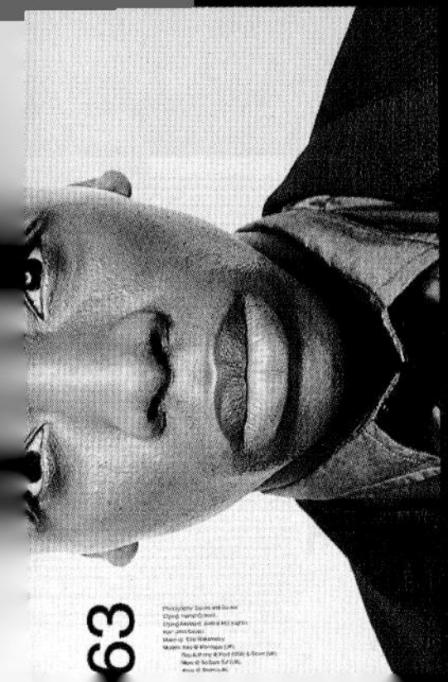

JOOP! DRAGON EMBROIDERED JEAN
AVAILABLE AT NEIMAN MARCUS
BEVERLY HILLS & DETOUR 425
WEST BROADWAY, NY.

DKNY ORANGE VEST
MACY'S HERALD SQUARE

GREY SWEAT SHIRT FROM THE
CENTER THRIFT SHOP 124 E. 28TH.

"I REMEMBER GOING TO KENSINGTON MARKET AND BUYING THIS HOUSE DECORATING BOOK FROM THE 70'S AND THE BLOKE I WAS WITH SAYING, 'THAT IS ACTUALLY THE BOOK OF BAD TASTE, ISN'T IT?',
ROUND AGAIN, IT LOOKS MODERN AGAIN. THE ONLY FRIGHTENING THING IS THE PACE WITH WHICH FASHIONS ARE BEING RECYCLED IN BRITAIN.

ACTUALLY, IT'S NOT JUST THE PACE, IT'S THE FACT THAT IT'S SO OBVIOUS WHAT'S

COMING NEXT. I MEAN, RIGHT NOW, YOU ONLY HAVE TO THINK, 'OKAY, WHAT CAME AFTER NEW WAVE?' YEAH, IT WAS NEW ROMANTICS:

THE HUMAN LEAGUE, SPANDAU BALLET, DURAN DURAN, AND ALL THAT. ACTUALLY, DURAN DURAN DO SOUND FUCKING BRILLIANT AGAIN! I HEARD 'GIRLS ON FILM'

GOD!' I TOLD

12

ANNIE ABOUT IT THE NEXT DAY AND SHE SLAPPED ME ROUND THE FACE. SHE SCREAMED AT ME: 'YOU'RE LOSING YOUR MIND!'" —

JUSTINE FRISCHMANN OF ELASTICA, RAY GUN #25, APRIL 1995

12
Issue 37. Ray Gun. June/July 1996.
Style Dps.
Art Direction & Design by Robert Hales.
Photography by Steen Sundland.
Styling by Cathy Dixon @ Streeters.

13
Issue 39. Ray Gun. September 1996.
Charlie Watts Sp.
Art Direction & Design by Robert Hales.
Photography by Davies & Davies.

Style
Page Nos

WHICH IS WHAT EVERYONE HAD THOUGHT UP TO THEN. SUDDENLY, I WAS LOOKING AT IT THINKING, 'THIS IS   THE BEST TASTE I CAN IMAGINE.' IT'S COME

PHOTOGRAPHER: STEEN SUNDLAND
STYLIST: CATHY DIXON AT STREETERS
HAIR: JONATHAN CONNALLY
MODEL: NINA AT WOMAN

THE OTHER NIGHT AT A PARTY AND I JUST THOUGHT, THIS IS   FOR TRISH MCEV

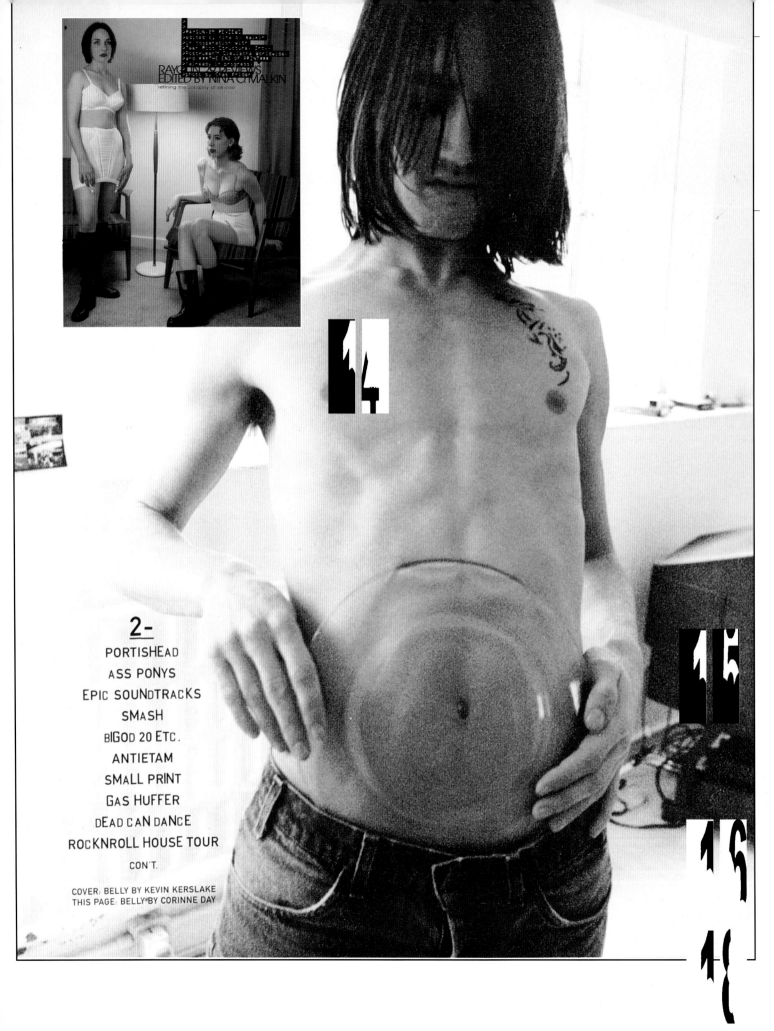

COVER: BELLY BY KEVIN KERSLAKE
THIS PAGE: BELLY BY CORINNE DAY

RAYGUN REVIEWS
EDITED BY NINA C. MALKIN
refining the uncanny of all coe

16
Issue 05. Blah Blah Blah. August 1996.
666 Style Dps.
Art Direction & Design by Neil Fletcher @ Substance.
Photography by Susan Gordon-Brown.
Styling by Toby Kay.

17
Issue 05. Blah Blah Blah. August 1996.
666 Style Dps.
Art Direction & Design by Neil Fletcher @ Substance.
Photography by Susan Gordon-Brown.
Styling by Toby Kay.

18
Issue 27. Ray Gun. June/July 1995.
Goths On Acid Style Dps.
Art Direction & Design by David Carson.
Photography by Corinne Day.
Styling by Tara St. Hill.

19
Issue 23. Ray Gun. Fe
Fashion Dps.
Art Direction & Design
Photography by Cori
ing by Tara S

14
Issue 29. Ray Gun. September 1995.
Reviews opener Sp.
Art Direction & Design by David Carson.
Photography by Chas Krider.

15
Issue 23. Ray Gun. February 1995.
Contents page.
Art Direction & Design by David Carson.
Photography by Corinne Day.

"I CAME OUT OF FASHIONABLE MUSIC, BUT MY THINGS WERE FAR MORE PHILOSOPHICAL AND PRODUCT WAS THE

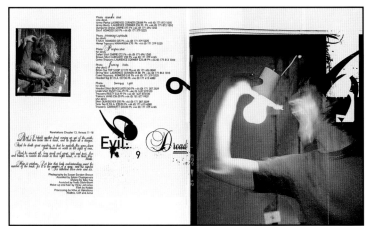

ST THING ON MY MIND. IT WAS ABOUT HOW TO MAKE FASHION THAT WASN'T FASHIONABLE AND MUSIC THAT WASN'T FASHIONABLE —— AND

WHEN YOU COMBINED THE TWO YOU HAD HYSTERICS. AT THE SAME TIME YOU CREATED SUFFICIENT ENERGY
WITHIN A DISENFRANCHISED PART OF THE CULTURE —— THE YOUTH LOOKING FOR REAL
VOICES —— TO CREATE THAT EXPLOSION. BUT, I'M AFRAID, IT BECAME A TEMPLATE
FOR PEOPLE TO IMITATE AND FIGURE OUT —— AND POUR SUFFICIENT WATER INTO THE
WINE." —— MALCOLM MCLAREN, HUH #8, APRIL 1995

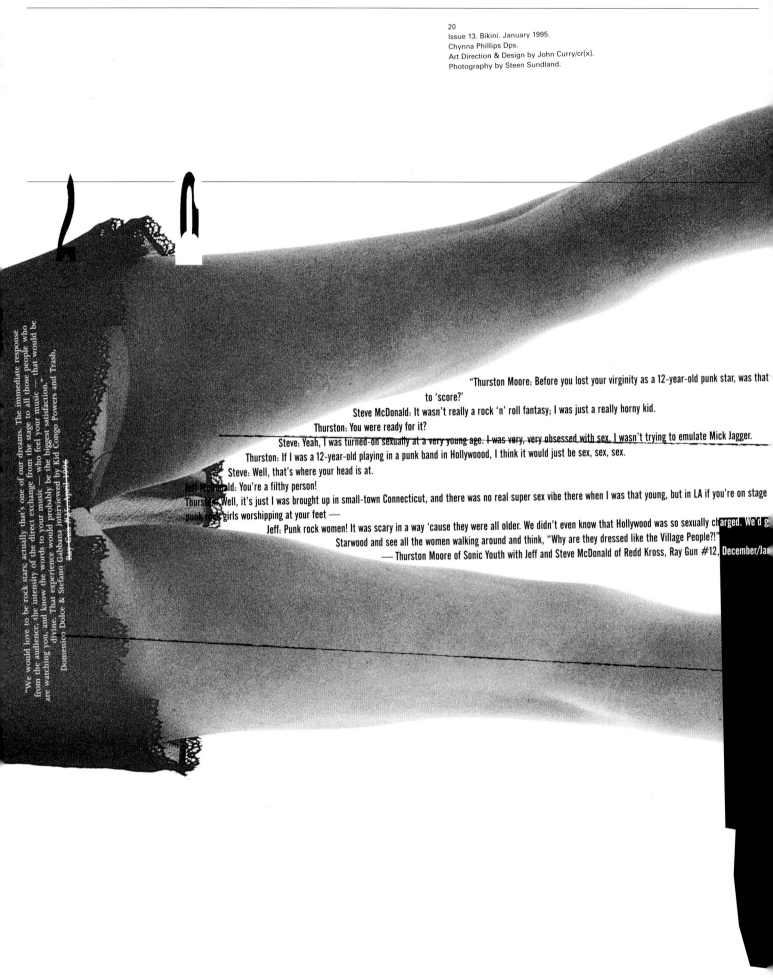

20
Issue 13. Bikini. January 1995.
Chynna Phillips Dps.
Art Direction & Design by John Curry/cr[x].
Photography by Steen Sundland.

"Thurston Moore: Before you lost your virginity as a 12-year-old punk star, was that to 'score?'

Steve McDonald: It wasn't really a rock 'n' roll fantasy; I was just a really horny kid.

Thurston: You were ready for it?

Steve: Yeah, I was turned-on sexually at a very young age. I was very, very obsessed with sex. I wasn't trying to emulate Mick Jagger.

Thurston: If I was a 12-year-old playing in a punk band in Hollywoood, I think it would just be sex, sex, sex.

Steve: Well, that's where your head is at.

Jeff McDonald: You're a filthy person!

Thurston: Well, it's just I was brought up in small-town Connecticut, and there was no real super sex vibe there when I was that young, but in LA if you're on stage punk rock girls worshipping at your feet —

Jeff: Punk rock women! It was scary in a way 'cause they were all older. We didn't even know that Hollywood was so sexually charged. We'd g[o] Starwood and see all the women walking around and think, "Why are they dressed like the Village People?!"

— Thurston Moore of Sonic Youth with Jeff and Steve McDonald of Redd Kross, Ray Gun #12, December/Ja[n]

"We would love to be rock stars; actually that's one of our dreams. The immediate response from the audience, the intensity of the direct exchange from the stage to all those people who are watching you, and know the words to your music — who feel your music — that would be divine. That experience would probably be the biggest satisfaction."
Domenico Dolce & Stefano Gabbana interviewed by Kid Congo Powers and Trash, Ray Gun #27, April 1996

21
Issue 13. Bikini. January 1995.
Chynna Phillips Dps.
Art Direction & Design by John Curry/d[x].
Photography by Steen Sundland.

22
Issue 35. Ray Gun. April 1996.
Dolce & Gabbana Dps.
Art Direction & Design by Robert Hales.

"Look at
fashion

models.

Eitzel,
Ray Gun
#34,
March   1996

They
stand
there,
pouting,
unhappy
as hell,
but God,
it's so
beautiful.
But we're
dour old
fucks;
there's
nothing
less wel-
come at
any
party....
But per-
haps I
suffer
from a
poor
self-
image

problem."

– Mark

23
Issue 12. Ray Gun. December/January 1994.
Styles Of Radical Will Sp.
Art Direction & Design by David Carson.
Illustration by Doug Aitken.

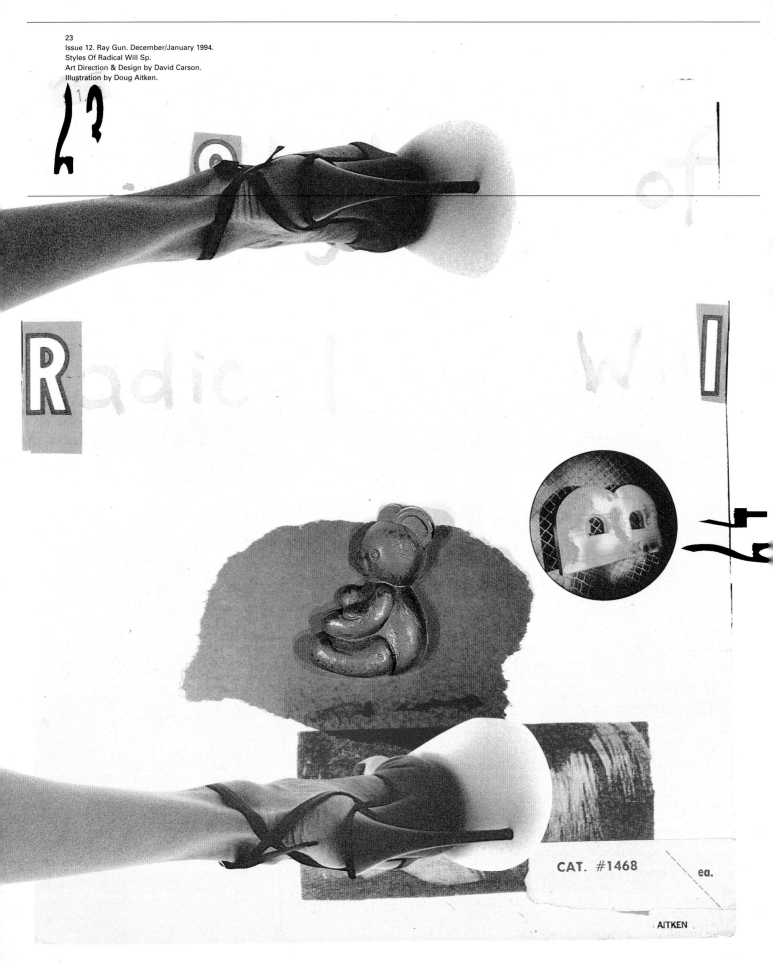

CAT. #1468   ea.

AITKEN

RAYGUNFASHIONBYDOUGAITKEN>>>

24
Issue 13. Bikini. January 1995.
Chynna Phillips Sp.
Art Direction & Design by John Curry/crlxl.
Photography by Steen Sundland.

25
Issue 01. Bikini. September 1993.
Don't Be In Fashion Dps.
Art Direction & Design by Scott Clum.
Photography by Trevor Graves.

"**feel the future of music is the**

Issue 01. Bikini. September 1993.
Don't Be In Fashion Dps.
Art Direction & Design by Scott Clum.
Page Nos
Photography by Trevor Graves.

114 / 115

27
Issue 24. Ray Gun. March 1995.
London Fashion Sp.
Art Direction & Design by David Carson.
Photography by Dave Stewart.

28
Issue 24. Ray Gun. March 1995.
London Fashion Sp.
Art Direction & Design by David Carson.
Photography by Dave Stewart.

cross-pollinated, hyper-hybrid sounds we're now hearing in hip-hop, and sectioned music gen-

res are no longer so sectioned. I find this to be a hopeful metaphor of culture as a whole. Maybe some politicians will, too. —

25

Todd Oldham,
Out of Control, 1996

26

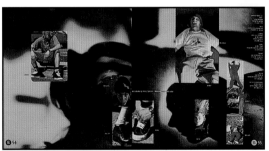

27

28

THERE ARE TOO MANY COLORS IN THE WORLD. COLOR MAKES ME TIRED

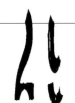

"SO WHAT WOULD THE MEMBERS OF THE BOREDOMS BE DOING IF THIS 'MUSIC' THING HADN'T WORKED OUT?

'MAYBE...HOMELESS,' STAMMERS EYE.

'MAYBE WORKING AT OFFICE,' ADDS HIRA.

'DOG BREEDER,' SAYS YOSHIMI WITH A LAUGH. 'I LOVE DOG.'

'JUST HANGING OUT,' CLARIFIES HIRA.

'YES,' AGREES EYE. 'SAME THING. HANG OUT.'"

— THE BOREDOMS, RAY GUN #38, AUGUST 1996

31
Issue 03. Blah Blah Blah. June 1996.
Supermodels take the Piss Dps.
Art Direction & Design by Amanda Sissons @ Substance.
Photography by Scott Lyon & Barnaby R-Caldbeck.

30
Issue 02. Blah Blah Blah. May 1996.
...ro-model Dps.
Art Direction & Design by Amanda Sissons @ Substance.
Photography by Larry Dunstan.

29
Issue 38. Ray Gun. August 1996.
Yohji Yamamoto Style Dps.
Art Direction & Design by Robert Hales.

Style
Page Nos
116/117

32
Issue 03. Blah Blah Blah. June 1996.
Supermodels take the Piss Dps.
Art Direction & Design by Amanda Sissons @ Substance.
Photography by Scott Lyon & Barnaby R-Caldbeck.

33
Issue 03. Blah Blah Blah. June 1996.
Supermodels take the Piss Dps.
Art Direction & Design by Amanda Sissons @ Substance.
Photography by Scott Lyon & Barnaby R-Caldbeck.

YOHJI YAMAMOTO IS THE KEITH RICHARDS OF FASHION – WEATHERED, DARK, QUIETLY PROPHETIC, IRREVERENT AND NEVER WITHOUT A CIGARETTE. HE IS A MASTER OF SCULPTING FABRIC AND... FAMOUS FOR DESIGNING CLOTHES WITH AN ODD, STOIC SEXINESS. AFTER NEARLY 25 YEARS IN FASHION, YAMAMOTO MEDITATES ON HIS JAPANESE ROOTS – AESTHETICS, ART, CULTURE AND FREEDOM.

RAYGUN: DEFINE THE TRADITIONAL JAPANESE AESTHETIC. **YOHJI:** IN ONE WORD, IT WILL BE "REFINEMENT." THE TRADITIONAL JAPANESE AESTHETIC COMES FROM FOREIGN CULTURES, ART WHICH WAS ORIGINALLY IN CHINA AND THE JAPANESE AESTHETIC. **R...** YOUR WORK? **YOHJI:** I DO... THE TRADITIONAL JAPAN... THOUGH, WHETHER I LIKE... "JAPAN INSIDE ME." CIR... BLOOD. IT HAS BEEN NO... PEOPLE QUITE OFTEN. **R...** CONTEMPORARY JAPANE... DIFFERENT? **YOHJI:** THE...

ART WHICH WAS ORIGINALLY IN CHINA AND THE JAPANESE ASIA, CHINA, KOREA AND INDIA FINALLY REACHED TERMINAL STATION – JAPAN (THE LAST FAR EAST ISLAND) – IT HAD BECOME "EXTREME REFINEMENT." "THE THINGS WHICH HAVE A F... WILL CERTAINLY BE DESTROYED." "THE OLD FAMOUS JAPANESE MINSTREL SUNG IN HIS SONG. THIS THOUGHT HAS CONTROLLED JAPANESE THOUGHT

THIS IDEA IS AT THE BASE OF THE TRADITIONAL KOREAN PENINSULA WHEN THE CULTURE OF

TRADITIONALLY WE LIVE OUR LIFE BEING OVERWHELMED WITH NATURE. A GOD DWELLS IN EVERY PART OF THE NATURAL WORLD. A HUMAN IS TRIVIAL IN THE FACE OF NATURE. THIS IDEA IS AT THE BASE OF THE TRADITIONAL

JAPANESE AESTHETIC IS AN "AESTHETIC OF CHAOS." BUT, IN THIS NEW AESTHETIC, THE TRADITIONAL JAPANESE AESTHETIC STILL THROBS CEASELESSLY. WESTERNERS HAVE EXPLAINED THE AESTHETIC AS "MYSTERIOUS"

IT'S THE EXACT OPPOSITE OF THE KINDS OF ART WE SEE IN MUSEUMS. **RG:** AND JAPANESE CULTURE... **YOHJI:** I STARTED THIS JOB BECAUSE I HAD A STRONG HATRED FOR "JAPANESE CULTURE." I CANNOT AGREE WITH

COLOR IN YOUR DESIGNS? **YOHJI:** THERE ARE TOO MANY COLORS IN THE WORLD. COLOR MAKES ME TIRED. COLOR FORCES SOMETHING. **RG:** YOU ARE A BLACK BELT IN KARATE – HAS KARATE INFLUENCED YOUR DESIGNS?

34
Issue 11. Ray Gun. November 1993.
London Fashion Sp.
Art Direction & Design by David Carson.
Photography by Wolfgang Tillmans.
Styling by Lutz Huelle & Wolfgang Tillmans.

RG28

"Steve Diggle,
Buzzcocks: The problem
is, people just give up.
People who had razor
blades and safety pins
all over the place are
now just pushing prams
down the street, and
you think, 'Fucking hell,
I thought punk mean
something.'
RG: Didn't punk invent
the concept of selling
out, say like leaving
England to make it in
America?
Pete Shelley, Buzzcocks:
No, that was Bob Dylan
when he went electric?"

"Style is the means by which individualism is packaged for consumption
and is purely a commercial concept. Style is a sense of belonging that
you can buy into. Style is categorization. Style is the political correctness of taste.
    How important is it? It is so important to those who believe in it that
the moment someone makes an effort to ignore it or stand against it, the
true believers immediately cry, 'How stylish! What style!' Anti-style thus
becomes a style itself and individual identity is once more co-opted into
global commercialism. Style is the junk food of culture."

— Billy Bragg, Out of Control, 1996

24

Photography
Melodie McDaniel

personal style

THIEVES 3

A   Shirts from **Camden Market**

NINA
PHIL
TIM

Hair
Ben Skervin

Make-up
Vicky Tringham for
Collection 2000

Styling
John Bland

Photography
Scott Lyon / Barney Roper

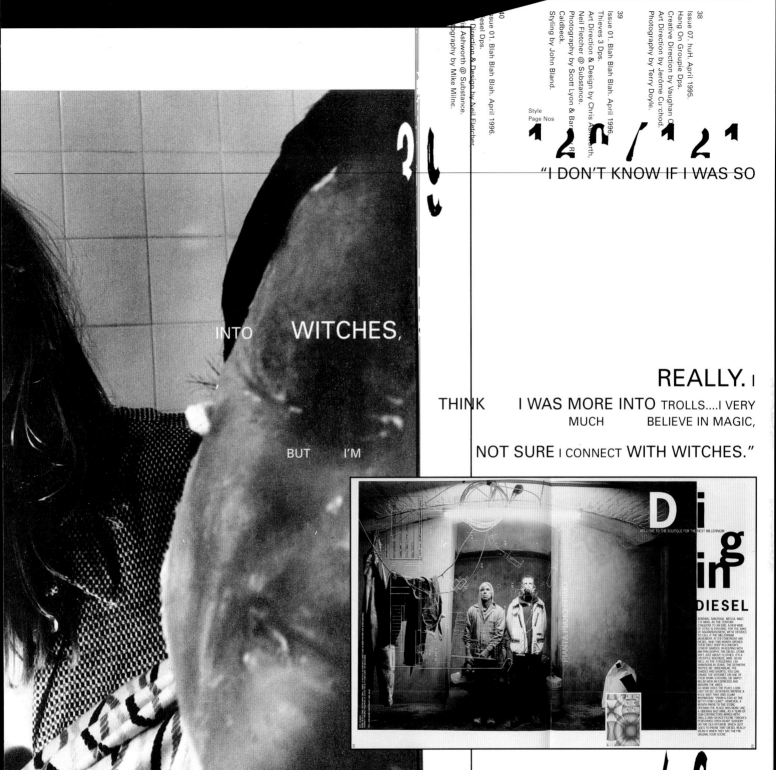

"I DON'T KNOW IF I WAS SO

INTO   WITCHES,

BUT   I'M

REALLY. I

THINK   I WAS MORE INTO TROLLS....I VERY

MUCH   BELIEVE IN MAGIC,

NOT SURE I CONNECT WITH WITCHES."

— KATE   BUSH, RAY GUN #14,
MARCH 1994

40

How to

sti pe

STIPE 12/11/96

it

/96 7:45 pm   Page 1 (2,2)

STIPE: I WENT TO ART SCHOOL BECAUSE

[UNIVERSITY OF GEORGIA]

BUILDING

MARK BLACKWELL: MAYBE WE SHOULD START BY TALKING A LITTLE ABOUT YOUR BEGINNINGS, MICHAEL....

MICHAEL STIPE: (DRAMATICALLY) IT WAS A SNOWY NIGHT IN THE WINTER OF 1960.... (LAUGHS)

BLACKWELL: AS FAR AS ART SCHOOL GOES.

STIPE: **I WENT TO ART SCHOOL [UNIVERSITY OF GEORGIA] BECAUSE IT WAS THE CLOSEST BUILDING DOWNTOWN AND I DIDN'T HAVE A CAR.** IT WAS EASY AND EXCITING AND MY INTEREST WAS IN PHOTOGRAPHY, ALTHOUGH THE PHOTO DEPARTMENT AT THAT TIME WAS NOT VERY EXCITING TO ME. THE MOST EXCITING THING WAS JIM HERBERT, AND HE NOW TEACHES FILM, BUT AT THE TIME HE JUST TAUGHT PAINTING, SO I MAJORED IN DRAWING AND PAINTING, WITH A MINOR IN ENGLISH LIT. **AND THEN I DROPPED OUT.**

BLACKWELL: WHAT WAS YOUR MOTIVATION FOR DROPPING OUT?

STIPE: THE BAND. I HAD TO MAKE A CHOICE BETWEEN SCHOOL AND THE BAND. I WAS IN MY FIRST QUARTER OF SENIOR YEAR WHEN I DROPPED. I WAS THE LAST BAND MEMBER TO LEAVE COLLEGE. I WAS LEARNING A LOT, BUT I WAS MAKING THE GRADES BY THE SKIN OF MY TEETH, AND THE STUFF THAT WAS REALLY STICKING WITH ME, IN TERMS OF AN EDUCATION, WAS — IT'S SO TYPICAL — THE MORE SOCIAL ASPECTS OF SCHOOLING, PARTICULARLY COLLEGE. A COMMUNITY LIKE THAT WAS AND STILL IS — THERE IN THE ART SCHOOL, OR JUST IN ATHENS — YOU'RE ABLE TO WORK SINGULARLY, IF YOU HAVE A SINGULAR VISION. BUT COLLABORATION IS ENCOURAGED AND IT'S NOT SOMETHING THAT'S FROWNED DOWN UPON IF THERE ARE, SAY, TWO OR THREE PHOTOGRAPHERS WHOSE WORK CLOSELY RESEMBLES EACH OTHER'S, AND THEY'RE OBVIOUSLY INSPIRED BY ONE ANOTHER. YOU'RE LEARNING FROM THE PEOPLE AROUND YOU, AND IT'S REALLY EXCITING.

BLACKWELL: HOW ABOUT YOU, CHRIS, WHAT WERE YOUR BEGINNINGS ART-WISE?

CHRIS BILHEIMER: THE SAME DEGREE, THE SAME SCHOOL, A FEW YEARS LATER. I GOT INTO THE ART PROGRAM BECAUSE IT WAS PRETTY MUCH, GROWING UP IN GRADE SCHOOL, THE ONLY THING I COULD DO. I WAS PERENNIALLY THE D+ STUDENT IN EVERYTHING BUT ART, AND I LUCKILY ENJOYED IT AS WELL, SO UGA WAS THE ONLY SCHOOL I APPLIED TO AND I BARELY GOT IN. I WAS A DRAWING AND PAINTING MAJOR. I TRIED TO GET INTO THE PHOTOGRAPHY DEPARTMENT, QUARTER AFTER QUARTER, AND I KEPT GETTING WAIT-LISTED AND FINALLY JUST SAID THE HELL WITH IT. AND THEN I DROPPED OUT, ALSO BECAUSE OF HIS BAND (LAUGHS), IN MY SENIOR YEAR.

BLACKWELL: HOW DID YOU GUYS FIRST GET TOGETHER?

STIPE: I'VE BEEN RACKING MY BRAIN....

BILHEIMER: I STARTED WORKING FOR YOU, JUST TAKING CARE OF PROPERTIES AND STUFF, LIKE CLEANING UP THE GRIT BUILDING, 'CAUSE IT WAS THE SUMMER AND I DIDN'T HAVE A JOB AND I WASN'T REALLY LOOKING TOO HARD TO FIND ONE. AND SO I JUST STARTED DOING ODD JOBS FOR YOU. WE MET THROUGH MUTUAL FRIENDS, I GUESS, SOPHOMORE YEAR, RIGHT AFTER THE *GREEN* TOUR. I'M A HORRIBLE MUSICIAN, SO THE THINGS THAT I KNOW HOW TO DO — LIKE TAKE PICTURES, AND I USED TO DO A LOT OF LIGHTING AT THE LOCAL 40 WATT CLUB — THAT WAS MY WAY OF BEING IN A BAND, BY PROXY. I USED TO MANAGE LOCAL BANDS AND BE INVOLVED IN THE LIVE PERFORMANCES AS MUCH AS I COULD, BECAUSE THAT'S WHAT EXCITED ME. I WISHED I COULD PLAY GUITAR OR PLAY DRUMS....

BLACKWELL: AT THIS POINT, HAD YOU WORKED WITH ANY BANDS GRAPHICALLY?

BILHEIMER: Even in high school, I used to do flyers and T-shirt designs and stuff for bands. And I was always pushing

bands and encouraging...setting up super 8 projectors, and projecting on pieces of plastic and screens, and just whatever to do something fun and to try and be involved. I was managing a band and I wanted to learn how to typeset flyers, so I learned how to use a Macintosh just so I could typeset, like, "SATURDAY." And I started designing stuff for anyone who would let me, for free. In the first three years I did design work, I maybe made about $250. It was just for the experience, and I always made sure to show Michael because I was a big fan of R.E.M. growing up. **THE FIRST CONCERT I WENT TO, WHEN I WAS 14, WAS THE *RECONSTRUCTION* TOUR.** And R.E.M. records and early U2

DOWNTOWN AND I [

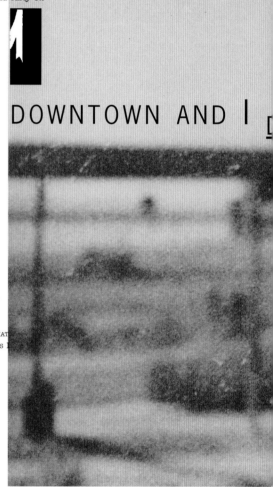

[UNIVERSITY OF

124/125

T WAS   THE CLOSEST

N'T

HAVE A CAR.

R.E.M.

NEW ADVENTURES IN HI-FI

REM – New Adventures In Hi-fi {CD Inlay}

STIPE: AN EXHAUSTING AMOUNT OF WORK TO GET SOMETHING OUT AND THEN YOU HAVE TO THINK ABOUT EVERY ... A LOT. IT'S AN

SINGLE SLEEVE AND EVERY AD. I MEAN, UNLESS YOU'RE THE TYPE OF BAND THAT WOULD JUST LEAVE THAT UP TO THE RECORD COMPANY. WE'RE NOT LIKE THAT, AND I

THINK IT'S LESS OF A MESSIAH COMPLEX ON MY PART THAN JUST...IT ALWAYS DID SEEM REALLY IMPORTANT THAT THERE BE SOME SINGULAR VISION AND THAT IT COME

FROM WITHIN AND NOT FROM OUTSIDE.

4
Drawing by Chris Bilheimer on Fed Ex package to Michael Stipe, later became REM T-Shirt

5
REM – T-Shirt
Photography by Kelly Sedei

records and Violent Femmes, those were my first influences, as far as, "Oh, this is what records are supposed to look like." You know, it didn't occur to me that, previous to that, pretty much everyone's record was a promo shot with a logo.

Stipe: (laughing) Then you absorbed the art work for *Fables of the Reconstruction* and never looked back.

Blackwell: So you were showing Michael your work?

Bilheimer: Yeah, I would always show him because he was one of the few people who actually gave a fuck about how a record sleeve looked. Then he and I drove 'cross country, and I got a call a couple weeks after we got back and was asked to just design one T-shirt for R.E.M. I was ecstatic, and then I turned the design in, and a week later they called me to come back in and they offered me a job.

Stipe: Was that before or after the computer stuff?

Bilheimer: It was after that.

Stipe: Chris had helped me kind of...illegally purchase a computer, I guess (laughs), and then showed me how to use it...because I never did read the manual, actually. I just needed it as a word processor. I was frustrated with typewriting.

Bilheimer: I got him a computer and a printer and showed him how to turn it on, type something, and turn it off.

Blackwell: Up until the point that you guys got together, did R.E.M. go through a lot of different art directors?

Stipe: Yeah. I tended to use the in-house people at whatever record company we were at. Through I.R.S., I worked alongside several different people. And then when we moved to Warner Bros. I was kind of assigned a guy in the art department there. He admired the work that I had done with I.R.S. and I thought his book of stuff was cool — Tom Recchion. So basically, I would have an idea and I would give it to him and he would make it happen. But it became more increasingly a full-time job. I had the patience for it, and I had the desire, but I didn't have the time really to do that and everything else....

Blackwell: How

6
REM – T–Shirt
Photography by Kelly Sedei

7
REM – T–Shirt
Photography by Kelly Sedei

How the Art Was Done and How It Got Us
Page Nos
126/127

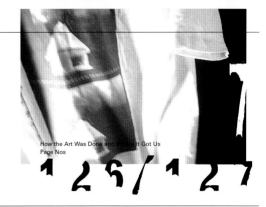

much energy would you wind up putting into it?

Stipe: **A lot. It's an exhausting amount of work to get something out and then you have to think about every single sleeve and every ad. I mean, unless you're the type of band that would just leave that up to the record company. We're not like that, and I think it's less of a messiah complex on my part than just...it always did seem really important that there be some singular vision and that it come from within and not from outside.**

Blackwell: Chris, your first R.E.M. record was *Monster*, right?

Bilheimer: Yes.

Blackwell: When you first got hired, did you have specific ideas that you proposed?

Stipe: What was that first T-shirt?

Bilheimer: The "Find The River" T-shirt. I think I got a three-word description of what you were looking for and I just went from there. But when I got hired to do *Monster*, the biggest thing I had done before that was like a Magnapop import single. And now I was gonna work on an R.E.M. record. I was so terrified at that point. I felt I was just sort of there to do what I was told. And it took probably halfway through *Monster* before I really felt comfortable to push my ideas, and my role developed from just doing the grunt work for Michael to having an influence through the process of making *Monster*.

Stipe: I had ideas, and I had people like Jem Cohen that I was using to take pictures, because I didn't want to do all the pictures. That just seemed incredibly egotistical to me. Jem was there and he's a great photographer, so we'd take pictures together. I'd say, "I like this and this and this," and Chris would have a suggestion, and I'd say, "Yeah, try it." He'd try it, and it would look great, so his role slowly evolved. We did the collaborative thing that I'm talking about, and I watched the stuff that he did evolve and knew that he had a good sense of his own eye. There was a point where I think (R.E.M. advisor) Bertis Downs realized that the amount of work it was gonna take to put together all the packaging for *Monster* was just phenomenally overwhelming, and it was all kind of on me, and it was just too much.

Bilheimer: As well as actually, like, writing the fucking record.

Stipe: Right. (laughs) As well as writing and recording the thing and whatever was going on in my personal life at that time.

Bilheimer: So I'd be there while he was trying to write lyrics for this record and I'd have to be, like, "Uh...hey...." Bugging him, "Hey, excuse me...uh...what do you want the cover to look like?"

Blackwell: I would imagine it was much more productive to have someone in-house, rather than someone at the record company Fed-Ex-ing or faxing things back and forth.

Stipe: Yeah, in-house. Not to denigrate the people that I've worked with. Tom Recchion is a great graphic artist, we had a great rapport with each other, but there was a problem with distance.

Marvin Jarrett: Very similar to our David Carson situation with *Ray Gun*. That's why I stopped working with David after three years, because of the distance thing. I wanted the rapport with the designers, and with me, and with the editors in-house.

Stipe: Well, when you're working on something like that, the simplest or stupidest thing can completely change the whole idea of what you're doing. The tiniest thing. It can be a gum wrapper on the table, and that's the answer. You all see it at the same time. And you go, "Throw it on the wall," and you throw it on the wall and it works. That's really hard to do with Fed-Ex and faxes and bad copies....

Bilheimer: Part of my designing sense comes from when we were driving across country; we'd drive by an old gas station sign and Michael would just go, "That's great." And things like that would stick in my mind, and pretty soon I got a pretty good sense of what attracted him to things.

Stipe: **And we took pictures in the hotel rooms, like, pre-dating those Calvin Klein ads that unfortunately shocked the nation. (laughs) Chris and I would take pictures of each other in these shitty hotels we stayed in across the country.....**

Bilheimer: **He has this God-awful picture of me in my underwear...deep shag carpeting, panelled walls, and I'm eating pizza in my underwear at four in the morning, going, "Do you really need to take a picture of this? Is this a moment we need to capture?"**

Stipe: Only after you saw the print did you say that. At the time, he was, like, helping me turn lamps over so I could get the right kind of lighting on the panelled wall.

Bilheimer: Like, "Okay sure. You're drivin'...."

Jarrett: Chris, you were talking about how you didn't feel that you were influenced by that many other record sleeves. It seems like maybe in America, that whole thing wasn't happening as much. In Britain — which Michael, you probably were influenced by — look at

Never Mind The Bollocks, and those really great sleeves that Vaughan Oliver did. Amazing stuff.

STIPE: I'm certainly aware of them. I'm trying to think of any direct influence....

JARRETT: Well I don't mean *direct* influence, like you would rip them off....

BILHEIMER: But stealing is an important part of designing. *Ray Gun* has always been a thing where, if you have to design something and you have 35 minutes to do it, you go running to the newsstand and usually you'll either be inspired by it or directly rip off something out of *Ray Gun*. That's how it's been ever since I've been designing. You know, if I felt incredibly apathetic and I didn't have an original idea and everything sucked, I'd literally go walk across and read *Ray Gun* without ever actually buying it from the newsstand. I'd just sit there and flip through it.

JARRETT: We need to get your $5.00 now.

8
REM – Bittersweet Me {CD Front & Back}

BLACKWELL: Michael, you've mentioned several times in the past about how you're such a big fan of magazines....

STIPE: Yeah, not a fan but a captive. They're really influential to me, in terms of design and photographs.

JARRETT: What magazines do you like?

STIPE: I'll read anything. I'll read *Dog Fancy* if that's what's available. I don't really read them, I just look at them. I mean, it's very Warholian to say, but that really is kind of how it is. I also do read 'em and that sometimes means that they accumulate around the house for years. I have piles of magazines at home that I haven't completely looked at.

BILHEIMER: A lot of times Michael will rip images out of magazines, as just, "This I think is interesting." And I'll tack it up onto my wall and....

STIPE: No I don't. I say, "Steal this, Chris." (laughs) But we're not supposed to talk about that. Ssshhhh.

BILHEIMER: I think the one thing you handed me during the whole time I was making *New Adventures In Hi-Fi* was the advertisement for the Alphabet cereal that had little candy letters, you know? And it was a

9362-43792-2

9
REM – New Adventures in Hi–Fi {Special Limited Edition}

This is the second in a series of CD singles released from "New Adventures In Hi-Fi". Each CD contains three extra tracks compiled exclusively for these single releases.

BILHEIMER: WELL, YOU'RE ALREADY SINGLED OUT ENOUGH

STIPE: I'M SINGLED OUT ENOUGH BECAUSE I'M THE SINGER, I'M THE FACE. BILHEIMER: YOU DON'T **NEED IT TO BE MICHAEL STIPE & THE STIPETONES.**

R.E.M.
BITTERSW

Kelloggs' photo shoot of things floating in milk. And that's just as valid an influence design-wise as anything out of *Ray Gun* or *Interview* or anything else.

JARRETT: Definitely, that's where some of the best ideas come from.

BLACKWELL: Cereal boxes.

JARRETT: When I was growing up, there wasn't MTV. The record jacket was really your link to your favorite band. You'd sit around in your bedroom and listen to music and you'd look at the record jacket. And now, the CD cover is not as substantial. Do you guys think that the jacket is as important, being that we have to look at it on a CD?

STIPE: **Something we were going for definitely with *New Adventures In Hi-Fi* was a record jacket that for 50 minutes or an hour you could just stare at, kind of almost in a meditative state, the same way that I would stare at the first New York Dolls record or *Radio Ethiopia* by Patti Smith — what an amazing cover that is — or *Killer* by Alice Cooper. You just go into a trance and you absorb it...and that's what we really wanted *with New Adventures*. And it is just fucking beautiful in 12-inch.**

BILHEIMER: And with the special limited edition book we did, we tried to make the booklet the size of a seven-inch, because CDs have killed big art.

Stipe: Big art. (laughs)

Bilheimer: Yeah, it just sucks when you have really

How the Art Was Done and Where It Got Us
Page Nos

beautiful imagery and it's the size of a cocktail napkin. You never get that sense of getting lost in the space of the photograph. It's easy to ignore. And you can't do that with record sleeves. Especially the old gatefold ones.

STIPE: With *Monster* we wanted something really pop and flat. Like really veneer. There was no question that there was nothing beyond what you were looking at, you know? We got the big stupid bear head with the crossed eyes and it was just black-orange-red; I mean, it's really offensive.

JARRETT: Where did you find that image of the bear head?

STIPE: On a balloon from the Tilley balloon company. The guy that actually drew the bear head came to one of the shows and I met him and shook his hand.

BLACKWELL: How much does the look that you want come from the content and the sound of the particular record?

STIPE: I think a lot.

BLACKWELL: I was wondering if Chris had the images in mind and then...he obviously has to hear what you're doing, Michael, before he can —

BILHEIMER: That's entirely Michael's area.

BLACKWELL: He somehow has to convey that to you.

BILHEIMER: Yeah. Usually, with the way the record industry is, they want a title and they want an album cover before they've even written half the damn songs.

Visually, we work the same way you guys work, where you don't want to set up too many rules at the beginning. You want to work through it and see where it goes. You let the function decide the form. And it's hard, because the record companies want it done before you really know what direction you're going in.

So I kind of have to defer to Michael on that. 'Cause it's all coming out — the lyrics, the music, the art, are all kind of being formed at the same time, and who am I to start deciding what direction visually it's going to go when it's all generated from him?

STIPE: But it's great to have someone to bounce that off of. He knows how I talk and he understands, usually, what I'm trying to say. It's not always that easy. He has his own sense and he also knows my sense of linking visual and audio, whatever that link is. So I could kind of project onto Chris and he could throw it back at me. Picking the photographs for *New Adventures*, you and I both went through all these contact sheets of mine. [R.E.M. guitarist] Peter Buck actually suggested it. I had come up with the idea of using some of my photos of landscape stuff, but I didn't want to give that to the band as an idea because I thought it would seem too much like "Michael's project."

BILHEIMER: **Well, you're already singled out enough.**

STIPE: **I'm singled out enough because I'm the singer, I'm the face.**

BILHEIMER: **You don't need it to be Michael Stipe & The Stipetones.**

STIPE: Right, exactly. I'm really sensitive about that. And I thought, "God, my pictures would look really cool with this music," but I kind of dismissed that and I was moving in a different direction altogether, and then Peter out of the blue said, "The artwork should be black and white landscapes, and it should

ET ME

LECTORS EDITION CD

1 0
Polaroid photography
by Michael Stipe &
Chris Bilheimer
Out of Control 1996

the size of the page or whether it's a horizontal or vertical image — if it doesn't work within that context, then the magazine isn't getting what it wants, and I'm not getting what I want because my photograph hasn't been well represented. If I can give it to you and you can crop into it and make it full bleed — my favorite term — the magazine gets what it wants and I wind up looking like this brilliant photographer, then everybody's happy. To be able to hand that over to Chris, as someone who's got a real distinct graphic sense, and say, "This is the picture. Do something here," and he will just crop the shit out of the photograph - I'd be like, "Hmmm," but it would work.
BILHEIMER: I try to be as *undesigny* as possible most of the time. One of the things I want to say before I go into that is, you were saying that they're unremarkable photographs. I think what's so special about them is, you know, 90 percent of what you see every day *is* unremarkable. And when you're spoon-fed your whole life Ansel Adams

look like those photos that you've taken, shooting out of the car. The whole package should be your photographs of traveling." And I was completely blown away, it was like he read my mind. And Chris took probably 70 pages of contact sheets with Ian McFarlane, who prints my photos for me, and he and Ian just picked out a bunch of stuff, and then we picked through those, and it just winnowed down to where we had 12 pictures, I think.
BILHEIMER: Originally, I picked like 20. And you maybe added one or two more, and then we just sat around for a few days and narrowed 'em down. It kind of just happened. After two or three days of just looking at these pictures and listening to the songs, it was pretty obvious which one should be the album cover. I remember you were sitting there and you had what ended up being the cover in your lap and **Peter walked by and just went, (offhandedly) "I like that one for the cover."** And we're cringing because

STIPE: No shit....
BILHEIMER: — because it's like we've been working on all this stuff for days, and then Peter just immediately goes, "Eh...that one."
STIPE: He's great for that, though. He called it. We had to work through it, we studied over it. He knew it. You're aware of this, but some of those pictures are wildly un-extraordinary. A lot of them are just total snapshots.
BLACKWELL: Yeah, I saw you doing it on tour, riding on the bus snapping things out the window.
STIPE: Yeah. And some of them are really un-extraordinary, but I'd say to Chris, "Crop, go into the picture, take what you want," and he would then pull from these really unextraordinary photographs a vista from the middle or the side and crop into it. **And when I've done magazine work I have encouraged the people that I worked with, as you well know, not to treat the photograph like this fine piece of art; it's not.**
BLACKWELL: I was surprised when you encouraged us to crop those photos of yours we ran in huH. A lot of people are really touchy about cropping images, you know, "This is my art. This is how I saw it."
STIPE: I think as a photographer one of my ace cards is my ability to frame something in a way that is really different from how other people might frame it. That being said, if I'm presenting it to a magazine, and it doesn't work well with the layout of that magazine or

AND WHEN I'VE DONE MAGAZINE WORK

I HAVE ENCOURAGED THE PEOPLE THAT I WORKED WIT

LIKE THIS FINE PIECE OF

ART;

IT'S

photographs, when you take a picture of one tree in the middle of a parking lot, or something like that, and it's presented, ' a photograph. It's a piece of art. You're supposed to look at it the same way you look at an Ansel Adams piece," I think it makes you rethink everything you see every day. I think that's influenced my photography a lot; you feel like you see thing little bit different than other people. Anyone can take pictures of sunsets, but it's trying to make people look at something they normally not look at, or think about in a different way, and that's what I learned growing up looking at R.E.M. r
BLACKWELL: I think *New Adventures In Hi-Fi*, out of all your records, the look of it goes about as well with the music as any of ever
STIPE: Yeah, I'm really proud of this pa
BILHEIMER: It's been pretty focused from the beginning. Everything involved with this record has a very similar look. I'm a big cohesiveness, this kind of single vision...without being redu

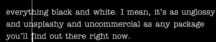
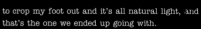

everything black and white. I mean, it's as unglossy and unsplashy and uncommercial as any package you'll find out there right now.

STIPE: And not in some self-conscious way.

BLACKWELL: Not like, "Here's what we have the power to do."

STIPE: Yeah. It doesn't look like cram mundaneness up your ass or down your throat. That, to me, is really important. That would be the last thing that I would want.

BLACKWELL: Was it atypical of Peter to come in and make a suggestion of how — .

STIPE: No.

BLACKWELL: It just seems that you, more so than the other guys, have had more of an interest in perhaps what things look like.

STIPE: But they always inform those choices. Always. Sometimes I really have to have my antenna up to get it, but in this case it was pure and simple. And, again, the extraordinary thing for me is that I'd had the idea but felt that it was far too egotistical and I wanted to be able to keep my interest as a photographer separate from R.E.M.. **But if you go back and look at every R.E.M. package, any photograph that isn't credited to someone, I took. I would never want to credit myself, because there's nothing worse than picking up a package and seeing someone's name 55 times on there.**

BILHEIMER: The first photos I shot of R.E.M. for this record, I was terrified because I'd never shot a band before. And it's funny...the photo we ended up going with in the record, I was picking up the 35mm, this kind of point-and-shoot camera, and it went off as I was picking it up. My foot is in the picture. I had

to crop my foot out and it's all natural light, and that's the one we ended up going with.

STIPE: No kidding. I didn't know that.

BILHEIMER: My damn foot's in it.

STIPE: That's a great picture.

Bilheimer: And once I saw that, I got really depressed at that whole session, because I realized that one picture, an accident, fully captured the feel that I missed with the other 900 photographs I took. I learned so much from that one photo session. Unfortunately, 99.9% of what I shot is pretty useless.

STIPE: I think if you have the eye or the ear to be able to recognize a good accident or mistake when it

YOU WELL KNOW, NOT TO TREAT THE PHOTOGRAPH

STIPE: This is taking the conversation and exploding it to Godzilla size, but, it might really be that, as a graphic creative team, Chris and I — given a very simple directive — thank you, Peter — Chris and I really rose above everything and created this body of work for this record that really is very extraordinary. But then again, it's a very simple idea. Very simple.

BILHEIMER: And there's something really refreshing about working so simplistically, you know, deciding to do

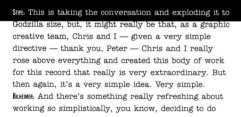

comes along, you can really learn quickly. For me that's one of the basics of collaborating. The cover of the single sleeve for "Strange Currencies," off of the last record, was kind of an interesting story.

BILHEIMER: Angie Grass had gone on this whole personal quest to photograph rotting billboards, just driving around and taking pictures of the billboards that are falling apart, where you see the last eight or nine different advertisements that were on it. And she literally grabbed her friend's camera and snapped it, the window was up, and it was raining, and she snapped this billboard as she was driving by. And processed it at one-hour photo out of her instamatic camera, and it's....

STIPE: She happened to show it to me, or you, in a week when we were trying to pull this sleeve together, and really trying to come up with something that didn't seem maudlin or like it was crawling out of its own butt, and here's this phenomenally beautiful photograph through this shitty, greasy window of this unbelievable billboard, and the colors are so like muted and saturated, it's just this astonishing picture. So we asked her if we could use it. And it's a beautiful sleeve.

BILHEIMER: There's something really special for me, going to Los Angeles, going into Warner Bros., and doing the same job as the art directors and knowing my budget was, you know, $75 to produce something, when they spend so much money on "real" photographers, when this instamatic print that she snapped off without thinking twice is equally if not more valid than if we'd hired God-knows-who. A big-name photographer.

STIPE: Ansel Adams.

BILHEIMER: Yeah, exactly. (laughs)

STIPE: Back from the grave.

BILHEIMER: There's just something wonderful about being able to walk in, in the middle of LA culture, and say, "This is what we want."

STIPE: (hick voice) "Here's our snapshot. We like it." (laughs) It's not like an us-versus-them kind of thing. It's not really that they desire to be in that kind of position, it's just the corporate-ness and everything.

BILHEIMER: No, I wasn't trying to knock them so much, but we're not limited to that.

STIPE: Right.

JARRETT: Do you bounce everything visual through Chris, even as far as, say, video directors go? Like, "Do you think Spike Jonze would be good for this?" Or is that a whole 'nother issue?

STIPE: That's probably a whole other issue. **Although we all get together and watch "120 Minutes" from time to time. (laughs) We look at videos and we usually lambaste and berate the people that made them and the people that are in them, just as I expect people do with our videos.** We all know what sucks and what doesn't. It's as simple as that. A video might not exactly be what it should be, but if you recognize, in the song, in the performance, or in the way it's put together, that there was some original thought, that there was some care taken, you see that it's no bullshit. You see it, it's cool. It doesn't have to be some sincere Sting-in-the-rainforest thing. I mean, not to take a jab at Sting, an unnecessary one, but you recognize heart when you see it, even if it's coming across on a TV set in the form of a music video amongst all this shit.

BILHEIMER: When picking photographers and picking video

directors, Michael's got a vested interest in it because it's actually *him*...you need to pick who's going to represent you the best. With videos and with still band photographers, I have very little input. I like it that way, because if I picked someone and you weren't happy with how you looked, I'd feel like a jerk.

BLACKWELL: Looking back, was there ever a period or instance where you feel you or the band didn't look right or didn't get presented right?

STIPE: It just, to me, seems like a series of horrible mistakes. (laughter) I just can't even think about it. But what I was saying about sitting around watching videos is, even outside of that official in-the-office work, the essence of the collaborative thing is absolutely there. And it's not like someone formed a school of collaborative thought in art and graphic design and music and decided that they would base it in Athens, Georgia. Or anywhere else. It's like life. You talk with your friends about things that are cool, and things that are not cool, and something that inspired you and something that had an innate sense of heart or realness to it, as opposed to like the fun shit that doesn't have any of that but it's kind of fun, as opposed to the stupid shit that is 80 percent of what's out there, that is just nothing. You talk about that stuff. And I know how Chris feels about different people that I work with or choose not to work with in the video world, and he knows how I feel about them, because we're friends and we talk about that.

JARRETT: Michael, do you usually say, "I'd like this particular director to do the video for this song," or do you just send it out to several directors and see what they come back with?

STIPE: It's almost always been that I find the person that I want, and I go to them, and that works.

JARRETT: What if they came back with a treatment that you hated?

STIPE: That's rarely happened. I've been super lucky. There've been a few times when it was a struggle, but it's usually worth it in the end, even if the thing doesn't get played or looked at that much. We haven't put anything out there that I think sucks. And it's thrilling to throw something at someone like Jim Herbert and say, "See what you can do with this." There are people like him and Jem Cohen that I've known all along and I just innately trust.

BILHEIMER: That's what was so fun on the tour, not having any constraints, really. With music

R.E.M. STRAN

THIS IS THE FOURTH IN A SERIES OF CD SINGLES FE

videos there's at least a cursory feeling of, "If we're

ONLY JIM HERBERT COMES TO YOU AND GC
REALLY WANT TO DO A FILM, FIVE MINUTES OF JUST FISH FLYIN
BOOTS,"

1
REM
Photography

by

Strange
Angie

Currencies

{CD

1
Front}
Grass

12
REM – Man On The Moon {CD Front}
Photography by Melodie McDaniel

How the Art Was Done and Where It Got Us
Page Nos

122/122

E CURRENCIES

NG SONGS RECORDED IN ATHENS, GA FOR GREENPEACE.

MAN ON
THE MOON
R.E.M.

"WELL, i
UT OF A PAIR OF

going to spend the money and do this, it should serve a purpose and actually promote the song." But with the films we used on tour, we didn't have to think about those things, we didn't have to follow broadcasting decency guidelines —

Stipe: It was a free-for-all.

Bilheimer: And there is nothing more fun than picking out these filmmakers and saying, "It's a free-for-all."

Stipe: "You've seen R.E.M. perform live, what would you like to see projected behind them? Give us ten ideas."

Bilheimer: And we don't have to say, "No, you can't film nude people," or, in Jim Herbert's case, "No, you can't film fish flying out of a pair of boots."(laughs) **Only Jim Herbert comes to you and goes, "Well, I really want to do a film, five minutes of just fish flying out of a pair of boots,"** and we're able to go, "Great, go for it." Or hiring Lance Bangs to film kids —

Stipe: Kissing parking meters....

Bilheimer: And part of that is being here. There's a pretty rich tradition here in Georgia with folk artists, and I almost consider myself a folk designer in a way because I don't...I've never taken a design class, I try not to look at what other people are doing, and just do what seems right. It's the same thing with Angie's photograph. That's all part of the collaboration culture of Athens, everyone just does it on their own without any kind of preconceived notions of making things into a career. It's fun to do things with other people, to have an experience, and to

share it.

Stipe: It's cool when it does blossom into a career, or even in Angie's case where she shows us the photo and we're, "Oh, my God, this is it," and we turned it into the single sleeve and she gets a big, fat check. It sounds almost smug, but it's what I've been saying all along in terms of R.E.M.: we didn't go into this to become mega-superstars, we went into it because we wanted to be in a rock band, and that was it. It is kind of wild how the story is very similar to Chris', and what he's saying is very true: I think, there's just a kind of genuine excitement about doing things and creating, and showing people stuff and getting their feedback and looking at what they're doing.

Jarrett: I think people sense that. Like, when I decided to do *Ray Gun*, my only goal was to make the coolest fucking magazine in the world. There wasn't any other ulterior motive. And then it was like, "Oh, if I could make a living at this, it'd be nice." And then things just sort of mushroomed. But I think people sense that, when you do something for some other reason.

Stipe: And that crosses over from music to art to graphic design to photography.

Bilheimer: **I have a career in graphic design, but if it ceases being fun, I'll quit. It's what I enjoy doing now, and that's always been the main thing behind R.E.M. I think, the day they stop enjoying playing songs together, they're going to quit.**

Jarrett: It would be interesting to hear what else influences you guys visually. Michael, you talked about the New York Dolls' first record cover...is there anything else that really stands out?

Stipe: Recently I've been really inspired by a lot of the color photographers that are doing work now....

Jarrett: Like who?

Stipe: Well, Wolfgang Tillmans.

Jarrett: Yeah, he's hot. Nan Goldin?

Stipe: Nan Goldin, and Nick Waplington and Philip-Lorca diCorcia. These guys, they're doing some amazing stuff. Larry Sultan, Richard Prince, those are the people that, for me right now, I just bristle with

At 23 years old I had to walk in to Warner Bros. and sit down with the president, the head of creative services. I had done it before. At 23 years old I had to walk in to Warner Bros. and sit down with the president,   the head

Warner Bros. put out that year.   Having never done it before.

1 2

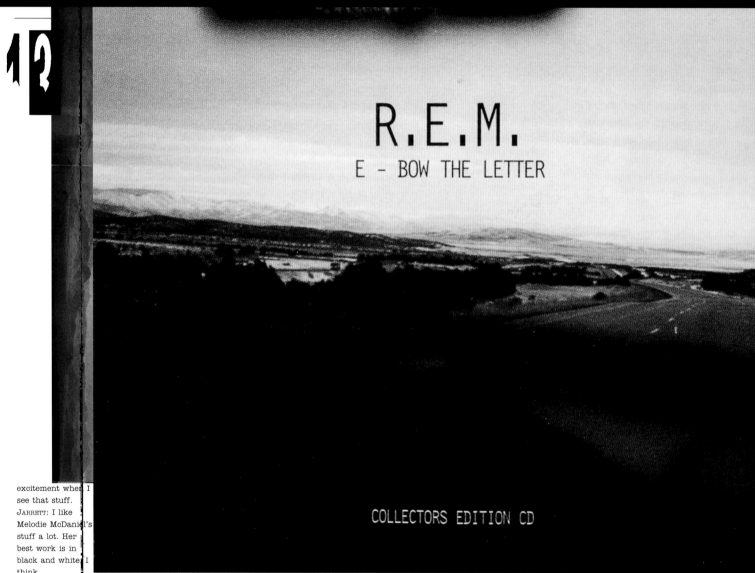

R.E.M.
E - BOW THE LETTER

COLLECTORS EDITION CD

excitement when I see that stuff.

JARRETT: I like Melodie McDaniel's stuff a lot. Her best work is in black and white I think.

STIPE: Yeah, she did some color stuff for us when we put out "Man On The Moon." She'd just broken her arm the day before, so she had trouble shooting, but she did some color stuff for us then that was real good. Chris, who are some of the people who have inspired you in the last three or four years? Outside of our circle of friends. In town it's like Lance Bangs, you, Jim Herbert, Jeff Luckey, Ian McFarlane....

BILHEIMER: Vaughan Oliver is obviously amazing. I don't think he's actually influenced my work per se — I don't think my design work looks anything like his — but there's someone who is very inspirational, you can immediately tell his work from two blocks away. I really feel like it's always distinctively his. Which I think

is a real triumph when you can do anything you want and it still looks like your work.

Stipe: Does he have a baby?

BLACKWELL: Yes.

Stipe: Did I put his baby's foot in my mouth?

BLACKWELL: Yeah, when I was doing that R.E.M. story in London for *huH.*

Stipe: Oh, okay. (laughter) I remember that.

BLACKWELL: Vaughan enjoyed that very much, by the way. He was pretty amused.

STIPE: **Well, he's got a good-tasting baby. Only later did I realize who that was.**

BILHEIMER: Once again, I really try not to look at what other people are doing that much.

to walk in and talk about putting out arguably the biggest record Warner Bros. put out that year. Having never of creative services. I had to walk in and talk about putting out arguably the biggest record

JARRETT: Do you want to keep yourself in this secluded little bubble?

BILHEIMER: (laughs) It's increasingly difficult. The more work I do, the more people I meet. In the last year I've been exposed to a lot more work, and I think if anything it's made me better. Another great designer is a guy from San Francisco named Rex Ray, who does High Risk, all the books for High Risk.

STIPE: That's a particularly inspired little press, I think. They haven't put out a shitty book yet.

BILHEIMER: I like Mike Mills' work. It's fun. I'm inspired by the way he fucks with things, the playful kind of way. I like his digging into pop culture and fucking with it. And making trite things beautiful and funny. I'm inspired by his philosophy of things.

STIPE: I've gotta go feed my dogs soon...and maybe I've talked too much...but I think it's really significant to say that what we've been talking about — in terms of a small community of people that inspire one another, and cross-inspire — that's the network that you set up, whether or not you're creating things. It reflects a much larger thing, which is what our lives become.

I don't want to get philosophical, but the point I'm trying to make is that this is not something that I think is specific to Clarke County, Georgia, or to Athens. I've been exposed to it in my travels, and it's one of the better things about maybe the way that I am and how I see things, but I always seem to fall into these groups of people. The same thing is going on in Ann Arbor and in Portland, Oregon; and in Olympia; Louisville, Kentucky; Madison, Wisconsin; Ithaca, New York; and somewhere in Providence, although we're not sure. (laughs) It's that thing we call life.

Of course, all those people don't have — and I'm thankful for this — magazines or books that are being published or necessarily even anybody paying attention to 'em, but it doesn't really have to go further than that community. That's enough.

BILHEIMER: I think once it gets out into that commercial level where business gets involved, it changes.

STIPE: That's true.

BILHEIMER: And there's no way around that. And I think what we do is fight against that as much as possible, get away with as much as we can. But it's so exciting that we can, every once in a while, expose someone's work to a greater number of people. It's one of the more gratifying parts of the job.

JARRETT: I think that's what's great about *Ray Gun*: we can constantly do that. *Ray Gun* really is sort of this community where we have great photographers, great artists —

BILHEIMER: And you're exposing them —

JARRETT: Exactly. And hopefully somebody will see their work and they'll get a job doing a record sleeve or whatever. People have gotten jobs doing their first videos through *Ray Gun*, and that's exciting.

STIPE: Speaking from a privileged position, I can't tell you how thrilling it is for me to be able to go to someone like Lance Bangs or Dominic DeJoseph, both of whom live in Athens, both of whom I think are

great filmmakers and do great work here, but haven't really had the opportunity to do something like a video for a huge band, and recognizing that they're ready to do that. And being able to say, "Do you want to do this?" That, for me, is so incredible. I'm going to someone I know who is inspired and talented and capable, and throwing a huge project at them, and know that they're going to be able to do it. Not only does that put a new slant and a new angle on the piece itself, and thus reflect upon the song or the piece itself, but you also turn to that world that we can see our place in, and say, "Look, here's a total unknown from my hometown who I think is really cool, and he's gonna direct the second single for us."

BILHEIMER: That's what you did with me. **At 23 years old I had to walk in to Warner Bros. and sit down with the president, the head of creative services. I had to walk in and talk about putting out arguably the biggest record Warner Bros. put out that year. Having never done it before.**

STIPE: I'm not going to say, "I knew you could handle it!" because that makes me sound like the Wizard of Oz —

BILHEIMER: I didn't know I could do it.

STIPE: You're capable, you're cool, you've got a good sense of what you do, and that's really all you need. Lance and Dominic and Jem, that's the stuff that, to me, is totally fucking grounded and totally thrilling. And when I look at their work I think of my work and it inspires it and it reflects it, so of course you would want there to be a collaboration.

JARRETT: Exactly.

STIPE: It makes perfect sense. Why go through the same video reels that every other band in the universe is looking at, the same 25 directors — not to slam them, because I've worked with them and I will again. But it's so nice to be able to say, "This is the world that I move through and that I'm really inspired by. This is how I want my work reflected, and these are the people that I want to see some wild, like, cross-grafting of two different worlds." In the case of "E-Bow The Letter," and in the case of "Bittersweet Me," that's exactly what I got, and I'm sure it'll be the same with "How the West Was Won" and Peter Care, on a different level, because Peter Care works within that world, but he's great. He's out there. He's marching to his own beat, and it happens to be one that I know the downbeat of, so it feels good. God...I feel like Ted Turner. (laughter) It doesn't feel right —

BLACKWELL: We can crop it if necessary —

STIPE: Please do.

BILHEIMER: You'd better go feed your dogs.

STIPE: Yeah, and pee. In that order.

Action

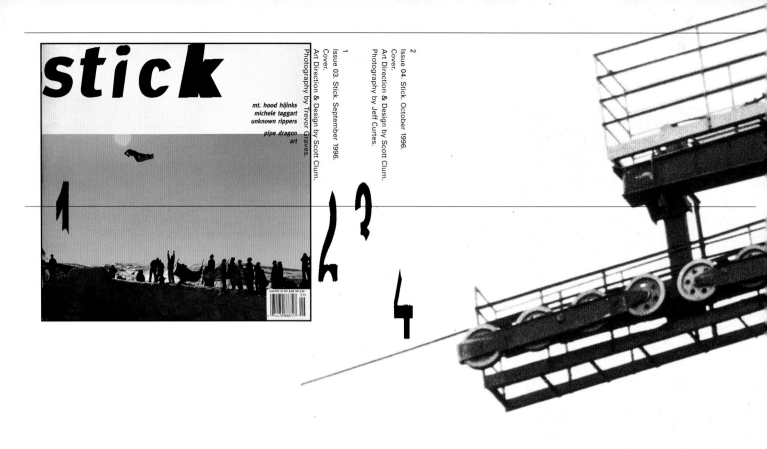

stick

mt. hood hijinks
michele taggart
unknown rippers

pipe dragon
art

1
Issue 03. Stick. September 1996.
Cover.
Art Direction & Design by Scott Clum.
Photography by Trevor Graves.

2
Issue 04. Stick. October 1996.
Cover.
Art Direction & Design by Scott Clum.
Photography by Jeff Curtes.

1

2 3

4

"I BELIEVE IN BEARING ARMS. PROBABLY GOING TO NEED 'EM THE WAY THINGS ARE GOING." – William S. Burroughs, Ray Gu

"You've got a fucking attitude and you can stick it right up your fucking arse!" – Johnny Rotten to Dave Allen, Ray Gun #34, March 1996

"Man, they shouldn't give a fat 23-year-old a gun to carry around in public."

"Macho-ness is so fucking ugly to me.

– Gibby Haynes of the Butthole Surfers, commenting on Park Police in a rest

So you can beat the shit out of me but can you do

TX, Ray Gun #37, June/July 1996

beautiful?" ——

lea of the Red Hot Chili Peppers, Bikini #8, February/March 1994

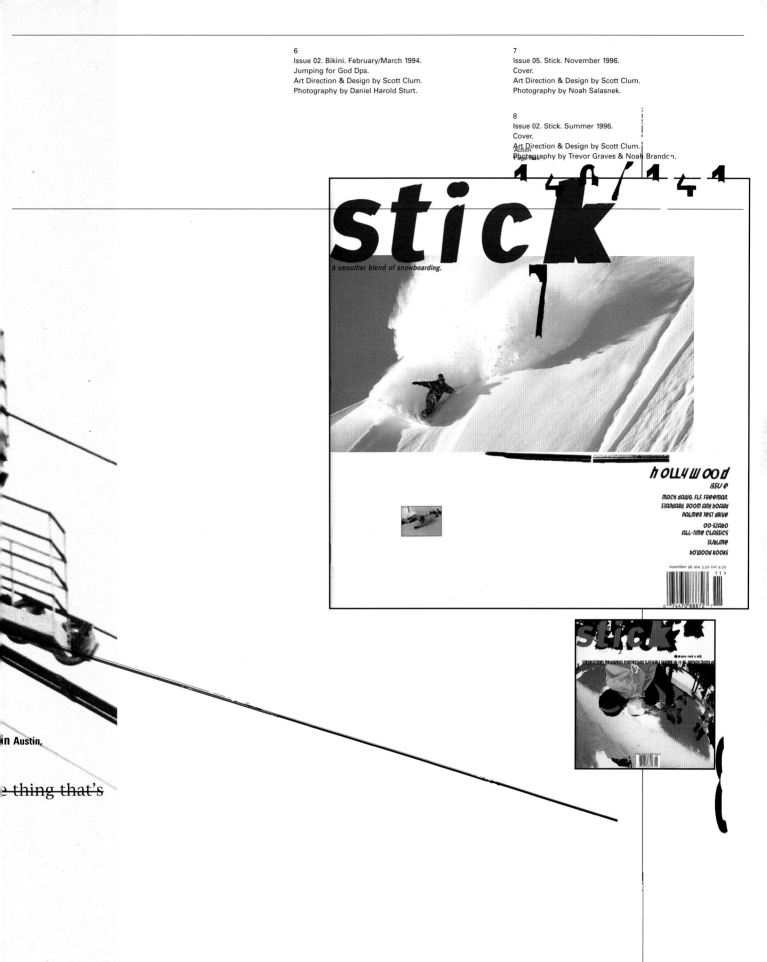

Action
page 143

stick

A smoother blend of snowboarding.

h oll4 w oo d
issu e

mack dawg. f.l.f. freeman.
standard. room and board
palmer test drive
oo-szabo
all-time classics
sublime
ho'wood kooks

november 96 usa 3.50 can 4.50
11 >

0 74470 88872 7

in Austin,

e thing that's

"I'M FINDING IT VERY
HARD TO
LIVE IN THE REAL WORLD
AT THE MOMENT.
I WAS INVOLVED
WITH THE POLICE FOR
THROWING PAINT ON THE
NEIGHBOR'S. I WAS
TRASHING EXPENSIVE
MACHINERY. I TRASHED
TWO PRETTY

"I don't want to be accepted into the great family of showbiz. You tend to kind of bland out
a bit once you've made it, because then you end up meeting these people,
and of course, you probably find out they're not such a bad person, really. So it was kind
of a stand against blanding out."
– Jarvis Cocker of Pulp, on tackling Michael Jackson at the Brits Awards.
Ray Gun #36,
May 1996

BIG THINGS. THEY WERE
ON THE LAND. THE FIRST
TIME I TOLD DORIAN SHE

W ENDY . POWELL

JUST FREAKED OUT.
SHE SAID, 'IT'S LIKE
£50,000,' I SAID, 'YEAH,
BUT IT WAS JUST THERE,
AND I WAS DRAWN TO
IT.' THE SECOND TIME, I
DIDN'T EVEN TELL HER."

JULIAN
COPE ON
ECOTAGE,
RAY GU N

9
Issue 01. Stick. Winter 1995.
New Zealand & Wendy Powell Dps.
Art Direction & Design by Scott Clum.
Photography by Trevor Graves (left: New Zealand)
& Douglas Winter (right: non-digital portrait of Wendy Powell).

10
Issue 01. Stick. Winter 1995.
Contents page.
Art Direction & Design by Scott Clum.
Photography by Trevor Graves.

Action
Page Nos

3 3 ,
F E B R
U A R Y
1 9 9 6

142 / 14 145

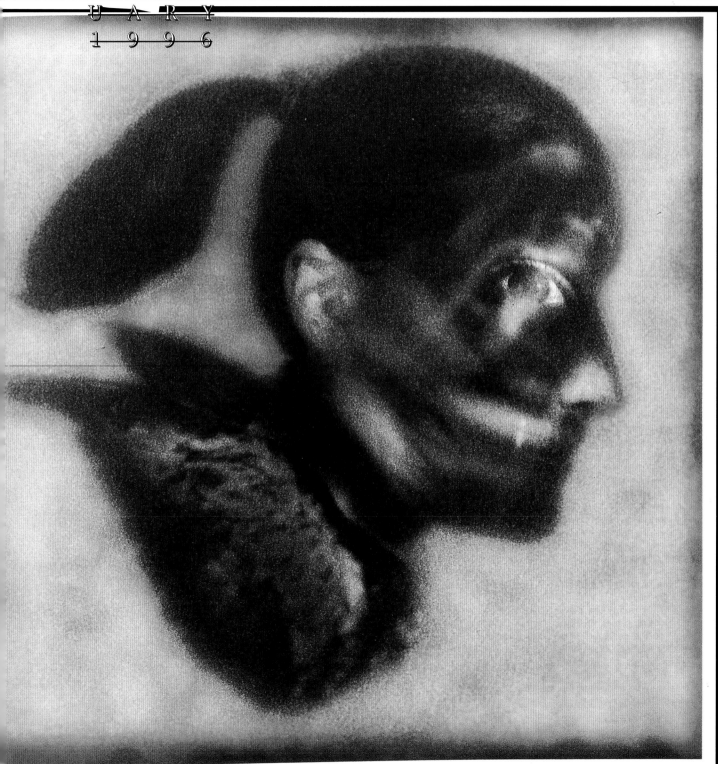

RTRAIT OF WENDY POWELL FOR STICK BY DOUGLAS WINTER.

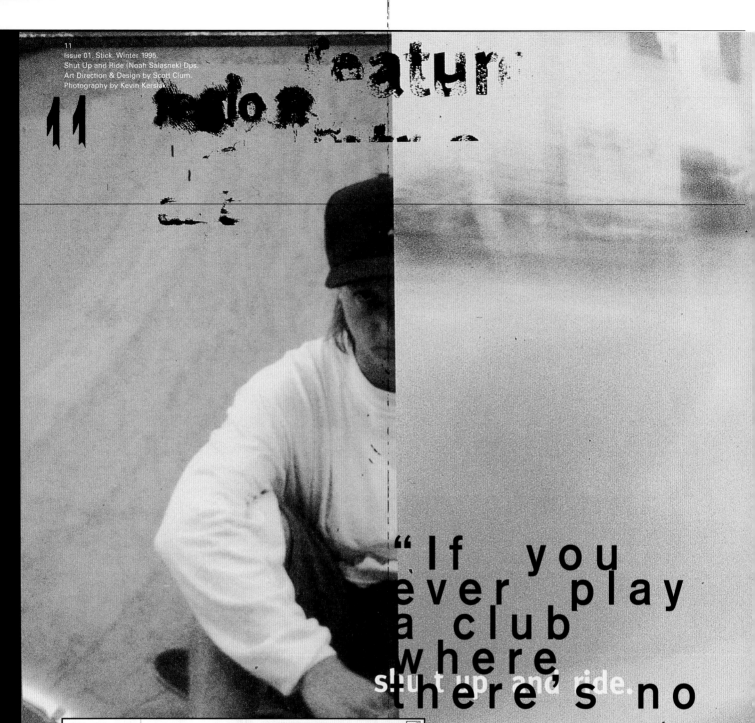

Issue 01. Stick. Winter 1995.
Shut Up and Ride (Noah Salasnek) Dps.
Art Direction & Design by Scott Clum.
Photography by Kevin Kerslake.

"If you
ever play
a club
where
shut up and ride.
there's no

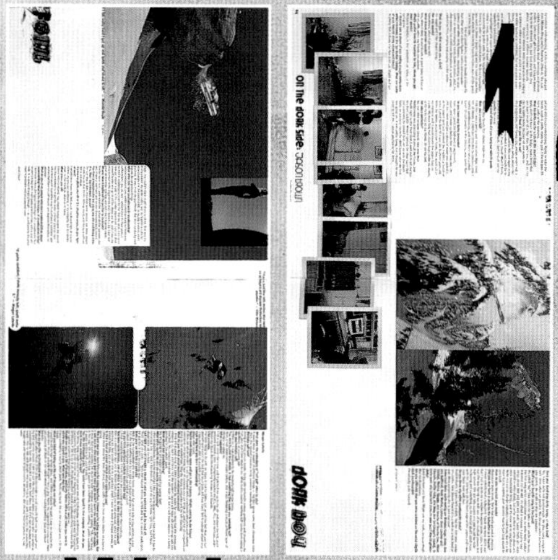

bouncers, there's never any fights.

Issue 05. Blah Blah Blah. August 1996.
Boardinsane Dps.
Art Direction & Design by Chris Ashworth @ Substance.
Photography by Rob Gracie/LifeStock.

Issue 02. Stick. Summer 1996.
Tuff enuff Dps.
Art Direction & Design by Scott Clum.
Photography by K. Gavin, Mark Gallup & Rich Van Every.

Issue 02. Stick. Summer 1996.
Jason Brown Dps.
Art Direction & Design by Scott Clum.
Photography by Trevor Graves.

Action
Page Nos

144/145

If there's no wars, you don't need an army. And if you don't have an army, you don't need the military budget. If you don't have the military budget, you can't be telling **people** where all these billions of fucking dollars are

And, so that's the mentality we're up against. Because we're dopers. We're pacifists

photographed by

Noah Salasnek

sequence. photographed

Mike Hauswirth

We're the epitome of pacifism, because when you're fucked up, your reaction time for getting angry is so fucking slow.

on the job side.

Tommy Chong with

Cypress Hill,

Ray Gun #34, March

1996

"We'd go in the service entry and up the escalator and these guys, this security force called Tokyo Patrol, would run up the stairs 30 floors and beat us to the top. We'd go out in the middle of the night and they'd be in the hall, practicing karate." – **Rick Neilsen of Cheap Trick on playing the Tokyo Budokan,**
Ray Gun #38, August 1996

MILLENN*IUM*MOD

Vexed Generation: post-Mod designers who turn M.o.D. hardwear into chemical-warproof scooter gear

threadhead: Lisa Verrico
bluetone: Terry Lewis

"Yo, look, man. You know what would bring people together aliens out here runnin' around... Chuck D of Public Enemy, huH #2, October 1994 Le' a thousand fuckin' big-headed automatically? aliens come down to earth. You know what I'm sayin'? A thousand big-headed

Issue 04. Blah Blah Blah. July 1996.
Millennium Mod Dps.
Art Direction & Design by Chris Ashworth & Neil Fletcher @ Substance.
Photography by Terry Lewis.

In September, thousands of scooter fans are expected to make the pilgrimage to Rome to celebrate Vespa's 50th anniversary. This month, just as many may descend on London's Hyde Park for The Who's comeback concert. And, who knows, at some point soon you may glimpse Oasis or Ocean Colour Scene in your rear view mirror, cruising along on their mopeds.

Yes, this year's scooter season is going to be crazier than ever, and cooler too. Why? Because this summer you can be seen astride one of Patrick Cox's customised Veleciferos [if you've got a spare three grand in a bowling bag under the stairs], wearing something from Vexed Generation's latest range [just a few used tenners in an old loafer].

Located in London's Soho, the shop's owners Adam Thorpe and Joe Hunter have come up with a collection of clothes designed not only to withstand modern, urban environments, but also specifically suited to two-wheeled travellers. Forget the Quad Mods' flimsy khaki parkas, Vexed Generation have designed a hard-wearing, ultra-functional, navy, '90s equivalent. Their lightweight, hooded, three-quarter length coats [complete with optional, detachable, furry lining] are made from high-tenacity, ballistic nylon, purchased direct from the Ministry of Defence.

"The M.o.D. use the material to make flakjackets and bomb disposal curtains," explains Thorpe. "It's coated with neoprene so it's waterproof, fireproof and knifeproof. We also add sub-aqua bomb disposal zips which are doubly strong and won't ever rust. Because the materials we bought are used in different types of land and air combat, when we approached the M.o.D. they asked for our exact specification. We said, 'Something very tough, but fashionable, and under £10 a metre'."

Clearly designed by devoted scooter fans, the parkas front fasten with a tail through the legs, which allows rainwater to run straight off, rather than pooling in your lap. Furthermore, every customer receives two metres of free velcro to wrap around objects such as mobile phones and wallets, for easy pocket access. Matching motorbike courier-style rucksacks, which strap across the chest, have velcro-lined pouches and pen-holders, while the trousers, which also crotch-fasten, have padded knees for extra protection and warmth.

Currently, Thorpe and Hunter are working on the ultimate Vexed outfit [for an exhibition at the Barbican in September] and, having persuaded Puma to relaunch the classic Puma State trainer, they're designing the sports company's exclusive, 'capsule collection' for the winter season.

Thorpe claims that the inspiration for Vexed Generation, which also houses record decks, video equipment and slide projection space, comes not only from the current state of the urban environment, but also from social claustrophobia created by the Criminal Justice Bill's stop-and-search laws and the rapidly-increasing presence of outdoor CCTV.

"We design clothes for the area in which we live," explains Thorpe. "When we started, there were six of us sharing a flat in the East End of London. Because it was on the edge of the Ring Of Steel, it was the first place to test out the CJB legislation and also to introduce widespread use of cameras on the street. Two years ago, we were walking down Commercial Road and suddenly none of us could breathe properly. We later found out that 300 people had been admitted that day to Whitechapel Hospital simply because the pollution had been so bad."

Consequently, Vexed Generation are using their shop to inform customers of some startling environmental and surveillance statistics. A TV in the whited-out window and luminous half-pillars around the walls display transparencies and slogans such as '160 Londoners die each year from urban smog' and 'Incidents of asthma have risen 500% in the last decade'. With this in mind, they are designing a fleece top which incorporates a face mask.

Moreover, the clothes themselves hang in a sealed perspex box and can be felt only by reaching through circular holes along each side.

Despite the futuristic feel of the surroundings and the materials used — as well as ballistic nylon, the designers favour rip-stop grid parachute fabric and silk/wool mix tonic, which takes on the appearance of liquid mercury under light — Vexed Generation insist that their clothes are simply contemporary.

"We've been accused of designing for a very bleak future," says Thorpe. "That's not true. Hoods and masks and protective fabrics are relevant today. In fact, they're absolutely essential for city life."

Oh dear, whatever happened to Parklife?

9 SCOOTERS

Action
Page Nos

15 / 146 / 147

Photography by Krystin Johnson.
Art Direction & Design by Scott Clum.
Action Sp.
Issue 02. Stick. Summer 1996.
18

Photography by Trevor Graves.
Art Direction & Design by Scott Clum.
Region Sp.
Issue 03. Stick. September 1996.
17

Photography by Trevor Graves.
Art Direction & Design by Scott Clum.
Mike & Dave Hatchett Sp.
Issue 05. Stick. November 1996.
16

"SEXUALITY IS PART OF THE UNCON-TROLLED SIDE, SOME-THING YOU CAN'T KEEP A HANDLE ON — THE MOST YOU CAN DO IS SUPPRESS IT, AND THAT'S WHEN THINGS START TO GET REALLY WEIRD. MUSIC AND SEX ARE INTER-TWINED. THE MUSIC I'M MAK-ING CALLS FOR SOME-THING LIKE SEX TO BE SUNG ABOUT OVER THE TOP OF IT — TO SING ABOUT GOING SHOPPING WOULD BE HORRIBLE!"

THESE HOLLYWOOD GUYS GET LOST LOOKING FOR THE C H O P P E R. THEY DON'T EVEN KNOW WHAT HIKING IS.

16

17

A CTION

15

—POLLY JEAN HARVEY, RAY GUN #6,   **MAY 1993**

19
Issue 33. Ray Gun. February 1996.
Contents page.
Art Direction & Design by Robert Hales
Photography by Steen Sundland

CONTENTS.33

20
Issue 03. Blah Blah Blah. June 1996.
Firestarters/Road Rage Dps.
Art Direction & Design by Chris Ashworth, Neil Fletcher &
Amanda Sissons @ Substance.
Photography by Bazza J (above) & Paul Cohen (below).

21
Issue 05. Blah Blah Blah. August 1996.
Fender Weekender Dps.
Art Direction & Design by Chris Ashworth & Neil Fletcher @ Substance.
Photography by Fela.

Action
Page Nos

WOMEN
IN DRAG:
FIRESTARTERS
→

DAVE
CLARKE:
ROAD RAGE
→

" D r u n k e n
b o a t   d r i v i n g.   I
j u s t   t o o l
ar   o   u   n   d   the
r i v e r   i n   c o m p l e t e
d a r k n e s s.   Something
seems really wrong about
drunk driving in a car.
But in a boat — I've done this a
million times — I'll just smash
into the bank, or I'll run the boat
aground, or run out of gas. It
doesn't really seem, at three in
the morning, like a bad thing. My
boat doesn't go fast enough to kill my
passengers." —

Dean Ween, Ray Gun #28, August 1995

"I'm not really competing. If I am, they can have it. I'm fat, got a small dick, I'm a bad player and I hate everything. So they're gonna win. But I watch MTV. I like that Coolio song. I'm down with it. All these guys wear their pants down around their ass. I've always done that. When will it be cool to start spilling food on yourself? That's when I'm gonna be fucking riding the wave." — Cris Kirkwood of the Meat Puppets, Ray Gun #31, November 1995

Fender weekender

Volkswagen fanatics. Result — Beetlemania! Then one of the wheels fell off.

The plan:15,000 pop fans in search of a surrogate Glastonbury Festival in a multiple pile-up with 15,000

than a burn-out teenage porn queen."
— Traci Lords on her album 1000 Fires,
Ray Gun #31,
November 1995

"I got to prove that I was something other

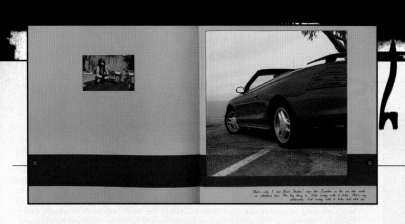

ray gun #27 *on the road again*

cover: björk by dave stewart

this page: illustration by blair thornley

Action
Page Nos

1 5 0 / 1 5 1

wheels of steel

48   49

50   51

"I never think where the shit's gonna go and that's why I think the people who do think about it are really suck-ass musicians that should all be shot, y' know. It blows. I don't think about it at all. I never thought about it. I just reacted. I acted and reacted. That's all. If you were playin' like 900-mile-an-hour music to a bunch of fuckin' New York critics sitting in folding chairs staring at you, you'd roll in broken glass too." —Iggy Pop with Perry Farrell, Ray Gun #35, April 1996

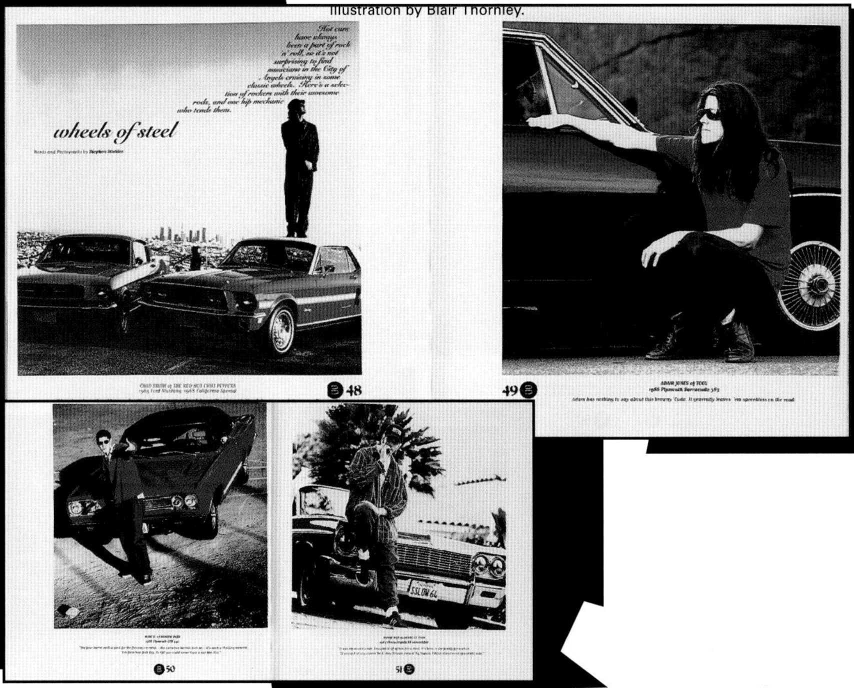

"We still play house parties, keggers. Those are my favorite gigs. You can't be a band of pussies and play those parties in Knoxville. The people will call you out. They can separate the crap from the real thing. You go at it like it's the last thing you'll ever do." – John Davis of Superdrag, Ray Gun #35, April 1996

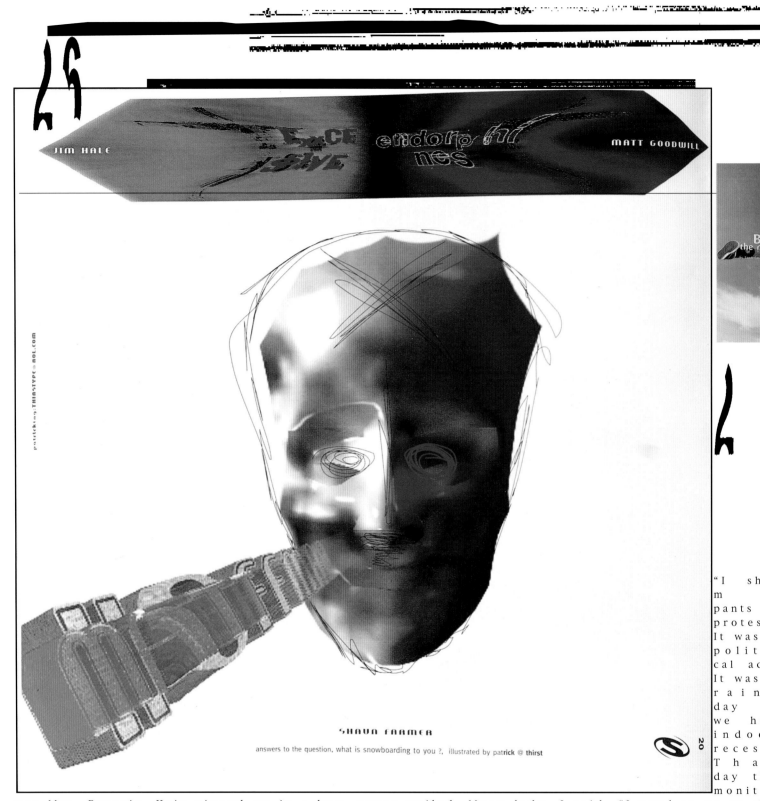

JIM HALE   endorphines   MATT GOODWILL

patrick @ THIRSTYPE @ aol.com

SHAUN FARMER

answers to the question, what is snowboarding to you ?, illustrated by patrick @ thirst

20

"I sh
m
pants
protes
It was
polit
cal ac
It was
r a i n
day
we h
i n d o o
r e c e s
T h a
day t
m o n i t

was Mrs. Francis. Hair pinned up in a bun, never smiled. Mean lady. I said, "I need to go to t
bathroom," and she's, like, "No, you wait 'til your teacher gets back." Well, recess was going to
an hour and when you gotta go, you know. So I had two choice
Leave and face the consequences of getting in trouble or underli
ing the injustice of this teacher-student interaction and shitti
my pants. So I went ahead and shit my pants and waited for r
teacher to come back and I told her that I'd shit my pants and to
her why. Mrs. Francis was publicly reprimanded. She had to cor
down and apologize to me in person." –

Greg Dulli of the Afghan Whigs with Chuck Cleaver of the Ass Ponys, Ray Gun #37, June/July 1996

Action Page Nos

1 5 2 / 1 5 3

"It's obvious that the American Dream is a top dream." —Shaun Ryder of Black Grape with Joe Strummer, Ray Gun #32, December/January 1996

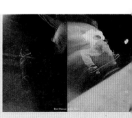

scream'n @ chickens

"Chicken is skateboarding. This is where you go when you know you're good"

IKINI

GOLDEN GLOVE BOXING

TEST DRIVE OF THE
STARS FEATURING
UGLY KID JOE'S
WHIT CRANE

BACKSTAGE WITH
REAL LIVE SHOW GIRLS

MASSIVE ATTACK
GETS IGNORED

HOW TO CHEAT
A PROFESSIONAL
LESSON

SEARCHING FOR
VEGAS BACKSIDE

EVEL KNIEVEL
AN HOMAGE

HOWGIRLS

"I just like to get back to my room, get buck naked, eat a couple of hamburgers and go to bed. That's my idea of adventurous." –

David Thomas of Pere Ubu, Ray Gun #7, June/July 1993

The Kristy Kronicles

Dweezil Zappa unleashes a probing interview on this savage blonde and meets his match

30
Issue 16. Bikini. July 1996.
Seiko Matsuda Dps.
Art Direction & Design by John Curry/mc2
Photography by Graham Kuhn.

3   1
Issue 12.   Bikini.   November   1995.
C   o   v   e   r   .
Design Direction by Scott Clum. Design by John Curry/cr[x].
Photography   by   Dave   Jensen.

32
Issue 16. Bikini. July 1996.
Kristy Swanson Dps.
Art Direction & Design by John Curry/cr[x].
Photography by Dave Jensen.

5 4 / 1 5 5

Nos

33
Issue 16. Bikini. July 1996.
Cover.
Art Direction & Design by John Curry/mc2.
Photography by Dave Jensen.

"Sex is an excuse for death.

We have sex because we die. If we didn't die, we wouldn't need to reproduce. So everytime you're aroused by a woman's hips or a flick of her hair, that's simply

because we are going to die. The whole thing is fueled by death."

Robyn Hitchcock, Ray Gun #5, April 1993

34
Issue 12. Bikini. November 1995
Gina Gershon Dps.
Design Direction by Scott Clum. Design by John Curry/cr[x]
Photography by Dave Jensen

BIKINI
action · film · cars · rock · roll

kristy swanson
the diva meets dweezil zappa
christina applegate
test drives a bitchin' camaro
daytona bike week '96
locals only: the so-cal surf wars
how to play the ponies
a day in the life of... pulp fiction producer lawrence bender
three's company's priscilla barnes
quien es mas macho? battle royale

July 3.95 CAN 4.80

chemical brothers salt gravity kills fuzzy seiko

"I'm really into the word 'grrrl.' 'Girl, 'slut', and 'dyke' all need to be taken back, and taken a

that use them as weapons. I think it's really disgusting that women made up a word and m

movement and now other people have told us what it means and given it a derogatory defi
me fucking mad. I'm not going to let a bunch of men who have decided that the word girl m

slave/slut/secretary take away a word that is completely different to me in every way."
— Kathleen Hanna of Bikini Kill, Ray G
December/January 1993

"Bruce McCulloch: Now this is my guess: The
thing that bugs you the most is when people
ask you about being a woman.
Juliana Hatfield: Oh, God. I hate it. I hate it so much.
Bruce: Especially 'cause you sort of rock. A little bit. Do
you get compared to other female artists? You're
never, I'm sure, compared to a man.
Juliana: I've been compared to Axl Rose before.
Bruce: In what context? That you get drunk and fucking trash things?
Juliana: Yeah, I like goin' on tour, gettin' fucked up and bangin chicks!" — Juliana Hatfield interviewed by Bruce McCulloch of "Kids In The Hall,"
Ray Gun #25, April 1995

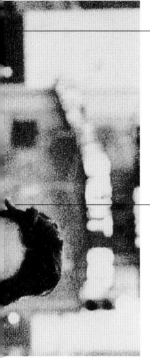

35
Issue 07. Bikini. January 1995.
Liv Tyler Dps.
Design Direction by Scott Clum. Design by John Curry/cr[x].
Photography by Lara Rossignol.

3   6
Issue   07.   Bikini.   January   1995.
Liv   Tyler   Dps..
Design Direction by Scott Clum. Design by John Curry/cr[x].
Photography   by   Lara   Rossignol.

37
Issue 07. Bikini. January 1995.
Cover.
Action
Design Direction by Scott Clum. Design by John Curry/cr[x].
Page Nos
Photography by Lara Rossignol.

155/157

y from the men

25

n. That makes

n   #2,

37

ACTION. FILM. CARS. AND ROCK N ROLL.

BIK'INI

Megadeth Motor Madness.

Quentin Tarantino:
another rare interview

Holiday Gift Guide.
electric socks n more!

Metallica House Tour: very scary

Heli Skiing. Chopper Rides, helluv cheap

Shoe Fashion.
gotta scrape the sh*t right off ...

Tijuana Bull Fights. a bloody mess

John Frusciante.
life after the Chili Peppers

Liv Tyler. best cover choice in t
by Thurston Moore

"Lately I've been feeling bad about myself because I don't think men flirt with me anymore. I used to be a very flirtatious girl. I used to be someone who would go into a room and get it all coming at me." – Liz Phair, Ray Gun #21, November, 1994

"YOU CAN'T FUCK TO INDIE ROCK."

– MARTIN DUFFY OF PRIMAL SCREAM, RAY GUN #16, MAY 1994

UMMM, E

THE SWEET STORY OF WHY YOUNG PRODUCERS LIK

"SO WE HEAD OFF TO THIS EXCLUSIVE CLUB IN NEW YORK WHERE SELVES USING BIC RAZORS — WE HAD CUTS ALL OVER. WE HAD HANGING OFF US. ANYWAY, THE MANAGERESS WAS THIS BEAUTIFUL ME AND HIM SMOKING A PIPE AND SHE JOINS US AND THEN START PLACE AND WE'LL DO IT PROPER.' SO WE GO TO HER GAFF AND GOT A BRA AND KNICKERS ON, COMING UP WITH THIS NAUGHTY HHUHHUH.' THEN HER FRIEND COMES HOME, WHO'S THIS OTHER WOMAN ALL DRESSED NICE.
AND THE NEXT THING, THEM TWO ARE FONDLING EACH OTHER AND BEZ, AND WE'RE SAT THERE GOING, 'LET'S HAVE SOME BEZ LOOKS AT ME AND SAYS, 'I'M JUST GOING TO THE DELI, WE GOT BOLLOCKED 'CAUSE WE MISSED THE SOUNDCHECK."

41
Issue 01. Bikini. November 1993.
Cover.
Art Direction & Design by Scott Clum.
Photography by Lance Staedler.

42
Issue 01. Bikini. November 1993.
Alyssa Milano Dps.
Art Direction & Design by Scott Clum.
Photography by Michael Muller.

38
Issue 18. Bikini. November 1996.
Cover.
Design Direction by John Curry/cr[x].
Photography by Kate Garner.

Action
Page Nos

BY **JOHN CRAVEN**
PHOTOS BY **DAVE JENSEN**
STYLING BY **AMANDA FRIEDLAND**
COVER SHIRT BY **ASH**

IEW MOVIE STARS FOR MAGAZINES THAT HARDLY PAY

Alyssamilano

she's the boss

WE'RE PLAYING. WE'RE REALLY SCRUFFY. WE GOT BALD HEADS WHICH WE SHAVED OUR-
BIG BLUE PARKAS ON, FUCKED-UP ADIDAS GAZELLE TRAINERS, REALLY SHITTY JEANS
WOMAN, RIGHT, WHO WAS ABOUT 35, A GOOD TEN YEARS OLDER THAN US. SHE SEES
PULLING OUT HER CHARLIE, BIG LINES, RIGHT. AND SHE SAYS, 'LET'S GO BACK TO MY
WE HAVE A SNIFF, AND SHE GOES OUT AND COMES BACK IN THE ROOM AND SHE'S JUST
TALK...AND WE'RE SAT THERE LIKE BEAVIS AND BUTT-HEAD GOING, 'HUH-HUH-HUH-
        FUCKING UPPERCRUST

AND SHE'S JUST GOT A BRA ON AND A PAIR OF FUCKING BOXERS RUBBING UP AGAINST ME
MORE COKE, 'HUH-HUH-HUHHHUHHUH,' AND THEY'RE FEEDING US LINES OF IT. AND THEN
RIGHT.' SO I LOOKS AT THEM AND SAYS, 'I'M GOING WITH 'IM.' AND WE FUCKED OFF. AND
Shaun Ryder of Black Grape with Joe Strummer, Ray Gun #32, December/January 1996

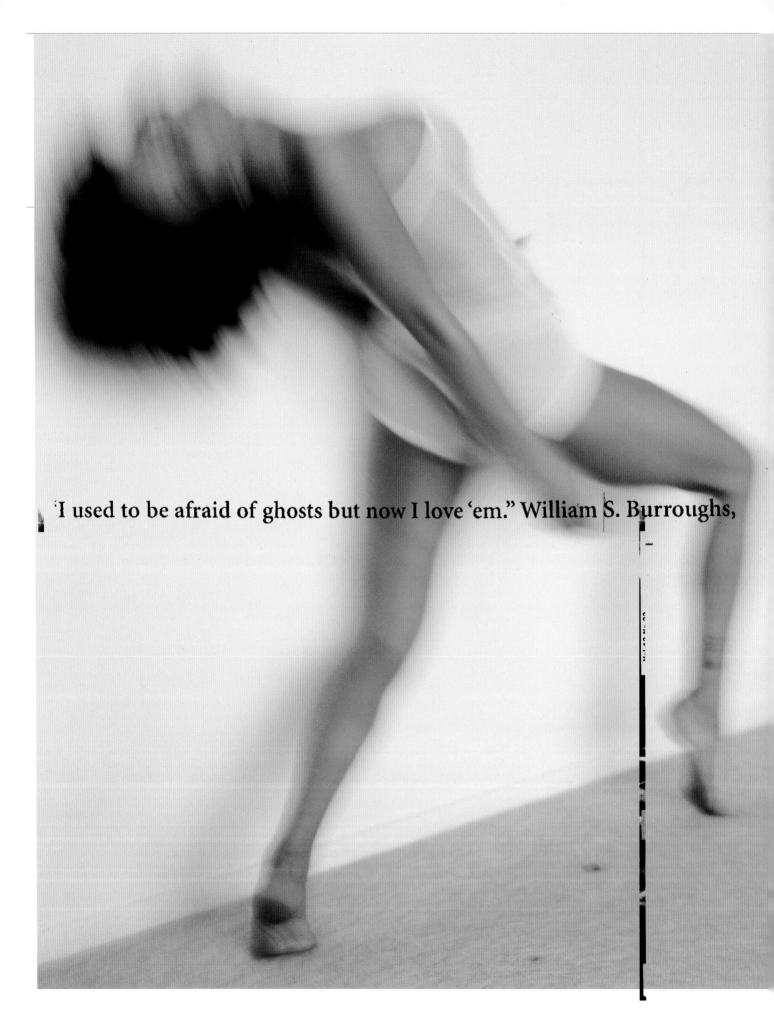

'I used to be afraid of ghosts but now I love 'em." William S. Burroughs,

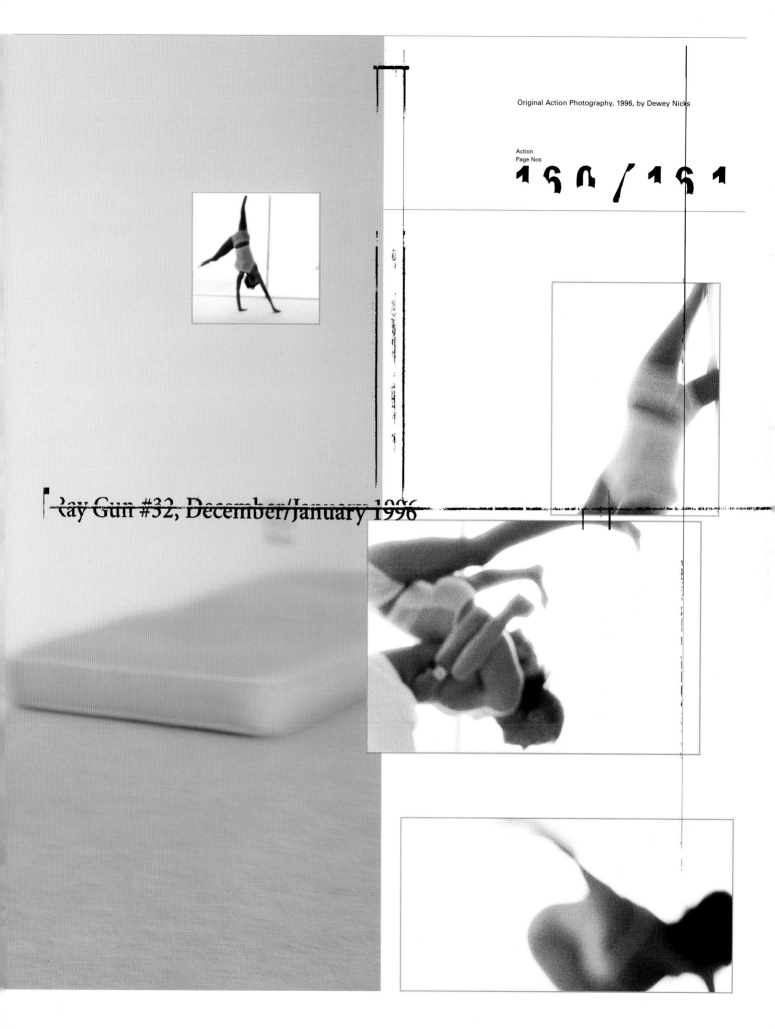

"People need to see the most ordinary things, but on television. They'll film themselves making a cup of coffee then watch it. It's that fascination of watching ordinary life. But once it's on telly, it's different. Our eyesight is so pure, what we perceive. But when it's on telly it gets that grainy quality. In fact, people prefer to see the grainy image. People find things more sexy when they're on bad quality film than when they're on 35 mil."

Damon Albarn of Blur, Ray Gun #32, December/January 1996

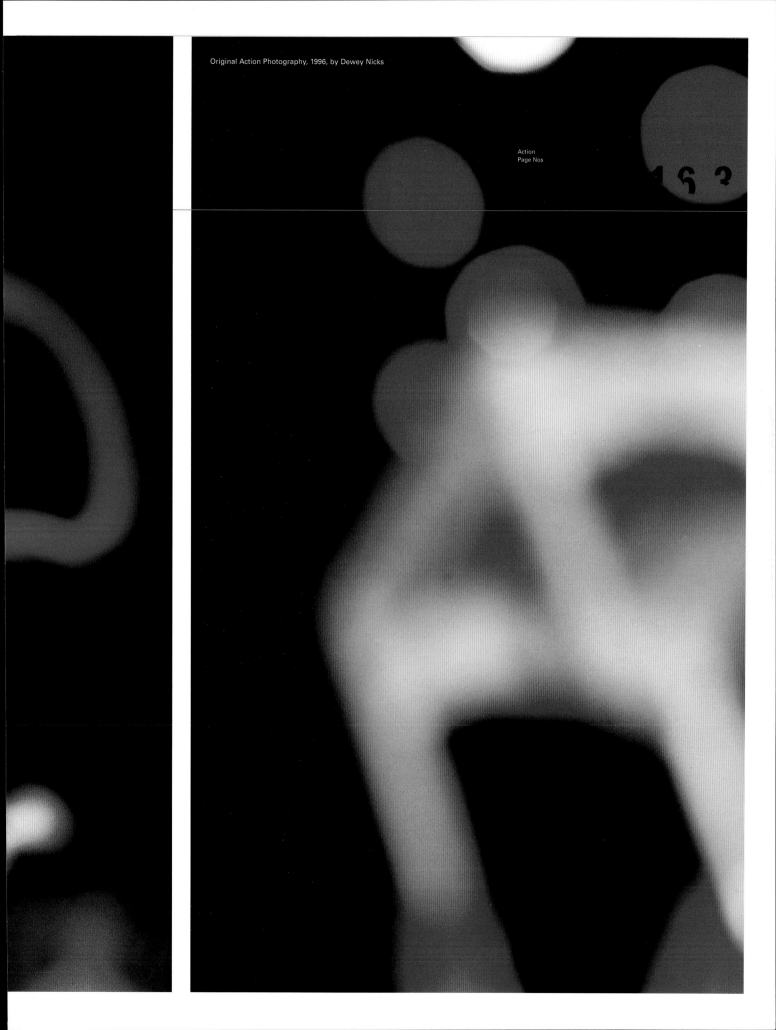

Original Action Photography, 1996, by Dewey Nicks

Action
Page Nos

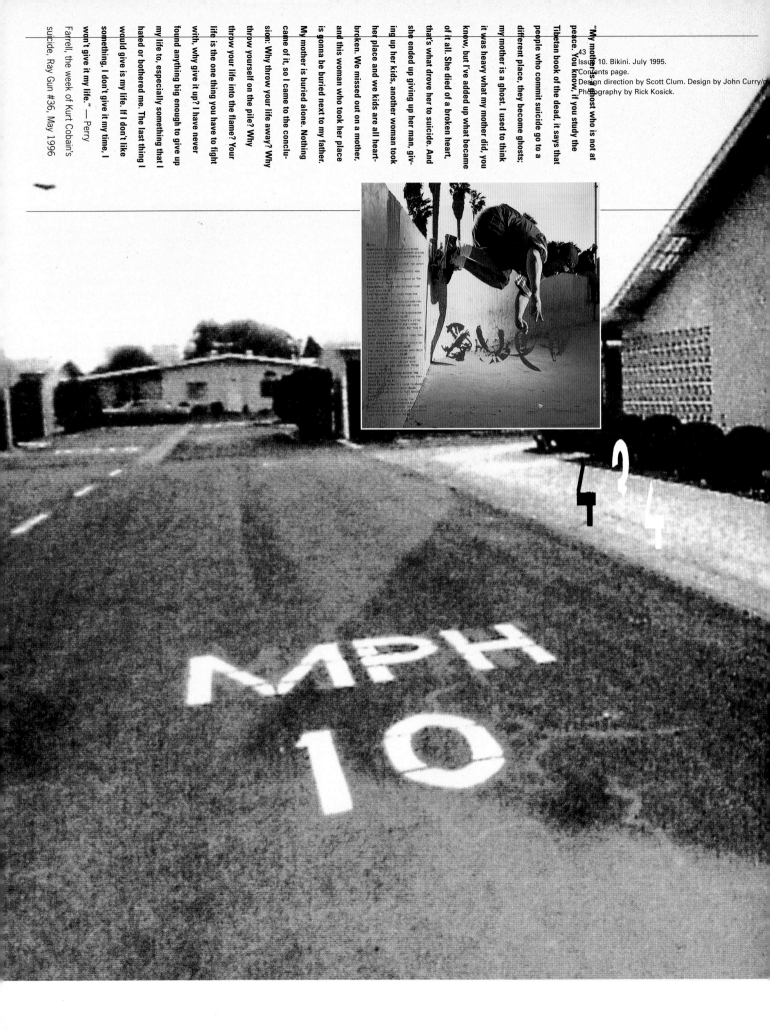

43
Issue 10. Bikini. July 1995.
Contents page.
Design direction by Scott Clum. Design by John Curry/r
Photography by Rick Kosick.

"My mother is a ghost who is not at peace. You know, if you study the Tibetan book of the dead, it says that people who commit suicide go to a different place, they become ghosts; my mother is a ghost. I used to think it was heavy what my mother did, you know, but I've added up what became of it all. She died of a broken heart, that's what drove her to suicide. And she ended up giving up her man, giving up her kids, another woman took her place and we kids are all heartbroken. We missed out on a mother, and this woman who took her place is gonna be buried next to my father. My mother is buried alone. Nothing came of it, so I came to the conclusion: Why throw your life away? Why throw yourself on the pile? Why throw your life into the flame? Your life is the one thing you have to fight with, why give it up? I have never found anything big enough to give up my life to, especially something that I would give up my life. If I don't like something, I don't give it my time, I won't give it my life." — Perry Farrell, the week of Kurt Cobain's suicide, Ray Gun #36, May 1996

44
Issue 14. Ray Gun. March 1994.
Leisure World Dps.
Art Direction & Design by David Carson.
Photography by Kathrin Miller.

Action
Page Nos

"i hope i die

before i get

old"   THE WHC

RAY GUN VISITS LEISURE WORLD. pho-

tography by kathrin miller

"PAUL: We're musicians. We make records, tour, and that kind of crap. It all seems so cut and dry. It's like digging a hole. You end up in the same place you started again.

KING: The whole music press, as far as what you're getting at, it's almost no win. If they talk about music it will bore us to tears, if you talk about the lore it will bore us to tears. The music press itself is a boring thing. It's like the Ceramics Press. Who cares? Go home! Quit reading Ray Gun magazine. Just look at the pretty pictures.

PAUL: Wipe your ass with Ray Gun magazine.

KING: That's right.

PAUL: Ray Gun magazine will probably be lucky if it makes it to my ass.

RG: But this is your lives.

KING: I know.

PAUL: Isn't that pitiful?

GIBBY: It's such a drag. It's causing me so much anxiety. I came to within an anxiety attack at the dentist the other day. I fucking went nuts. I shit in my chair.

RG: Was that 'cause of the dentist or 'cause of your life?

GIBBY: 'Cause of my fucking life.

GIBBY: 'Cause of the psychoanalysts yet.

KING: Capitol Records hasn't coughed up the psychoanalysts.

PAUL: In fact, they're holding back the psychoanalysts.

KING: Everybody sits around, waits for big juicy tidbits to roll out of your group therapy. It sucks.

GIBBY: Who hasn't?"

RG: I take it you've been.

GIBBY: Fuck group therapy, man. Everybody sits there blubbering about your fucking father's penis. I hate group therapy. You're sitting there blubbering about your fucking father's penis. I hate mouth. They don't give shit away, you're sitting there blubbering about your fucking father's penis. I hate mouth. They don't give shit away.

Gibby Haynes, King Coffey and Paul Leary of
The Butthole Surfers,
Ray Gun #37,
June/July 1996

1
Issue 21. Ray Gun. November 1994.
Pieces of Liz Dps.
Art Direction & Design by David Carson.
Photography by Kevin Kerslake.

2
Issue 21. Ray Gun. November 1994.

Art Direction & Design by David Carson.
Photography by Kevin Kerslake.

Out of Control (C)
Page Nos

3
Issue 21. Ray Gun. November 1994.
Contents page.
Art Direction & Design by David Carson.
Photography by Kevin Kerslake.

198/199

RAY GUN

cover+ this page: liz phair by kevin kerslake

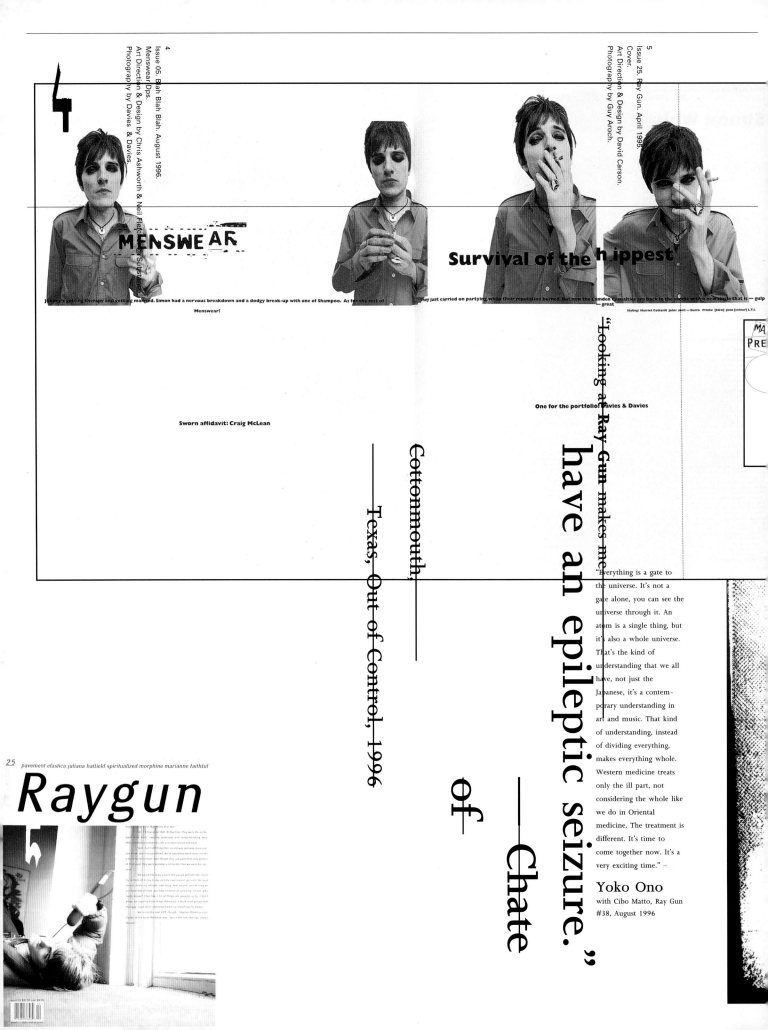

4

Issue 05. Blah Blah Blah. August 1996.
Menswear/Dps.
Art Direction & Design by Chris Ashworth & Neil Fletcher @ Substance.
Photography by Davies & Davies.

5

Issue 25, Ray Gun. April 1995.
Cover.
Art Direction & Design by David Carson.
Photography by Guy Aroch.

MENSWEAR

Survival of the hippest

Johnny's getting therapy and getting married. Simon had a nervous breakdown and a dodgy break-up with one of Shampoo. As for the rest of Menswear!

they just carried on partying while their reputation burned. But now the Camden casualties are back in the saddle with a new single that is — gulp — great

Styling: Harriet Cotterill John: shirt — Burro Prints: [b&w] Jane [colour] L.T.I.

Sworn affidavit: Craig McLean

One for the portfolio: Davies & Davies

Cottonmouth,

Texas, Out of Control, 1996

"Looking at Ray Gun makes me

have an epileptic seizure.

—Chate

of

"Everything is a gate to
the universe. It's not a
gate alone, you can see the
universe through it. An
atom is a single thing, but
it's also a whole universe.
That's the kind of
understanding that we all
have, not just the
Japanese, it's a contem-
porary understanding in
art and music. That kind
of understanding, instead
of dividing everything,
makes everything whole.
Western medicine treats
only the ill part, not
considering the whole like
we do in Oriental
medicine. The treatment is
different. It's time to
come together now. It's a
very exciting time." –

Yoko Ono
with Cibo Matto, Ray Gun
#38, August 1996

25 *pavement elastica juliana hatfield spiritualized morphine marianne faithful*

Raygun

6
Issue 11. Ray Gun. November 1993.
Manic Street Preachers Dps.
Art Direction & Design by David Carson.
Photography by Colin Bell.

7
Issue 25. Ray Gun. April 1995.
Pavement Dps.
Art Direction & Design by David Carson.
Photography by Guy Aroch.

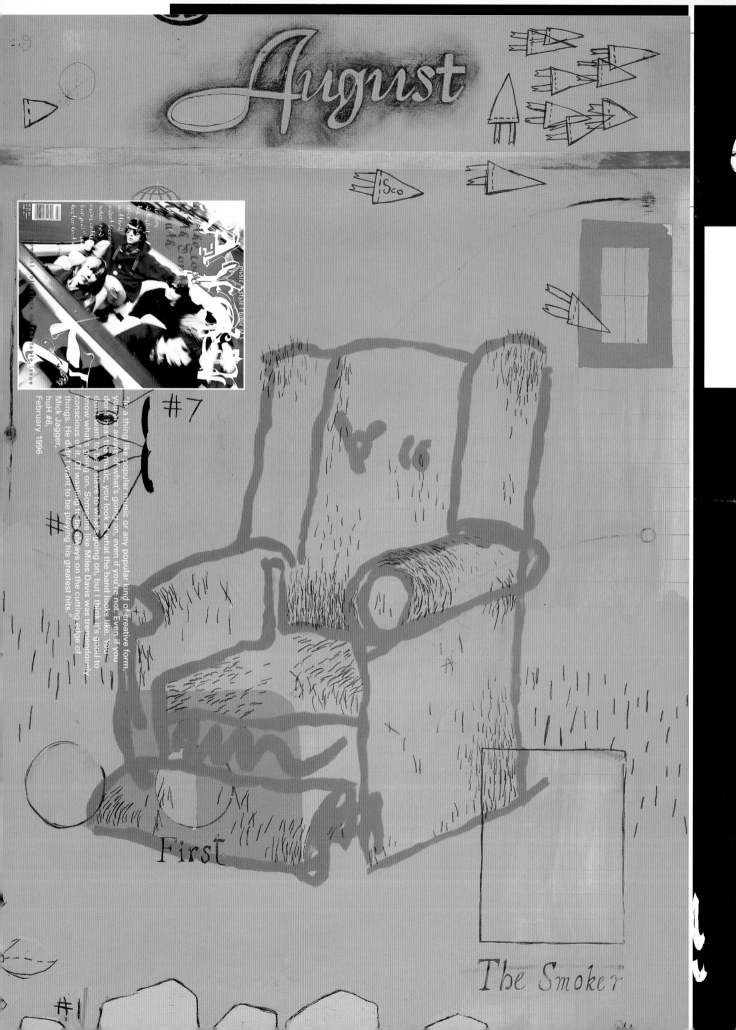

8
Issue 07. Ray Gun. June/July 1993.
Cover.
Art Direction & Design by David Carson.
Photography by Michael Lavine.

Out of Control {C}
Page Nos

172/173

10
Issue 05. huH. January 1995.
The Cranberries Dps.
Creative Direction by Vaughan Oliver.
Design by Jerôme Curchod.
Photography by Cynthia Levine.

Cranberry Fields Forever

ust another fruit group
really have the juice?
rough the band's bog.

How does that cranberry commercial go? Sweet-tart? Yeah, that pretty much sums up the cranberries. You can't miss the sweetness of their sound, which ranges from the vaporous melodies of their 1993 single "Dreams" to the passionate, lovesick sound of last year's ballad "I Can't Be With You." And if any other song were more sugary than the overplayed "Linger," well, we'd all be needing insulin shots about now.

he dark side is lingering on the cranberries' new album, No Need To Argue, in the subtle minor chords,
ry war-protest song "Zombie," and, especially, in the cranberries' decidedly-tart Irish attitudes – the
ey hide away when it's time to go on stage to sing, one more bloody time: "You've got me wrapped
your finger, do you have to, do you have to let it linger?"

, we're pretty sick of that song," admits guitarist Noel Hogan, making his already-soft voice almost
le, as if to disguise the complaint. "I mean, it's been five years we've been singing that song.
mes, we are just going through the motions, y'know." He makes a sour face, then reverts back to his
s position, hunched and squirming ever deeper into a leather sofa. You get the feeling that, if it were
e, he would allow his ever-present Marlboro to suck him up, rather than vice-versa, just so he could be
re but in the spotlight.

is fellow bandmates, bassist Mike Hogan (Noel's younger brother) and drummer Feargal Lawlor, Noel
than happy to allow vocalist Dolores O'Riordan take center stage. If only she would.
es, 25, petite and platinum blonde, is the magnet for the fans and the press, but she shies away from both
on stage, when she dons a long dress and seems to float above the crowd, swaying to the almost beatless

phy by Cynthia Levine

11
Issue 09. huH. May 1995.
Peter Murphy Dps.
Creative Direction by Vaughan Oliver.
Design by Jerôme Curchod.
Photography by John Dunne.

'You know that low-frequency lobster radar deep in the bottom of the ocean I've got some of that."

11

—— Brian Wilson to Matthew Sweet, Ray Gun #33, February '95

Burning Down Bauhaus

Was the silence of goth just a moody blunder or was Peter Murphy simply bred to brood. Todd. C. Roberts finds the lobster master of darkness out negotiating with the sirens.

Photography by John Dunne.

Issue 04. Blah Blah Blah. July 1996.
Nicolette Dps.
Art Direction & Design by Chris Ashworth & Neil Fletcher @ Substance.
Photography by Valerie Phillips.

14
Issue 18. Ray Gun. August 1994.
Rock for Choice Dps.
Art Direction & Design by David Carson.
Illustrations by Eric Lynn, Nicky, Beregausky.
Photography by Lance Mercer.

13
Issue 32. Ray Gun. December/January 1996.
Oasis Dps.
Art Direction & Design by Johnson & Wolverton.
Photography by Davies & Davies.

12
Issue 32. Ray Gun. December/January 1996.
Strummer/Ryder Dps.
Art Direction & Design by Johnson & Wolverton.
Photography by Davies & Davies.

"I'll tell you a story. I walk into 2120 S. Michigan Ave. in Chicago, Chess Records. And there's a guy painting the ceiling. And they're like, 'Oh, you might like to meet this guy. This is Muddy Waters.' He wasn't selling records at the time. They had him painting the goddamn ceiling. So, there's Muddy Waters, right, and he's got whitewash like dripping down his face. And I'm meeting God, you know what I mean? And he said, 'Hear you guys cut some of my songs. Thank you very much.' It's like (whistles), 'Grow up, boy. This is life.'"

— Keith Richards

huH #18, February 1996

She was on a weird ragga tip with nascent junglists Shut Up And Dance. Then she provided the candyfloss soul stuff for pioneering trip hoppers Massive Attack after Shara Nelson did a runner. Now Nicolette's released this year's Dummy/Debut/Maxinquaye*, a classic dance-pop crossover album which proclaims: **dubnorentwithmyheadman**.

(*delete whichever ones you don't have)

16

Issue 22. Ray Gun. December/January 1995.
Content page.
Art Direction & Design by David Carson.
"Baby Keith" by Cordy Swope.

RAY G UN 22

ACTUAL LETTERS
SONIC BOOM
SOUL COUGHING
LISA GERMANO
GOLDEN PALOMINOS
LORDS OF ACID
TOM JONES
BARRY WHITE
SMALL PRINT
DIGABLE PLANETS
ROYAL TRUX + KEITH
RICHARDS
GO-GO'S
FATIMA MANSIONS
IGGY POPS BIG CHIEF
SOUND IN PRINT
SHADY
COMPULSION
REVIEWS

cover: keith richards photographed for Ray Gun
by alan messer .(615.256.1019)
this page: baby "keith" by cordy swope.

16

1 7
Issue 09. Ray Gun. September 1993.
Urge Overkill Dps.
Art Direction & Design by David Carson.
Photography by Lisa Spindler.

1 8
Issue 14. huH. October 1995.
C o v e r.
Creative Direction by Vaughan Oliver.
Design by Jerôme Curchod.
Photography by Davies & Davies.
Cover logo photo by Kees Huber.

1 9
Issue 21.
h u H
May 1996.
C r e a t i v e
Direction by
V a u g h a n
O l i v e r.
Design by
J e r ô m e
C u r c h o d.
Photography
by Davies &
D a v i e s.
Cover logo
design by
T i m o t h y
O' Donnell.

1 7

"I wonder about all those alternative bands that say they were influenced by the MC5. Well, give me the opening spot on your tour! Kick out the tours, motherfucker!" —
Wayne Kramer with John Sinclair. Ray Gun #42,
December/January 1997

"I don't wanna be just another dead guy." — Scott Weiland of Stone Temple Pilots, huH #22,

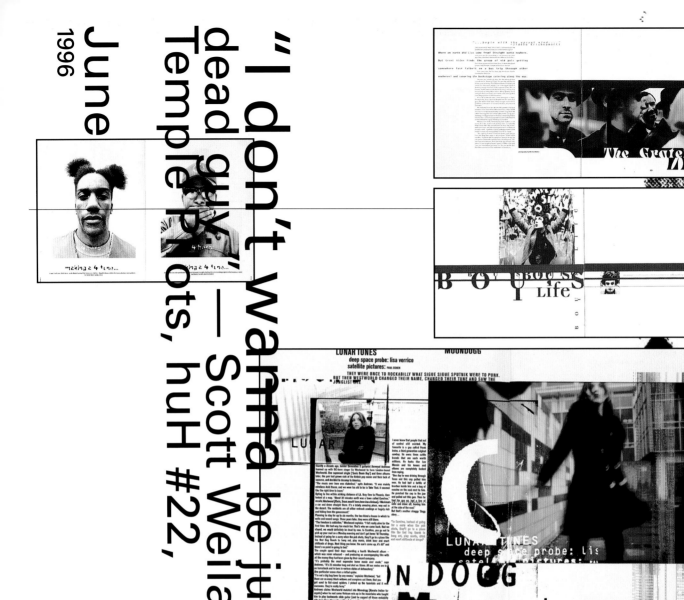

"You know they have the Cannabis Cup every year in Amsterdam, where they judge the best dope. What a fuckin' joke. You travel all that way to get stoned. I can do that at home. They gave me all this shit. They had to carry me home. And he's like, 'Oh boy. We got Chong here, the king of the dopers. He's really gonna show us how to party.' Half-hour later, I'm laying in the bed going, 'Lur-r-r-r-r.'" –

Tommy Chong with Cypress Hill,

Ray Gun # 34,

March 1996

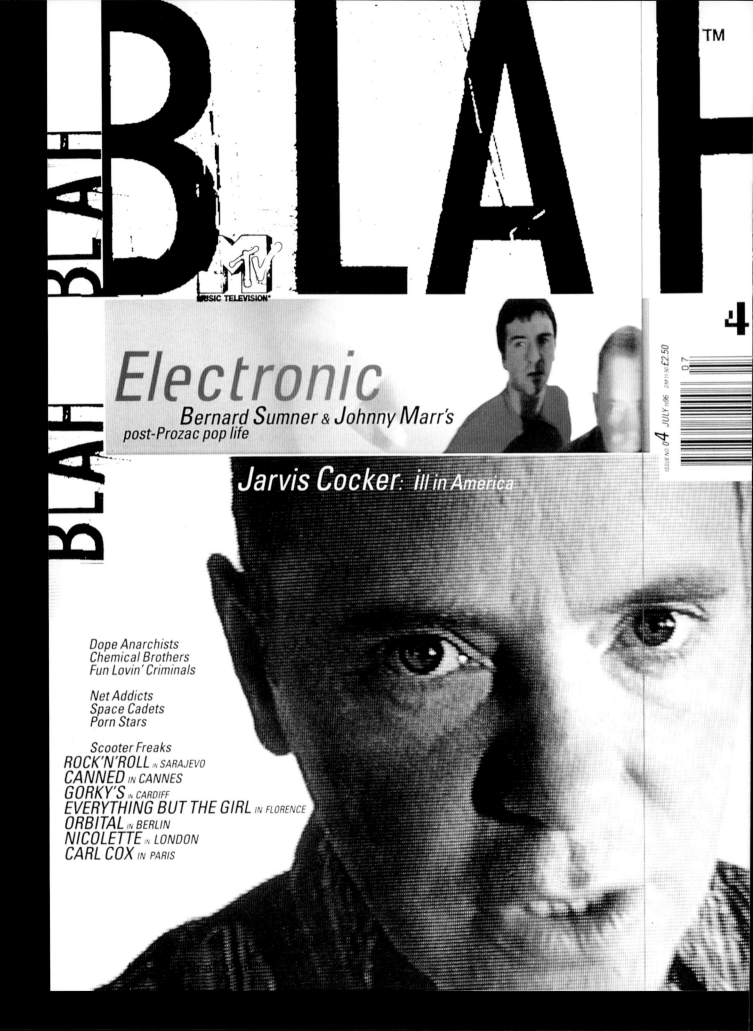

BLAH
BLAH
BLAH
BLAH

™

MTV
MUSIC TELEVISION®

4

Electronic
Bernard Sumner & **Johnny Marr's**
post-Prozac pop life

ISSUE NO. 04 JULY 1996 DM 11.50 £2.50

07

Jarvis Cocker: *ill in America*

Dope Anarchists
Chemical Brothers
Fun Lovin' Criminals

Net Addicts
Space Cadets
Porn Stars

Scooter Freaks
ROCK'N'ROLL IN SARAJEVO
CANNED IN CANNES
GORKY'S IN CARDIFF
EVERYTHING BUT THE GIRL IN FLORENCE
ORBITAL IN BERLIN
NICOLETTE IN LONDON
CARL COX IN PARIS

27
Issue 04. Blah Blah Blah. July 1996.
Cover.
Art Direction & Design by Chris Ashworth & Neil Fletcher @ Substance.
Photography by Peter Anderson

29
Issue 02. Ray Gun. December/January 1993
Burning Spears Dps.
Art Direction & Design by David Carson
Photography by Steve Sherman.

28
Issue 05. Blah Blah Blah. August 1996.
Neneh Cherry Dps.
Art Direction & Design by Chris Ashworth & Neil Fletcher @ Substance.
Photography by Spiros Politis.

Out of Control (C)
Page Nos

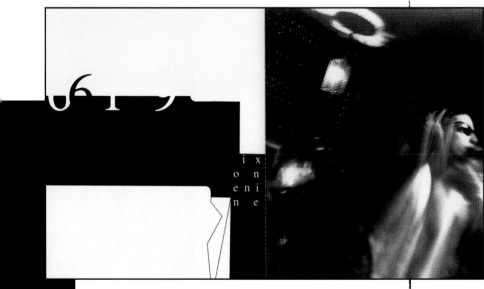

"We didn't realize the forces we were up against and how serious they were. The status quo is a monster, not a bunch of toy soldiers you can blow over. America is entrenched. The revolution is not military, it's cultural and economic. The revolution has to be an evolution." —

Abiodun Oyewole
of the Last Poets,
Ray Gun #37, June/July 1996

p u l p

"We are　a civilization of people taping each　other."

Mission: Impulpable

...ritpop double-act were so popular they sold eight ...ckets in Dallas. This time around there's —

30
Issue 04. Blah Blah Blah. July 1996.
Pulp Dps.
Art Direction & Design by Chris Ashworth & Neil Fletcher @ Substance.
Photography by Shawn Mortensen.

more interest in the guy that jerked-off Jacko. But is Jarvis too ill to thrill?

pulp faction: Mark blackwell pulp action: Shawn Mortensen

33 PULP

Christopher Walken, Bikini #10, June/July 1995

31
Issue 02. Blah Blah Blah. May 1996.
Afghan Whigs Dps.
Art Direction & Design by Neil Fletcher @ Substance.
Photography by Ann Giordano.

32
Issue 02. Blah Blah Blah. May 1996.
Oasis Dps.
Art Direction & Design by Chris Ashworth & Neil Fletcher @ Substance.
Photography by Joseph Cultice.

Out of Control {C}
Page Nos

112/113

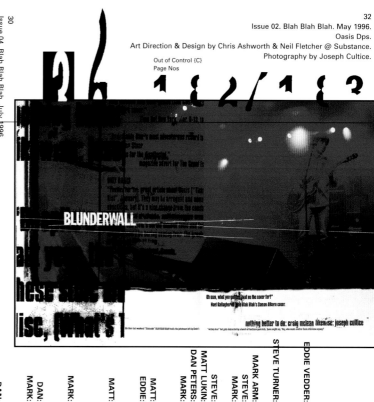

BLUNDERWALL

"Oh man, what you getting Jacko on the cover for?"
Noel Gallagher on Blah Blah's Damon Albarn cover.

nothing better to do: craig mclean likewise: joseph cultice

EDDIE VEDDER: "I'm gonna get back on the vinyl check, 'cause I'm interested if you'd express your love for vinyl over any other format. Is that true?

STEVE TURNER: I don't think any of us have the ears that can hear the differences between CD and vinyl.

MARK ARM: My ears are pretty much shot.

STEVE: All he hears is like a muffled rumbling.

MARK: That damn super-fuzz. I wish you never discovered that thing.

STEVE: Every record just sounds like this: "Sheeeeeeeezzzzhh!"

MATT LUKIN: Unless it's folk.

DAN PETERS: Everybody's using those damn fuzz pedals these days.

MARK: Even that damn new Bon Jovi record's got distorted vocals all the way through it, is he singing through an amp?

MATT: But vinyl has got the bigger pictures.

EDDIE: I think that it's a shame that they're not going to know what they're missing. With vinyl you get to read the cereal box while eating your cereal.

MARK: Sometimes they get the booklets. It's a hell of a lot easier to roll joints on the gatefold of an album than on a CD, though. You need one of those fuckin' Aerosmith Pump fold-out posters to be able to roll a joint with a CD.

DAN: Like [Rush's] 'All The World's A Stage' is a classic pot record, just because it folded out three times and you had two creases to catch the seeds in.

MARK: There's a naked dude on it.

DAN: Oh, that's the part I didn't like. What are these Canadians trying to do to me, as a young impressionable junior high school student?

Loaded full of pot and making you look at naked men."

— Eddie Vedder interviews Mudhoney,
Ray Gun #24, March 1995

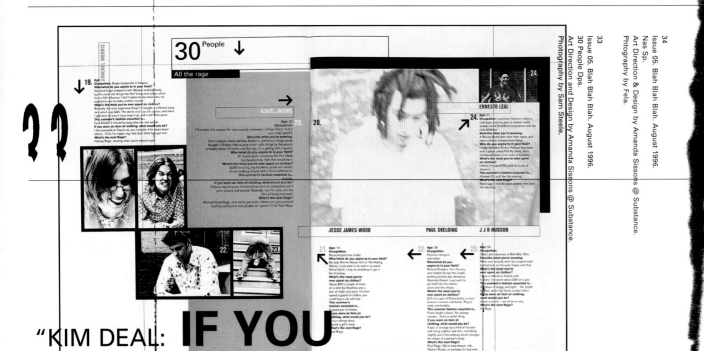

34
Issue 05. Blah Blah Blah. August 1996.
Nas Sp.
Art Direction & Design by Amanda Sissons @ Substance.
Photography by Fela.

33
Issue 05. Blah Blah Blah. August 1996.
30 People Dps.
Art Direction and Design by Amanda Sissons @ Substance.
Photography by Sam Steele.

30 People ↓

All the rage

"KIM DEAL: IF YOU COULD CHOOSE ANY PROFES- SION OTHER THAN A MUSICIAN WHAT WOULD IT BE?

J MASCIS : PRIEST.

KD: DO YOU BELIEVE IN GOD?

JM: SURE.

KD: I wish I did. I really do. That would be great. Mascis. Is that a

naughty but nas

Nas Escobar, lyrical poet, Mafioso hoodlum, king of Queens

KD: **NO SHIT?**

36
Out of Control.
Original Illustration.
Caty Bartholomew. 1996.
"Howdy Doody."

Out of Control (C)
Page Nos

German name?

JM: **WELL, I THINK IT'S
MAYBE GREEK IN ORIGIN BUT IT'S BEEN
IN ITALY FOR
THOUSANDS OF YEARS. LIKE ONE
OF MY**

JM: **SHIT, YEAH.**
KD: Really. That's why you
wanted to be a priest, to kind of
continue the family career.
JM: I really don't want to be a
priest.

KD: **IT'S JUST YOUR SECOND CHOICE.**
JM: **EXACTLY."**

— KIM DEAL OF BREEDERS
AND J MASCIS 0F DINOSAUR JR.,
RAY GUN #20,
OCTOBER 1994

ELDERS WAS A POPE.

37
Issue 02. huH. October 1994.
"Jelly Bean Elvis."
Creative Direction by Vaughan Oliver.
Design by Jerôme Curchod.
Jellybean art by Mark Blackwell.
38
Issue 38. Ray Gun. August 1996.
Boredoms Dps.
Art Direction & Design by Robert Hales.
Photography by Katsumi Omori.

Out of Control (C)
Page No

pills, thrills, and belly aches

Max Fahlström
direct Pav Modelski

One minute you're a cardi'n'slippers couple for the armchair generation. The next you're in intensive care. To rub it in, your label drops you. Before you can reach for a razor blade you have a smash hit around the globe and everybody loves you. It Must Be Great™ being... Everything But The Girl

Twelve months ago Ben Watt and Tracey Thorn couldn't get arrested in publicity terms and, they would concede, they didn't deserve to be.

Having spent the best part of a decade churning out a familiar mix of light, jazz-flavoured bedsit pop, they had become increasing immaterial. They were boring themselves and us shitless.

"It's true and I have to say people were right. I don't think we had much to offer back then," agrees Ben Watt with the benefit of hindsight. "We had become irrelevant to the music scene."

That was before Todd Terry transformed Everything But The Girl into a supremely relevant, shiny '90s pop machine with a remix of 'Missing'. Now a new era has dawned for the duo, a fact confirmed by the success of last month's impressive new album, Walking Wounded. Suddenly, Everything But The Girl are hip, quotable and in demand, thus making stage of us all.

"I find it ironic that now we get the NME and the Maker ringing up to do us," grins Ben over a horrifically expensive beer in the bar of the palatial Villa Medici hotel in Florence. "It is hard not to be smug," says Tracey from behind her fringe, "but it's pointless holding a grudge. I'd rather pretend to be magnanimous even if I don't really feel that way about it."

It could all have worked out very differently after their record company, Blanco Y Negro, dropped them after more than a decade of service, topping off a miserable couple of years during which Ben contracted a deeply unpleasant and life-threatening illness, Churgh Strauss Syndrome. And this after the duo delivered the remixes of 'Missing'.

Realising they had fallen into a rut, the pair had begun to look at ways of regenerating themselves, commissioning remixes of that song and tinkering with a new approach to their music inspired by Tracey's link-up with Massive Attack (on their Protection album) and Ben's new-found love of drum'n'bass.

The Man, though, wasn't having it. Later when I talk to Geoff Travis, who signed them back in 1988 to the Warner's-controlled Blanco Y Negro, at the office of his new Trade Too label in London, he confirms the story. "The plan we had to reinvent them was taken with a pinch of salt by some of the people at Warner's."

Travis remains close to the duo and can take some of the credit in helping them forge their new direction after introducing them to the wonders of Spring Heel Jack's There Are Strings LP, but at the time it was a tough decision.

"It wasn't a heat of the moment thing," he expands. "It was more like when you have a long relationship with a girl and it sort of peters out. You remain good friends but it's time to call it a day," he says, sounding like he is describing the scenario from one of their b-sides rather than the day he told them they were sacked.

So Everything But The Girl were out on their ear and there were no obvious options.

"I thought about taking it all back to scratch, signing with an indie and slogging it out on the road," says Ben shifting uncomfortably in his chair at the memory, "but I just couldn't face that and it wouldn't have worked anyway." Fate intervened. Their parting shot for Warner's, 'Missing', hovered in the top reaches of charts around the world for months. The label ended up with a huge hit and no band.

The success confirmed to Watt that his new direction was the right way to go. Drum'n'bass had rekindled his enthusiasm for music.

"We're not just ripping it off," he says in defence of their adoption of the style. "I genuinely love the stuff. I've called it futuristic bossa nova because that's what it sounds like to me, that's where we meet and I think this album brings something new to the party."

Not that Walking Wounded is a drum'n'bass album.

"No, it's not a drum'n'bass album," agrees Ben. "I've never claimed it was some jungle project. I don't want to set myself up as a drum'n'bass guru."

Why, though, didn't he make the leap into programmed sounds earlier when Hesse was permeating the indie scene?

"Well, I didn't like many of the bands who added dance music to their music, and while I liked some of the early garagey stuff like Turntable Orchestra, I didn't think it would work with our sound then."

Ben's DJing is a nascent thing that he has kept low-key. His first foray occurred in March at New York's Fez club with Howie B under the appropriate heading Anatomy Of Melancholy. "I'd wanted to do some DJing for a while, so I asked Howie B," remembers Ben. "We went over to New York and set up a little night there. He came on and did his thing for a couple of hours and then I came out and did mine, mixing drum'n'bass and stuff like bebop. James Lavelle came along and was very encouraging, which made me very happy because he's achieved so much and has such a great ear. Tricky popped in, too, but you never quite know what's going on in his head."

'Missing' eventually sold over two million copies, paving the way for their current, packed out European tour. They must be pretty rich if the Vila Medici is typical of the quality of their overnight stops.

"Obviously, we don't have to worry too much, but I don't know what we're worth on paper," says Ben, vaguely. "Shit, how much does this place cost anyway?" he asks, staring around at the sumptuous drapes, rococo pillars, and renaissance-style frescoes.

"We certainly spend a lot more now, particularly when we're on the road, because of my condition. I have the digestive system of a sparrow. This is as much as I can eat," he says, exaggeratedly twiddling a cheese nibble. "I'm also on drugs to control the condition because there's a danger it could recur, though the idea is to take down the dosage as my immune system recovers. Fortunately, I can drink alcohol because it's absorbed through the stomach lining," he adds, reaching for his Becks.

There was a rumour that part of his medication included Prozac.

"No, I'm not on Prozac, I never even received any counselling to deal with what was happening, that was why I had to start writing a book — to make some sense of it all." An account of his illness, entitled Patient, is due to be published in September. It contains some great insights into the British health system and some excellent moments of black comedy.

"There were some quite scary moments when a nurse was trying to get this old guy to walk after he'd had an operation on his leg. He was whining and saying he couldn't do it and we were all sitting there thinking, 'Look, can't you leave the poor old geezer alone, he can't do it'. But she was saying, 'Come on Mr Jackson it's part of your rehabilitation, you've got to get onto your feet'. He just stood there going, 'I just can't move, I'm trying but my legs are stuck'. And the nurse goes, 'Try lifting the chair leg Mister Jackson — it's on your dressing gown!'

"Every so often a patient would be brought in with a heart attack. It was surreal and funny at the same time because I was constantly barfing and it became quite surreal. Tracey and my mother were just passing these bowls in a chair for me to chuck up in.

"There was another point when a nurse was trying to get this old guy to walk after he'd had

3   9
Issue 04. Blah Blah Blah. July 1996.
Everything But The Girl Dps.
Art Direction & Design by Neil Fletcher @ Substance.
Photography by Pav Modelski.

"EYE says Boredoms is a feeling. Boredoms is touching something, but Boredoms itself is not the object. It's just more like becoming nothing. Not like Boredoms break up — we keep doing it, but it's the same as doing nothing. And so Boredoms itself is becoming nothing, because it's something like Big Bang Theory. In space you start with nothing. If you start thinking about 'nothing means nothing,' then you have to ask yourself, 'So what is the space?' Nothing has the most power. It makes Boredoms something. It's very difficult to explain what the nothing is. Before Big Bang there was nothing. Boredoms' want to become that nothing, not nothing nothing. Everything starts from there. If we have some goal, we're going somewhere else than where we want to go. We just want to be somewhere. But we don't really know what we have to do or where we have to go." — EYE Yamataka of the Boredoms (via translator),

Ray Gun #38, August 1996

40

Issue 32. Ray Gun. December/January 1996.
Blur Dps.
Art Direction & Design by Johnson & Wolverton.
Photography by Stefan Ruiz.

BLUR

41
Issue 08. huH. April 1995.
Oasis Dps.
Creative Direction by Vaughan Oliver.
Design by Jerôme Curchod.
Photography by Michael Wong.

Out of Control (C)
Page Nos

42
Issue 14. huH. October 1995.
R.E.M. Dps.
Creative Direction by Vaughan Oliver.
Design by Jerôme Curchod.
Photography by Davies & Davies.

43
Issue 26. Ray Gun. May 1995.
Contents page.
Art Direction & Design by David Carson.
Photography by Melodie McDaniel.

26

2/1

43

— Henry Rollins with William Gibson, huH #2, October 1994

cover: beasties + luscious by ari marcopoulos
this page: henry + issac by melodie mcdaniel

44
Out of Control.
Original Illustration.
Gary Baseman. 1996.

45
Issue 06. Ray Gun. May 1993
PJ Harvey Dps.
Art Direction & Design by David Carson.
Photography by Colin Bell.
Illustration by Geoff McFetridge.

Issue 06. Ray Gun. May 1993.
Baseheads Dps.
Art Direction & Design by David Carson.
Photography by sk©id

Out of Control (C)
Page Nos

"My mother had really

long hair. She wore all those Moroccan bracelets and things. I was the only child, *living in a house with seven adults. They all had long hair and listened to Jimi Hendrix* all

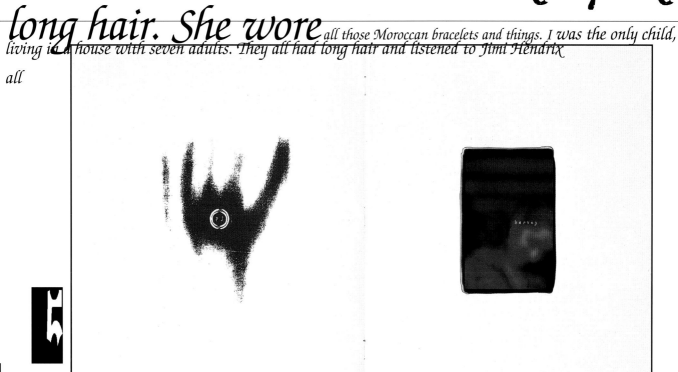

day long, and everything was painted purple, so   I'm alle   rgic to purple now.
They had all these dreams and wild plans — you know, 'Let's live o
n an air-

things like that, which is
brilliant
for a kid.
Can you imagine being
brought up by seven
grown-ups
who all hate work and all
they want to
do is

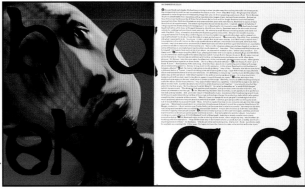

play games with you all the time and tell you stories and make kites? It took me ages as a child to learn to be
interested in other people because my head was so busy and so interesting."

— *Björk, Ray Gun #27, June/July 1995*

here   went

47
Out of Control.
Original Illustration.
Val & Bob Tillery. 1996.
"Hungry Dog Studio."

48
Issue 13. Ray Gun. February 1994.
Al Jourgensen Dps 1.
Art Direction & Design by David Carson.
Photography by Michael Grecco.

Out of Control {C}
Page Nos

19 2/1 9 3

The tutor they gave me smoked pot.
I never wanted to
leave. I'm in
this mental hospital
for drug abuse
at the age of 14, getting free
drugs from the
doctors. They
alternated between
thorazine and tuinals. That's
where I really grew up sexually. They separated the girls
and the guys on the
third and fourth floors, but
on the fifth
floor was
the ping pong table
and rec room.
It was just like One

Flew Over
the Cuckoo's Nest.
We'd play

Issue 13. Ray Gun. February 1994.
Al Jourgensen Dps 2.
Art Direction & Design by David Carson.
Photography by Michael Grecco.

poker

al

You can call him
al Jour-
gensen
by Kather-
ine tur-
man

stry, Jourgensen   of

with the orderlies, I'd win and
they'd give me
bathroom privelages.
I had a tutor

who turned me on to Naked Lunch, Charles
Bukowski, all this shit.
This was heaven! Every Saturday, we'd have meetings with parents and
psychiatrists and the patients
and it was just a bunch of white suburban kids. We all loved it;
we weren't nuts, we were just being kids. So on Saturday,
all the kids would act like schizos. My
parents caught on after
a few months. But I was wiling to stay there until the day I died.
Sex, drugs, and really decent literature." –

Gun #13,

ruary   1996

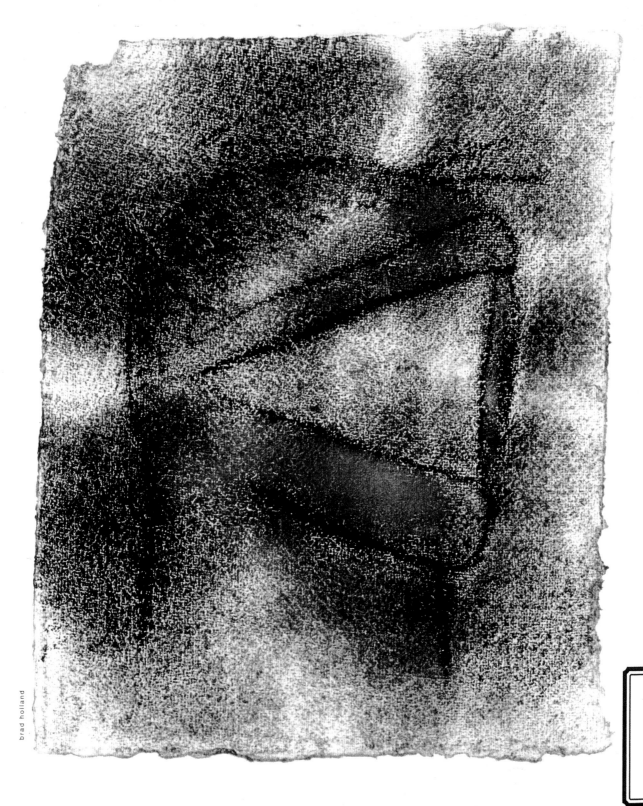

brad holland

50
Issue 30. Ray Gun. October 1995.
The Residents Dps.
Art Direction & Design by David Carson.
Illustration by Brad Holland.

51
Out of Control.
Original Illustration.
Eric White. 1996.
"A Place in the Sun (explained)"
Out of Control (C)
Page Nos

1ɔ4/1

RAY GUN #30, OCTOBER 1995

- H A R D Y   C O X,
S P O K E S M A N   F O R
T H E   R E S I D E N T S',
C R Y P T I C   C O R P O R A T I O N.

THEY FEEL THAT YOUNG PEOPLE ARE NOT AS IN TOUCH WITH THE WEALTH OF MUSIC THAT IS COMING OUT OF AMERICA. THE WEALTH OF REALLY INTERESTING AND REALLY DIFFERENT IDEAS."

EUROPEAN CULTURE AND MUSIC. THEY HAVE A PROBLEM WITH THE EAST COAST IN GENERAL BECAUSE IT STILL CLINGS SO TIGHTLY TO EUROPE. THEY FEEL THAT REAL MUSIC AND REAL CULTURE WENT WEST WITH THE PIONEERS.

"THE RESIDENTS REALLY BELIEVE THAT AMERICA IS THE CULTURAL HOTBED AND DRAW A VERY STRONG LINE AWAY FROM

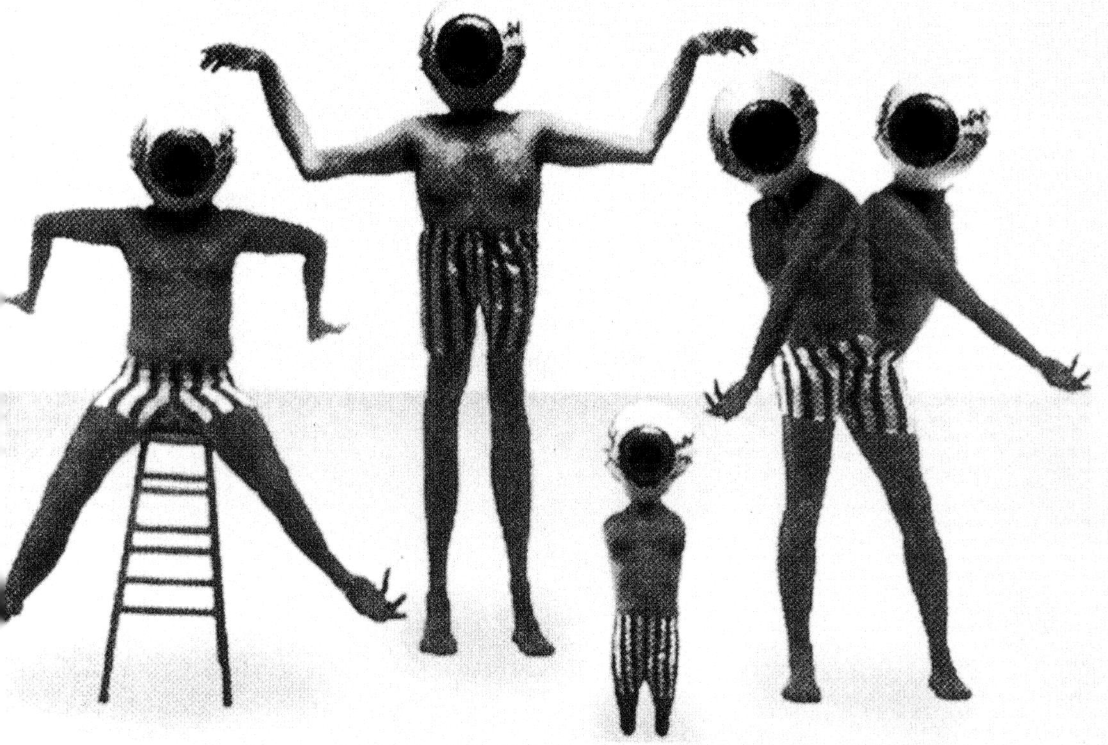

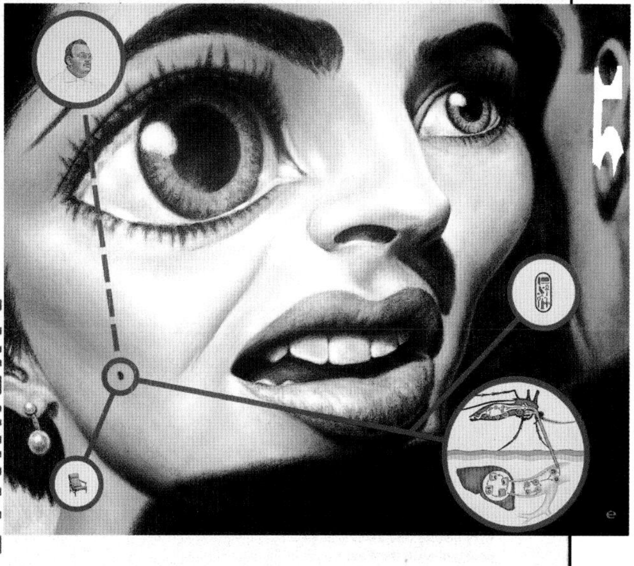

30

AUTHOR:

RAYGUNMAGAZ

Spencer H. Abbott

52
Issue 23. Ray Gun. February 1995.
Belly Dps.
Art Direction & Design by David Carson.
Photography by Kevin Kerslake.

54
Issue 02. Blah Blah Blah. May 1996.
Sleeper Dps.
Art Direction & Design by Chris Ashworth & Neil Fle[tcher]
Photography by Kevin Westenberg.

"I do think that the biggest
goal of religion is, more than
explaining the origins of
authority or explaining g[od]
is explaining time. How c[an we]
be here for only a short f[ime]
when that would be so
meaningless? Do our lives
more meaning? How does [it]
work?"1994.

– Laurie Anderson, huH #3, November

53
Issue 11. Ray Gun. November 1993.
Swervedriver Dps.
Art Direction & Design by David Carson.
Photography by Stefan Ruiz.

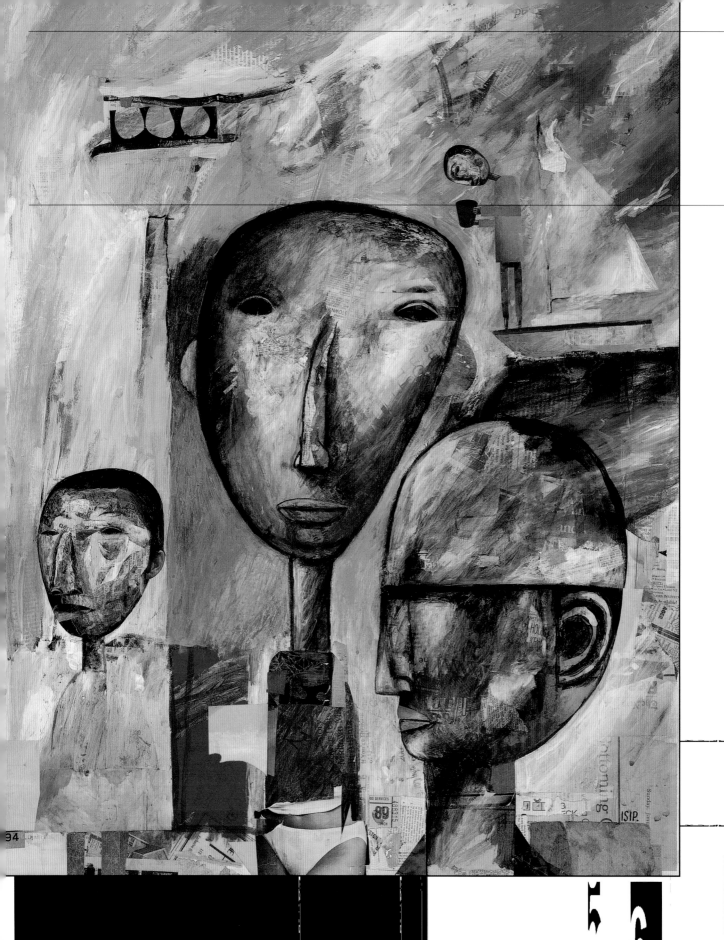

"I spend hours on the internet almost every day, but I have to say that 99.9 per cent of everything that I find is of absolutely no value to my life. It's just like another drug. I know it's stupid and pointless, but I still stay up all night surfing around because that's the way I use things. I use external things to fill up the big hole that there is inside." — Robin Guthrie of the

Cocteau Twins, Ray Gun #36, May 1996

56
Out of Control.
Original Illustration.
Jordin Isip. 1996.

57
Issue 04. Blah Blah Blah. July 1996.
Electronic Dps.
Art Direction & Design by Chris Ashworth & Neil Fletcher @ Substance.
Photography by Peter Anderson.

Out of Control (C)
Page Nos

1 ((/ 1 ((

'The secret about the Cocteau Twins, about what makes us who we **are, is.... What? Yes, yes, oh** my

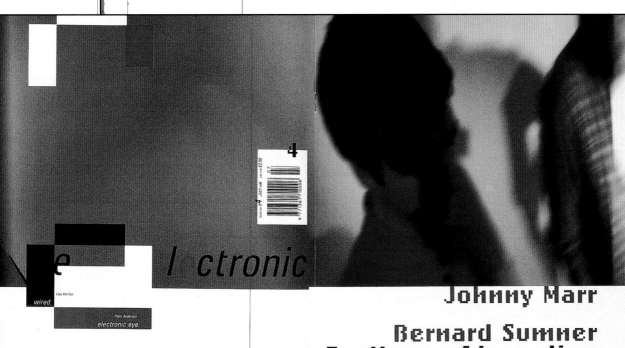

e l ctronic

wired:
Lisa Verrico

Peter Anderson
electronic eye:

4

07
9 771361 710006

Johnny Marr

Bernard Sumner
Brothers of invention

Separately, they were the architects of some of the greatest British music ever made.
Together, they're trying to do a bit more than that. Ladeez and genmelmun, cleaned-up, wised-up and trussed-up in some nice
Safeways pants, the supersonic duophonic Johnny Marr and Bernard Sumner.

God, I've completely lost whatever it was I was going to say. It was a paradox, I think. It was there, it was so clear,

and now it's gone." — Liz Fraser of the **Cocteau Twins,**

"MOBY: I ascribe to belief systems that draw a lot of fanatics: Christianity, vegetarianism, environmentalism. **I'm a Christian, but I don't**

MOBY: I ascribe to belief systems that draw a lot of fanatics: Christianity, vegetarianism, environmentalism. I'm a Christian, but I don't like other Christians. I'm a vegan, but I don't like other vegans. I love dance music, but I tend not to get along with dance enthusiasts.

ALEX PATERSON { *THE ORB* } : Hey, you sound like me! — **Ray Gun** #26, May 1995

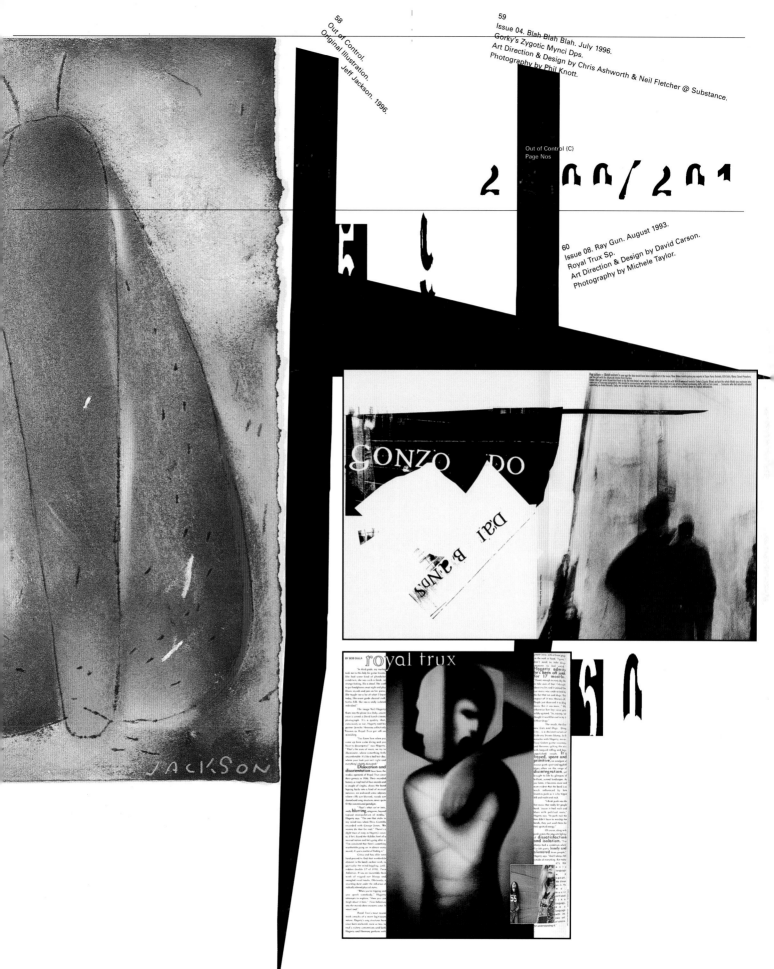

58
Out of Control.
Original Illustration.
Jeff Jackson. 1996.

JACKSON

royal trux

61
Out of Control.
Original Illustration.
Jason Holley. 1996.

62
Issue 02. Blah Blah Blah. May 1996.
Babylon Zoo Dps.
Art Direction & Design by Chris Ashworth & Neil Fletcher @ Substance.
Photography by Pav Modelski.

Out of Control {C}
Page Nos

aspects. We put music behind it — organ music, sixties music, wierd stuff

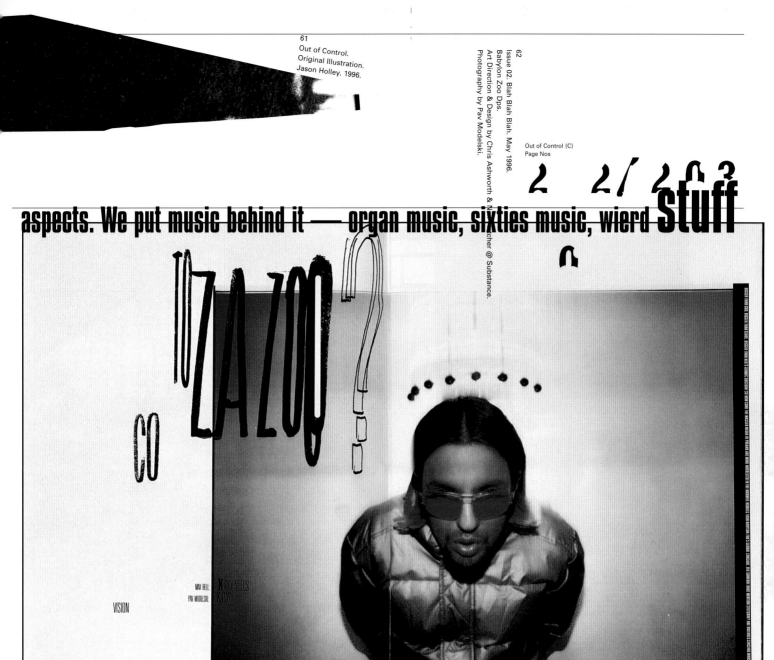

VISION

WHAT IS THIS ZOO?

MAX BELL: X RAY SPECS
PAV MODELSKI. X-RAY

— and then I read these pieces. It's hilarious, and also very poignant. I'm proud of it."

Exene Cervenka on "The Unabomber Manifesto: Selected Excerpts Read by Exene Cervenkova," Ray Gun #34, March 1996

63
Issue 01. Blah Blah Blah. April 1996.
Damon Albarn/Irvine Welsh Dps 1.
Art Direction & Design by Neil Fletcher @ Substance.
Photography by Phil Poynter.

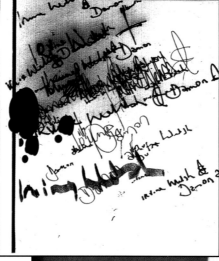

64
Issue 01. Blah Blah Blah. April 1996.
Damon Albarn/Irvine Welsh Dps 2.
Art Direction & Design by Neil Fletcher @ Substance.
Photography by Phil Poynter.

65
Issue 22. Ray Gun. December/January 1995.
Compulsion Dps.
Art Direction & Design by David Carson.
Photography by Michael Wong.

66
Out of Control.
Original Illustration.
B Bartholomew. 1996.
"Fight."

– **Damon Albarn of Blur with Irvine Welsh, Blah Blah Blah #1, April 1996**

"Masel' and this Dutch writer went to this bar in Amsterdam. It's in the red light district and it's like a stag-night bar. The women get these bananas and stick them up their fannies and the guys eat the bananas. So what we did was we went in there and we decided to stick these bananas up our arseholes and get photographed on the bar, both together. At that time I really wanted to kick off in Amsterdam — the books were getting translated into German and French and Italian. The pictures have never been published. Yet...."

"It's Europeans," Damon nods. "I did this thing for a German magazine and I had a really bad hangover and I had a really smelly feet, and I'd just taken my shoes off and I was at the Landmark Hotel on Euston Road in London. It was a day of press and I had really smelly feet.' And the room was really smelly. And David Bowie walked through the door with Brian Eno and there was this terrible smell! So the first thing I said was: 'Uh, really sorry about the smell. And David haven't put any odour-eaters in and I've got really bad, smelly feet.' And he must have thought, 'Who the fuck is this?'

"Anyway, it didn't last very long and he left very quickly. But then I had this German photographer waiting to do pictures, and because my hangover was so bad and I was dwelling on the fact that I'd made such an idiot of myself in front of David Bowie I said, 'I'm gonna go and have a shower,' and he said, 'Khan I take a voto or you in the shower?' And I said, 'Yeah'. And I let him take photos of me soaping up me dick.

He hasn't printed them yet. So Irvine's got a banana up his arse and I've got a soapy dick!"

NOW IT'S YOUR
TO DRY UP AND BLOW
OH ROBERT YOU ARE A REAL MAN AFTER ALL!

the JESUS LIZARD

The honest, hardworking members of the Jesus Lizard have a dirty little secret. They've earned a reputation for being a collection of ear-pummeling, nut-waggling, hell-raising noisemaniacs, and it's a rap the band often lives up to. But there's something else about these loud Chicagoans that doesn't seem to get talked about as much as it should: At present time, the Jesus Lizard happens to be one of our nation's finest, fiercest rock 'n' roll bands.

Forget about assigning the Lizard to some neo-psycho-post-punk cubbyhole or some alternative/quasi-grunge garage. The thrill they've delivered across such albums as Head, Goat and Liar is quintessential, primal rock 'n' roll wallop; equal parts sex, danger, comedy, dementia and showmanship. Most recently, the band has released the Lash EP, which collects four large-sounding live cuts with a couple of sizable new tunes (also available as a triple set of singles). Sweaty, stinking, thrilling stuff. Rock stuff.

"That's how I like to think of us," says crooner David Yow. "as just a rock band. Obviously, there's some punk rock in our sound and some other stuff. But Mac here never gave a shit about punk rock." Yow gestures toward drummer McNeilly as the two partake of cold beverages prior to a headlining show at LA's Whisky-A-Go-Go. "He's a hippie. He listens to Poco and the Little River Band." Cartoonish cackles ensue and Yow celebrates the jovial mood with a slug from a bottle of Old Bushmill's whiskey. (He also offers the bottle to well-wishers outside the tour van with the invitation, "Would you like a sip from my bottle of urine?" The offer is declined.)

"We got called 'hardcore' in reviews," says McNeilly, "and that just doesn't fit with what we think of ourselves or what we think hardcore means."

Certainly the band, which includes guitarist Duane Denison and bassist David Sims, can play loud and fast if they choose to. And to the uninitiated, song titles like "Mouth Breather," "Slave Ship" and "Deaf As A Bat" might sound like they belong to fairly standard hardcore venom bullets. But the Lizard has range. Their repertoire includes the cracked-skull, "La Grange"-shuffle of "South Mouth," the gap-toothed country jig of "Rope" and the unsensible rock-slide of "Nub". Further, the band doesn't exist simply to vomit forth rage and menace in town after town. For nearly five years, the Jesus Lizard have been lighting up club and concert stages not with bilious angst but with invigorating, rock-solid entertainment spectacle.

"People miss the humor," Yow explains. "There are the ones that catch on, but too few get it—99 per cent of our reviews talk about what an insane maniac David Yow is. But I think I'm more like a court jester, or just a plain idiot, than any kind of a dangerous, threatening madman. We take our music very seriously, but not ourselves."

Mac agrees: "We're a band playing rock music in clubs. That says a lot right there about how serious we are as people. You shouldn't listen to our stuff as serious, heavy music. It's hilarious. Well, it's pretty funny."

The ball thing is funny. Like Elvis with his scarves or Gene Simmons and the tongue, Yow has a trademark gesture he bestows upon audiences when the spirit moves him: He pops his testicles out the fly of his jeans and performs what he refers to as "tight and shiny." Before the Whisky show, he says that he's tired of being called on to air his nuts and doesn't want to do it anymore. But as he hits the stage that night, the Bushmill's has weakened his resolve, and it's clearly an expectant and appreciative crowd. As the band opens with the pounding riff from Lash 'n 'Glamorous," Yow faces McNeilly's drum riser, puts a hand to his crotch and then wheels around with what looks like a hairy nectarine on the end of his fist.

No scrotum could hope for a better backing band.

McNeilly and Sims are as locked down and powerful as a rhythm section can get, and Denison plays with a beguiling combination of power and precision. Jesus Lizard songs can hit a listener with all the brute force of a fist to the face, but they are also packed full of admirable craft and musicianship.

"I get a chuckle out of bad reviews," says Yow, "because they're often written by somebody who just hates everything about us. There was one that began by saying that Duane didn't know how to tune his guitar. Now that's hilarious, because Duane can play circles around Joe Satriani's little midget ass."

"Duane's a surgeon," McNeilly says solemnly.

To the steamrolling sound that the band kicks up, Yow adds some of the most brilliantly twisted images you're likely to find this side of a bad dream. A sad pygmy weeps while he snuffs you in "The Art of Self-Defense." The little messy stinky girl laughs at the singer's breaking bones in "Perk." An autoerotic suicide is discovered with a trowel up his ass in "Rope." Yow clearly takes great pride in the pictures he conjures and says he prefers his abstract approach to straightforward storytelling.

"It's definitely more important what the words sound like than what they're actually saying," he says. "I spend a lot of time with instrumental tapes of new songs trying to figure out what should go where. If a listener gets strong images from the final result, that's great. But I-the songs are about."

On one of the new singles, Yow turned to higher literature for inspiration. When he became stuck for lyrics to a bridge, he began to flip through his wife's Dante's Inferno. The word "farting" caught his eye. "I believe it's from Canto —," explains: "With farting tongue pressed tightly to his teeth. He blew back with the voice of an asshole.' It was perfect. I had already titled the song 'Deaf as a Bat,' so 'an asshole' seemed perfectly regal. I would hope the band took it in that particular song."

Yow's comedic abandon, Denison's skill... and the giant grooves of Sims and McNeilly are c... audience member at the Whisky—none other than... tion has its exciting band, and they're it," the g... "They create a fantastic frenzy. They make Elvis... ass shows.

The band is well-pedigreed. Yow and S... Austin outfit Scratch Acid, and Sims went on to... Rapeman. The two reteamed and recruited Denis... the Lizard's debut Pure EP in 1989, with Albini... band's recorder. McNeilly came over from Phan... solid lineup since. The band has done battle with... al in the videos for "Nub" and "Puss" (a feature... part of a split single with Nirvana). They've also... overtures of a number of major labels, preferrin... Touch and Go. And through it all, they've gotten better and better at putting...

"We just played the Garage in London," says McNeilly, "and appar... end of the show, which fucked up the monitor system. After the show, the... and the light guy were standing on stage laughing, saying 'Brilliant! Fuckin... They said they'd have us back any day."

"We managed to completely mangle these three-foot steel pipes th... up as a stage barricades," Yow recalls. "They were completely bent and tw... caused $2,000 of damage. People were flying off the stage, and the club's... got messed up. I usually don't notice too much, because I'm focused on the... I like to see the kids' faces when they hop up on stage and they have that kn... in their eye just before they jump. It's a great little animal ritual. At this sh... was some bleeding, but nobody got badly hurt. It was an impossible situation... well."

Yow says that it doesn't take much for him to get psyched up when he... plays, but a bit of liquid courage never hurts. "For live shows, I like to be... ed with a little alcohol," Yow says. "I don't like to be drunk with a capital... happens sometimes and I usually end up getting pissed off at myself. And t... guys in the band get pissed off, too. We don't want to be too ragged."

Lubrication is definitely in process a couple of nights later as the b... holds forth at a non-musical record store appearance prior to a club show... Beach. Yow is scaling the record bins with a magic marker in hand, trying... where he can deface a Henry Rollins poster. McNeilly happily signs a pair... sticks for an eager punkette, while Denison dutifully signs 8x10s at the fr... counter. Sims skulks about, Budweiser in hand.

Back at the club's bar, Yow needs further loosening up and gene... offers to buy shots of whiskey for a small clump of friends. Somehow Yow... with two shots in front of him. The first one goes down easily, but after th... the singer looks pale.

He demurs politely and strides off towards the restroom for a quick power-puke. When he returns, he is refreshed and inspired.

"We played some shows with the Jim Rose Circus Side..." says. "And I was embarrassed to ask Jim about a lot of his... but he was more than happy to explain them. I showed him 'tight and shiny'... before the singer can demonstrate the legendary "his drinking red wine fro... The show that night hits a phenomenally high energy level. McNeilly ru... possessed, Sims is perspiring madly, Yow spends as much time prostrate across th... hands of the audience as he does on the stage proper. Only Denison seems cool as a... ening our guitar lines. Crowd and band seem to reach an epiphany during "Puss"... speaking in tongues or kicking up extraterrestrial cable channels, but he's maxin... congregation. And it's clear from the looks of bliss and uplift on the faces around th... this show is as close to holy communion as secular ci...

Afterwards, the band is a confident and glowing one without excess. McNeil... moment and tries to explain his satisfaction. "Too many bands just leave you saying... Not that everybody has to be wild, but there has to be something special there may... that's what we try to give. We love what we do. When our music works well, it trans... And I hope it takes the crowd apart, too. Maybe that sounds pretty cosmic, but it su...

Yow is a sharp guy, a friendly guy, and funny as hell, but after the show... stripped to the waist, drenched in sweat and helped to a corner, the look on his face... bottle—"the look of a rock 'n' roll warrior who's just performed his highest cere... band had to pull it to come together now," he whispers. "But when it does, it's s... sound is good, we play well and the audience has a blast. It's r...

67

"I had this conversation with John Cage, when

he discovered this horrifying fact

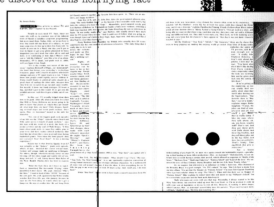

that there are more living people on earth now than there are people who have ever lived on this planet. Isn't that a frightening thing? It's a lot of people

with plans. It's a lot of
dreams. It's a lot of desire
walking around. It's overwhelming, sometimes. You
just look around on the
streets. All these people
wanting things. It's
exhausting.

67
Issue 13. Ray Gun. February 1994.
The Jesus Lizard Dps.
Art Direction & Design by David Carson.
Photography by Michael Wong.

68
Issue 13. Ray Gun. February 1994.
Disclaimer Dps.
Art Direction & Design by David Carson.
Photography by Greg Allen.

Out of Control Cc
Page Nos

205/207

69
Issue 21. Ray Gun. November 1994.
Blues Explosion Dps.
Art Direction & Design by David Carson.
Photography by Kevin Kerslake.

The whole aovernment needs one massive douche."—

Zappa, Ray Gun # 30, October '95

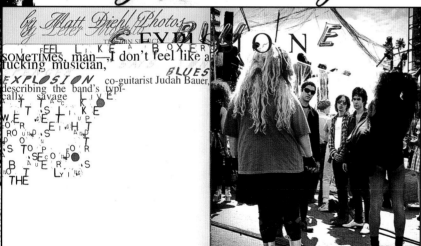

by Matt Diehl Photos

I FEEL LIKE A BOXER

SOMETIMES, man—I don't feel like a
fucking musician,

BLUES EXPLOSION co-guitarist Judah Bauer,
describing the band's typi-
cally savage LIVE

Laurie Anderson, huH #3,
November 1994

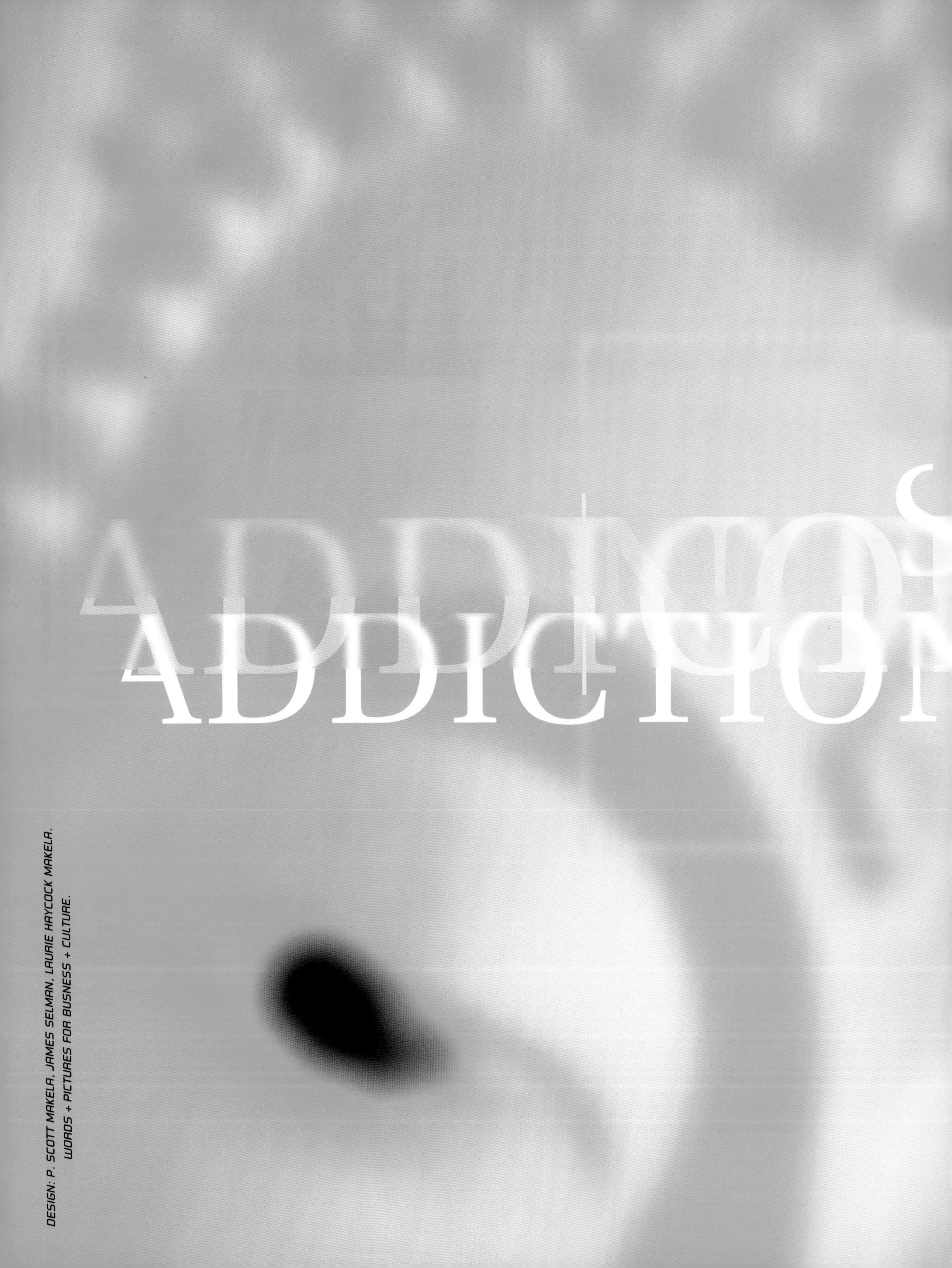

ADDICTION

ADDICTION

DESIGN: P. SCOTT MAKELA, JAMES SELMAN, LAURIE HAYCOCK MAKELA.
WORDS + PICTURES FOR BUSNESS + CULTURE.

70
Out of Control.
Original Illustration.
P Scott Makela. 1996.

71
Out of Control.
Original Illustration.
Polly Becker. 1996.

72
Out of Control.
Gene Ween. 1996.

Gene Ween

Out of Control (...
Page Nos
2/10/211

1. Do you believe in heroes? How do they affect youth culture?

I, I could be king, and you, you would be Queen..

2. What were your childhood aspirations? What is the most important thing you want to create or achieve now?

I wanted to be a mother fuckin hustler, you better ass somebody...

3. What is style and how important is it? How does "image" come into play in your creative process?

Style is everything. Dean and I have an extensive wardrobe furnished by _____ of Tokyo _____ wong lee

4. Where do you get your information? TV, newspapers, a particular journal, internet groups, or word of mouth?

T.V. always TV

Do you feel like you are more or less informed about your world than your parents were about theirs? -

im more informed, They're cable selection wasn't nearly as extensive

5. What is the ultimate in recreation? Do you prefer indoor sports or outdoor? Tell us about your ultimate vacation, real or imagined.

Reef Diving off the coast of Brisbane at the end of every May

6. Are you engaged in political or social causes today? Is activism a priority?

actively involved in the Pro-smokers forum.

7. Do cars matter? Are cars style? What does "the road" mean to you?

Cars matter, cars are style, im gonna hit the fucking road, mang.

8. What one piece of art (album, movie, book, artifact, etc.) has most influenced your work or thinking? Is there one artist with whom you identify most closely? Why?

America's greatest hits, once you go America, you never go back

9. Is cynicism good?

Sure

10. Are you a believer in academia? Would you take classes, or go back to school full time, at this stage in your career?

I am planning on taking some for Technical classes in Plumbing. Those guys can make a shitload of money

11. How do drugs affect your life now? Are they useful to you? Are they dangerous?

only users lose drugs

12. Is your sexuality an important issue to your work in public? Do you feel pressure to identify yourself in this way? Are people tolerant of your true self?

There is always a strong sexual element in ween. Every night is Saturday night

13. Is it important that art, in its widest sense, have a message, or that artists "say something"?

no, music should serve to soften the blow, any blow.

14. What is the future of music? Who or what is the best indicator about where music is going?

Jungle Grunge

15. If there's a burning question we skipped, please ask it and answer it.

7

2

Post-it® Fax Note   7671   Date / # of pages
To RANDY BODKASTA   STEPHANIE HARTT
Co./Dept. PAYGUN   Co. N/L/M
Phone#   Phone #
Fax #   Fax #

Thanky

73

Issue 15. Ray Gun. April 1994.
Cover.
Art Direction & Design by David Carson.
Photography by Davies & Starr.

74

Out of Control.
Original Illustration.
Fly. 1996.

73

the END of PRINT" bible of music + style

R AYGUN,

15

soundgarden e n
o TOOL o l
e BEYOND e d
BRAND NEW HEAVIES
table of contents
m a MASTHEAD a d
LETTERS r s
sound in print

april'94
$3.50 usa
$3.50

"Where do the prayers go? Are they held by gravity on the rim of space? You know, where all these space shuttles crash into the old prayers floating around like abandoned satellites?"
— Robyn Hitchcock, huH #11, July 1995

"I've always believed in God and the possibility of life after death, but as something that must be fought for, like everything else. I can relate much more to a dedicated Cassock than to an atheist. Atheists bore me."

William S. Burroughs, Ray Gun #32, December/January 1996

"I'm sorry to say, everybody, I still read the Bible every morning." – Nick Cave, Ray Gun #34, March 1996

75
Issue 40. Ray Gun. October 1996.
Tricky Dps.
Art Direction & Design by Robert Hales.
Photography by Spike Jonze.

"It's a gimmick of a
gimmick. It's a
parody of a parody.
And anybody who
thinks I'm blind
to that, that I'm not
intelligent enough
to see that, they're
missing the point
more than they
think I'm missing
the point. That's the
funny part of it,
when people say,
'Marilyn Manson is
a gimmick.' It's
a mockery of gim-
mickry in itself.
Besides, if I wanted
a gimmick that
would make me suc-
cessful, I'd be like
Hootie & The
Blowfish or Pearl
Jam, because they're
very easy to swal-
low." Marilyn
Manson, huH #26,
October 1996

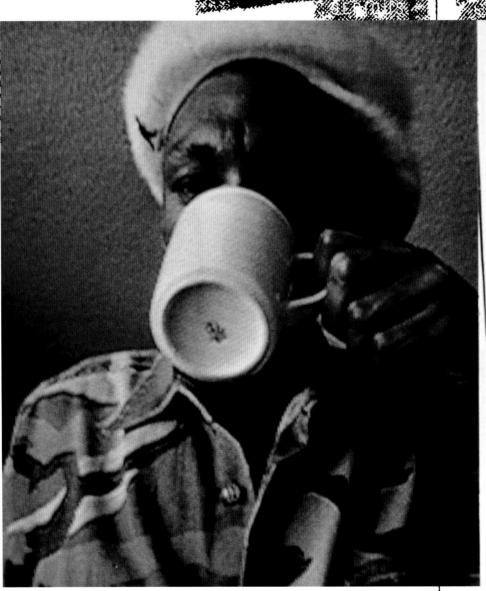

GONE INTO
SET YOUR

I WANT T
EVERYTH
GOING T
JUNGLE,
BECAUS
YOU BE
JUNGLE,
MAKE JU
IF YOU
MAKE JU
YOU WO
IT ANY

75

76
Issue 40. Ray Gun. October 1996.
Cover.
Art Direction & Design by Robert Hales.
Photography by Spike Jonze.

SLAYER NEVER CAME ALONG, I WOULD HAVE

7   7
Issue   26.   huH.   October   1996.
C   o   v   e   r
Art Out of Control Direction   by   Jerôme   Curchod.
Design Page Nos   by   Scott   Denton-Cardew.
Photography by James & Matthew.

214/215

MEDICINE. PROBABLY PSYCHIATRY.

TOM ARAYA OF SLAYER, HUH #2, OCT 1994

BE THE BEST AT

G. IF YOU'RE

BE THE KING OF

AT'S ONLY

'M GOING TO LET

E KING OF

ECAUSE I DON'T

GLE MUSIC. BUT

S ME OFF, I'LL

GLE MUSIC AND

T BE THE KING OF

RE.

4TH ANNIVERSARY ISSUE

RAYGUN

MUSIC + STYLE 40

TRICKY

ELECTRONIC
STEVE EARLE
DRUM & BASS
METALLICA
& ANTON CORBIJN

ISSUE 40
OCTOBER 1996
$3.50 USA
$4.50 CAN

PRINTED IN USA

76

77

huH
marilyn manson

78
Out of Control.
Gibby Haynes. 1996.

79
Out of Control.
Original Illustration.
Mike Mills. 1996.

1. Do you believe in heroes? How do they affect youth culture?

I believe in bondage gear

2. What were your childhood aspirations? What is the most important thing you want to create or achieve now?

TO RULE the world and fly. WEIGHTLESSNESS

3. What is style and how important is it? How does "image" come into play in your creative process?

Style is a balding tennis player.

4. Where do you get your information? TV. newspapers. a particular journal. internet groups. or word of mouth?

Do you feel like you are more or less informed about your world than your parents were about theirs?

*THERE IS MORE PRINTED MATERIAL CONCER
THE FEMALE ORGASM NOW!*

5. What is the ultimate in recreation? Do you prefer indoor sports or outdoor? Tell us about your ultimate vacation. real or imagined.

*THE RIDE at the STATE
FAIR WHERE YOU BECOME a CRICKET.*

6. Are you engaged in political or social causes today? Is activism a priority?

NO NO

7. Do cars matter? Are cars style? What does "the road" mean to you?

CARS aren't everything they are the only thing

8. What one piece of art (album. movie. book. artifact. etc.) has most influenced your work or thinking? Is there one artist with whom you identify most closely? Why?

COCO PUFFS

9. Is cynicism good?

Its a better DISEASE to HAVE than MOST

10. Are you a believer in academia? Would you take classes. or go back to school full time. at this stage in your career?

COLLEGE is girls

11. How do drugs affect your life now? Are they useful to you? Are they dangerous?

DRUGS WILL GET YOU

12. Is your sexuality an important issue to your work in public? Do you feel pressure to identify yourself in this way? Are people tolerant of your true self?

*SEX IS MY toLL booth.
I WILL BE IN JAIL.*

13. Is it important that art. in its widest sense. have a message. or that artists "say something"?

THE best painting has already been mad

14. What is the future of music? Who or what is the best indicator about where music is going?

SOUND. The SMELL OF RUBBER.

15. If there's a burning question we skipped. please ask it and answer it.

*IF My dog CAN EAT FLIES
SO SHOULD I.*

Tha

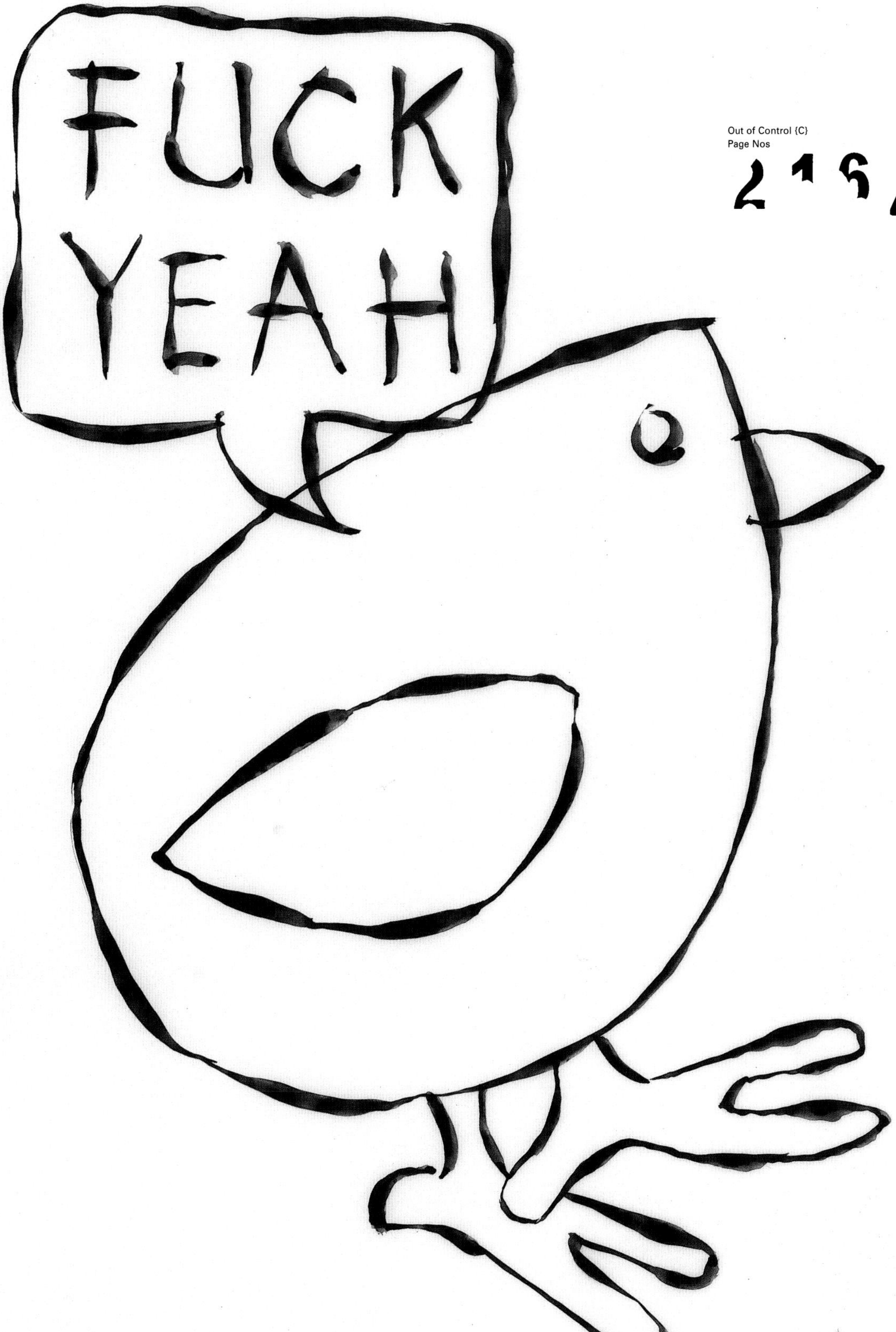
FUCK YEAH
MM

80
Issue 41. Ray Gun. November 1996.
Cover.
Art Direction & Design by Robert Hales.
Photography by Melodie McDaniel.

"It was really close to Halloween. Me and Greg Lisher were walking

81
Issue 41. Ray Gun. November 1996.
John Cale Dps 1.
Art Direction & Design by Robert Hales.
Photography by Guy Aroch.

out of this bar in San Francisco. It was

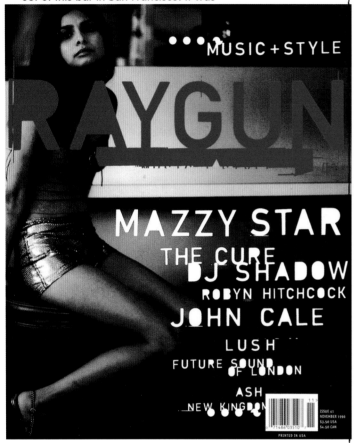

really late. Right then this cop car comes racing down the street and just screeches to a halt in front of us. There are two

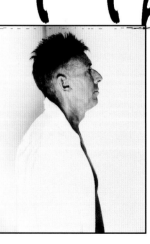

82
Issue 41. Ray Gun. November 1996.
John Cale Dps 2.
Art Direction & Design by Robert Hales.
Photography by Guy Aroch.

83
Issue 41. Ray Gun. November 1996.
Contents page.
Art Direction & Design by Robert Hales.

Out of Control (C)
Page Nos

218/219

41

CONTENTS

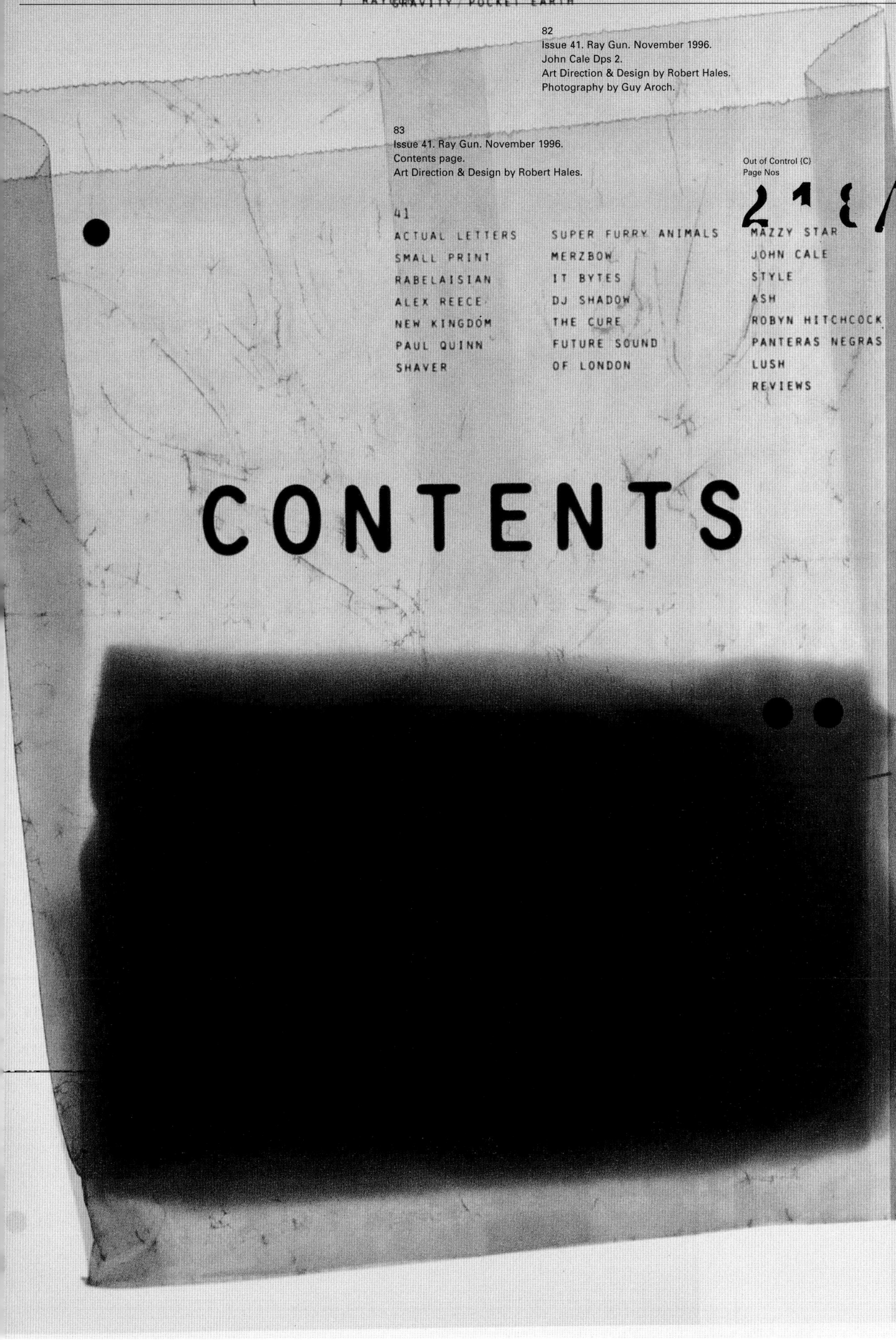

cops in the car, and the cop on the passenger side rolled down the window, and he was wearing this pig snout mask, and the cop driving was wearing bug-eye glasses where the eyeballs are hanging out. And then they just totally drove off. I mean, God, that's like one of the highlights of my life. Is that good? Is that bad? I don't know."

David Lowery of Cracker, Ray Gun #36, May 1996

{?

Issue 25. huH. September 1996.
Cover.
Creative Direction by Vaughan Oliver.
Art Direction by Jerôme Curchod.
Design by Scott Denton-Cardew.
Photography by Doug Aitken.
Cover logo photo by Timothy O'Donnell.

84

25

4

$2.95 usa $3.50 can

09 >

0 71486 03512 1

this is a magazine about music. you know, like, bands and stuff.

huH

sponge
wax ecstatic
in detroit rock city
with KISS september 96
by mark blackwell & jim greer

85

Issue 24. huH. August 1996.
Cover.
Creative Direction by Vaughan Oliver.
Art Direction by Jerôme Curchod.
Design by Scott Denton-Cardew.
Photography by Danny Clinch.

86
Issue 41. Ray Gun. November 1996.
The Cure Dps.
Out of Control (C)
Art Direction & Design by Robert Hales.
Photography by Doug Aitken.
Pages 223

The **present** of music is the past re-examining bits and pieces of what's been discarded in the haste of the late 20th century, and sticking them together

in a slightly different way. If there is a future, I wonder how much louder and is a future, I wonder how much louder and more brutal it can become. It might be hordes of telepathic Christians holding hands and vibrating in silence in front of crucifix PAs. Or it might be ripped off from whatever black musicians come up with next.

— Robyn Hitchcock, Out of Control, 1996

87
Issue 41. Ray Gun. November 1996.
DJ Shadow Dps.
Art Direction & Design by Robert Hales.
Photography by Torres & Barr.

"When we played our music in '66 or '67, we were talking about things that were happening in our lives that were real, and our crowd was focused on what we were singing about and how it related to their lives and how they interpreted it. And there was a closeness between us, because the music industry hadn't gotten so big — it wasn't the 'music industry.' It wasn't Dow Chemical; it was like a drug store. But these bands — Pearl Jam, Nirvana, Nine Inch Nails, Smashing Pumpkins — they're similar to what I remember feeling between the Doors and their audience and Buffalo Springfield and their audience and Love and their audience and the Byrds, in their original state, and their audience. These kind of relating points between these bands and their audiences are very similar to bands today and their audiences. There's a direct connection between the two. And it hasn't really happened much since." –

Issue   27.   huH.

November   1996.

Cover   x   2.

Art   direction   by

Jerôme   Curchod.

Design   by   Scott

Denton-Cardew.

Photography   by

Alice Wheeler.

the
shadow
knows...

Neil Young, Ray Gun #28, August 1995

"THAT'S WHAT
BOOKS ARE,
REALLY. TALKING
TO GHOSTS. IT

THE WAY THAT
THE DEAD TALK
TO THE LIVING."

Document2 31/10/96 6:37 pm Page 1 (1,2)

TO THE LIVING

LAURIE
ANDERSON, H
#3

THE

!!

S

!!

224/225

RAYGUN

JAMES + D'ARCY
OF SMASHING
PUMPKINS AND
THE NEW WAVE OF
ARTIST-RUN
LABELS

91
Issue 42, Ray Gun, December/January 1997.
Cover.
Art Direction & Design by Robert Hales.
Photography by John Scarisbrick.

90
Issue 32, RayGun December/January 1996.
Last Page.
Art Direction & Design by Johnson & Wolverton.

LAS

2

UH PAGI

POYNOR

POYNOR

it's a trap

I'm leafing through a magazine and the ad that stops me is arresting even by the hyperkinetic standards of contemporary ads. At first glance it's just a jigsaw of black and white fragments. There's a photograph of a deserted street or city square cut at angles, with a shadowy figure breaking out of one side into the white of the page – he finds two or three echoes in patches of blackness around the edge. There are scrawled numbers (they could be measurements), a hand-drawn arrow, an illegible rubber stamp, and the main type is fuzzy, suggesting with the other details that this could be a fax. Running up the side there's a third layer, a word-processed message with phrases crossed out.

The main copy, I now see, is posing a dilemma: the man hiding at the back of the photo is looking out for an enemy sniper. I'm standing where the shadowy figure is standing and the man is counting on me to send soldiers to help him. And so is the sniper: it's a trap. It is also, I now realise from the logo tucked away in the corner, an officer recruitment campaign – 1990s style – for the British army.

It's possible, though unlikely, that the creative team which put this ad together has never seen a copy of *Ray Gun*, but even if they haven't there is no better word for the ad than *Ray Gun*-esque. It uses design devices that aren't unique to the magazine, but which *Ray Gun*, more perhaps than any other source, has turned into a fashionable graphic signature of the 1990s. The ad's typography isn't particularly weird or unusually distressed (nor, these days, is much of *Ray Gun*'s) but the engagingly raw, excitingly immediate, loose-fitting assembly of its components would not look out of place in the pages of *Ray Gun* itself.

So here in a snapshot, as bluntly as I can spotlight it, is the central conundrum about this in many ways remarkable magazine. In the space of just four years since its launch in November 1992, a

design language heralded inside and outside the design world for being "radical," "subversive," "revolutionary," "innovative" and in every sense ground-breaking has been so thoroughly assimilated by the mass media that it can now seem an appropriate mode of address for an organisation as *un*subversive, *un*revolutionary and completely establishment in outlook as the army.

How did we get here?

For a magazine which has generated such apocalyptic claims about the future of communication in our time – even running the tagline "end of print" on its cover for a while – *Ray Gun* has been subject to little analysis, as either media presence or design construct. Design journalism and the mainstream newspaper, magazine and television coverage that fuelled art director David Carson's ascent have tended to treat *Ray Gun* as though it exploded fully-formed from nowhere, equipped with a set of design precepts that no other designer, in his or her wildest dreams, had ever imagined. If *Ray Gun*'s design was granted a prehistory at all in such celebratory accounts, it extended only as far back as the six issues of *Beach Culture*, Carson's previous vehicle as art director. Carson's own book, *The End of Print*, attempts to reinforce this view of the designer as a creative genius who has, according to its cover blurb, "single-handedly changed the course of graphic design". While the magazine's look was always the work of many hands – type designers, graphic designers, photographers and illustrators were given a great deal of freedom – the book makes no attempt to explore or explain these collaborations. When it comes to the prehistory, it is largely silent.

The disavowal of history is appropriate to a product as post-modern as *Ray Gun* – and I want to return to this – but it does nothing to explain how David Carson was able, in the commercial arena, to build on earlier developments. This is arguably less a matter of specific influences (though these could be traced) than of the creative possibilities these precursors opened up. This isn't the place for a detailed examination of the graphic design of the 1980s, which has been extensively catalogued elsewhere, but a handful of examples will make the point. The intense subjectivity and private symbolism of fellow Californian April Greiman's work anticipates Carson's emotionally-charged atmospherics by a decade and she, too, was criticized by some for producing "art" in the guise of design. At *The Face*, Neville Brody deconstructed the

conventions of magazine sign-posting and page-layout several years before Carson began his own dismantlings at *Beach Culture*. In the designers it featured and through its own endlessly mutating format, Rudy VanderLans' *Emigre* magazine (also based in California) mounted a vigorous – and continuing – exploration of experimental approaches to type design, typography and page structure. Just as seminal was the decisive engagement with literary theory pursued, throughout the 1980s, by graduates of Cranbrook Academy of Art. *Ray Gun* is a commercial heir of their commitment to deconstruction, the vernacular

DESIGN?

ALTERNATIVE DESIGN?

what *is* radical about the design is not so
much its intrinsic content as the transposition
of a televisual atmosphere to the static medium of print, as print struggles frantically to catch up
and compete with the computer and the TV screen

and "anti-mastery" – the deliberate flouting of professional notions of correct design – and a number of Cranbrook designers went on to contribute to it.

As a cultural phenomenon, though, *Ray Gun* has an even more significant immediate precursor in the shape of MTV. Seen from this vantage point, *Ray Gun*'s radicalism may not appear quite so radical. Or rather, what *is* radical about the design is not so much its intrinsic content as the transposition of a televisual atmosphere to the static medium of print, as print struggles frantically to catch up with and compete with the computer and the TV screen. The justifications offered by Carson and others for *Ray Gun*'s design were, as a result, repeatedly framed in terms of the screen's – and specifically MTV's – viewer satisfactions and agenda. *Ray Gun* readers, ran the mantra, belonged to the "MTV generation," they'd grown up with it as kids and teenagers, their brains had been in some way "rewired" by the experience, they were able to process much larger quantities of simultaneous "information" than earlier generations could handle and they wouldn't accept, let alone deign to read, anything that didn't offer something approaching televisual levels of intensity and excitement.

There are close parallels between the ways that *Ray Gun* and MTV engage their audiences. In a much-cited observation, David Byrne suggests that Carson's work on *Ray Gun* and other projects communicates "on a level beyond words . . . that bypasses the logical, rational centers of the brain and goes straight to the part that understands without thinking."[2] Twelve years earlier, MTV executive Bob Pittman, speaking to *Rolling Stone*, had used strikingly similar language to explain the station's way of grabbing its viewers. "Our core audience is the television babies who grew up on TV and rock & roll. The strongest appeal you can make is emotionally. If you can get their emotions going, [make them] forget their logic, you've got 'em."[3]

MTV's aim, from its earliest promotions, was to give everything a larger-than-life quality, or what

its programming manager called a "weird edge." But the channel's debut, in 1981, proved to be a false start. MTV's on-air image didn't look right – it was too stiff, too formal, too close in style and tone to conventional television. After a rethink, bright, "phony" lights were abandoned for "shitty" lighting, tele-prompters were banished, and veejays were told to adlib around the scripts. If they made mistakes that was fine because mistakes would look real. "It took a little while," *Rolling Stone*'s Steven Levy noted, "but MTV finally got what it wanted – a well-designed studio that looked like something casually thrown together, scripted patter that sounded like it was made up on the spot, an ironclad format that proceeded like a random chain of events . . . ."[4]

Ray Gun got it right from the start. It was a highly designed object – "Alternative by design," as a first-issue mission statement put it – while appearing completely informal and almost dangerously spontaneous, as though a suitcase of Dadaist poems, scribbles and family photographs had been upended across the pages and stuck down where they fell. You didn't need a degree in design (though many *Ray Gun* readers did have, or were getting, degrees in design) to enjoy the brutal relish with which its typography broke every so-called rule in the book. Typos. Negative leading. Hand-scrawled headlines. Weird new mangled fonts. Colliding columns of text. Letters drifting so far apart that you had to piece them together yourself to make words, while others clumped in tight strings or massed in threatening black clouds that obliterated verbal meaning and linear sense. And holding this graphomaniac chaos together: a synthesising collage sensibility that fairly screamed the word "ART." In 1992, *Ray Gun* looked like nothing else on the newsstands, including rivals such as *Spin* and *Rolling Stone*. For its readers, it offered compelling signs of authenticity, appearing to promise a publication that was non-corporate, irreverent, self-expressive and free.

Ray Gun's problem as a publication for its first three years was that a design so blinding made it hard to see where its editorial vision lay, or even

whether it had one, beyond letting the designer do his own thing. In that sense, editorial director Neil Feineman's clarion call, "Raw by choice. Immediate by necessity. Alternative by design," was more prescient than he could have known at the time. If *Ray Gun* had something genuinely new, something *alternative* to say about the "alternative" musicians it featured alongside more mainstream stars, it came to seem that this lay less in the editorial conception or writing than in the functioning of the design itself. On a production level, working from his own studio rather than the publisher's offices, David Carson had an exceptional degree of control. It was the designer's decision, for instance, not the editors' or publishers', to put the words "end of print" on the cover. Often Marvin Scott Jarrett wouldn't even see proofs before the pre-press stage. Most of the media attention *Ray Gun* received in its first two years came from the design press and this focused, inevitably enough, on the designer's "interpretations" of the content. Their appropriateness was taken for granted, rather than demonstrated by analysis, because these observers weren't, in truth, particularly interested in *Ray Gun*'s editorial content, or how it might relate to the history of thinking, writing and publishing on popular music. For these design-world onlookers, the design *was* the content. Whether they were academic theorists of graphic design as a form of authorship, or just straight-forward sensation-seeking design fans, *Ray Gun* was a timely, highly public demonstration – a vindication even – of what experimental graphic design could accomplish, given the chance.

Yet there are small signs, in *Ray Gun*'s first editorial, of another agenda struggling to break free: "We still believe that music and the people who make it can change the world. Have to, in fact. Because if we don't, no one else will." This is a revival of a form of rhetoric that hasn't been voiced with total conviction since the 1960s and was last heard, with any stridency, during the heyday of punk. For many music critics and fans, this view of rock as a radical binding force and agent of social and political transformation had been blown apart by the tribal fracturing of the audience in the post-modern 1980s and, not least, by the coming of MTV. It was not an ideology that *Ray Gun* was able to sustain with any conviction (Feineman left after four issues) and it was ironically rejected, towards the end of his own time there, by the magazine's designer: "graphic design will save the world right after rock & roll does."[5]

Here again, there is a parallel with the evolution and critical perception of MTV. "Unlike the activist sixties rock coalition," noted a sceptical *Rolling Stone*, "the MTV coalition is essentially passive. Their function is to sit still, watch the commercials and buy the products, not change the world."[6] Critical accounts of the channel's programming in the 1980s tended to assess it in the gloomiest terms. According to these commentators, MTV's post-modernism, its mesmerising play of surfaces, its denial of everything except the perpetual present, its "'schizophrenic' abandonment of rational, liberal-humanist discourse which creates a nihilistic, amoral universe of representation," would so enrapture viewers that the real world of real problems would cease to register with its audience at all. More recently, though, cultural critic Andrew Goodwin has challenged this reading of MTV's supposedly ahistorical, apolitical, asocial aesthetic by suggesting that there are in reality two MTVs. Pointing to the channel's response to cause-rock events such as Live Aid and Amnesty International's Conspiracy of Hope tour, he discovers the persistence within its output of a "classic Romantic rock ideology" that combines "traditional notions of rebellion . . . with a new sense of social responsibility and philanthropic concern."[7]

Ray Gun's seductive play of surfaces is nothing if not thoroughly post-modern, but the sense that there might be two *Ray Guns* and that the magazine is searching for some deeper

commitment has strengthened of late. An editorial in issue 33, written by managing editor Dean Kuipers, doesn't go quite as far as Goodwin (Kuipers points out, in fact, how rock has "moved away from mass social movements"), but there are clear signs that the editors are trying to rethink *Ray Gun*'s editorial policy and subtly reposition the title. Even before David Carson's departure after 30 issues, *Ray Gun* had begun to embrace in its design a quieter, more reflective mood which Marvin Scott Jarrett liked to describe as a "new simplicity." Layouts were cleaner, dysfunctional typefaces thinner on the ground. This streamlining (with outbursts of the old head-banging) has continued over the last ten issues following the appointment – with issue 33 – of British art director Robert Hales. "We have a new commitment [sic] to content and readability in the design," notes Kuipers. The effect of cooling the design temperature has been to increase the magazine's appearance of authority and consequently to put new emphasis on the writing itself: now it has no choice but to deliver.

Kuipers identifies the prevailing *Ray Gun* message as "constructive anarchy," with a passing nod to the Russian anarchist Peter Kropotkin's idea of "mutual aid." "[R]ock 'n' roll continues to offer the possibility of personal transformation," he suggests, "precisely because it is *not* organized and not led. In fact, you might get more out of rock now, more that pertains to you personally, than ever before." And *Ray Gun*'s place in this? "[W]e want to help you with your revolution," he concludes. How will they do it? By hearing a good song and "passing it along."

Whether the magazine can somehow resolve the tension between what its form seems to express and what it would perhaps like to believe in remains to be seen. In magazine publishing terms, *Ray Gun* is the quintessential Avant-Pop product. Avant-Pop, writes American literary critic Larry McCaffery, "combines Pop Art's focus on consumer goods and mass media with the avant-garde's spirit of subversion and emphasis on radical formal innovation."[8] It is the product, he explains, of the "coevolution" of the artistic avant-garde and mass culture – rock music, TV, films, and advertising – so that by the early 1980s, with the arrival of MTV, they were mutually supportive, exchanging "information, stylistic tendencies, narrative archetypes, and character represen-tations." Many of the formal strategies of Avant-Pop, as defined by McCaffery, were present in *Ray Gun* from the start: sampling; collage principles; digressive, improvisatory structures; surface textures; the seductive, information-saturated feel

of advertising; the pace, surrealism and visceral impact of punk and MTV; a painterly emphasis on the emotional and aesthetic intensity of the creative act. McCaffery is surely right when he suggests that the marriage of the avant-garde and mass media is entirely logical because hyperconsumer capitalism's unquenchable demand for "the new" is exactly the same need that has always driven the avant-garde.

Is *Ray Gun*'s readership ready for a return to meanings you might have to think about (if that's what Dean Kuipers is hinting at), or did it prefer the immersive, seductive, kinetic sensationalism of Avant-Pop graphics? *Ray Gun* may have succeeded briefly in being "alternative by design," but the design was never used by the magazine as an instrument of opposition or critique and at the close of the twentieth century, with the death of the artistic avant-garde, in the context of mass-market hyperconsumption, in a newsstand title packed with lifestyle advertising aimed at a wealthy audience, it perhaps never could have been. By the time these radical visual ideas reached *Ray Gun*, they had come a very long way, and the speed with which they jumped the page gutter to become advertising shows just how close they were by then to the end of their journey. In an age of hyperconsumption, *Ray Gun*'s design dilemma is the same one that faces any artist trying to locate a position of resistance in a culture that can accommodate and commodify just about anything you throw at it.

I can see the sniper. Now how do we avoid the trap?

another agenda

Pop product

struggling to break free

01 For a crash course in recent graphic design developments see: April Greiman, *Hybrid Imagery: the fusion of technology and graphic design*, London: Architecture Design and Technology Press, 1990; Jon Wozencroft, *The Graphic Language of Neville Brody*, London: Thames and Hudson, 1988; Rudy VanderLans and Zuzana Licko, *Emigre: graphic design into the digital realm*, New York: Van Nostrand Reinhold, 1993; Hugh Aldersey-Williams et al., *Cranbrook Design: the new discourse*, New York: Rizzoli, 1990.

02 Lewis Blackwell, *The End of Print: the graphic design of David Carson*, London: Laurence King, 1995, unpaginated.

03 Quoted in Steven Levy, "Ad nauseam: how MTV sells out rock & roll," *Rolling Stone*, 8 December 1983, p.33.

04 Levy, *Rolling Stone*, p.34.

05 Quoted in Blackwell, *The End of Print*, unpaginated.

06 Levy, *Rolling Stone*, p.78.

07 Andrew Goodwin, "Fatal distractions: MTV meets postmodern theory," in *Sound & Vision: the music video reader*, eds. Simon Frith, Andrew Goodwin and Lawrence Grossberg, London and New York: Routledge, 1993, p.46 and p.63.

08 Ed. Larry McCaffery, *After Yesterday's Crash: the Avant-Pop anthology*, New York: Penguin, 1995, pp.xvii-xix.

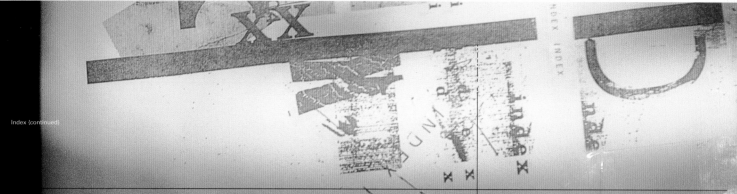

Index (continued)

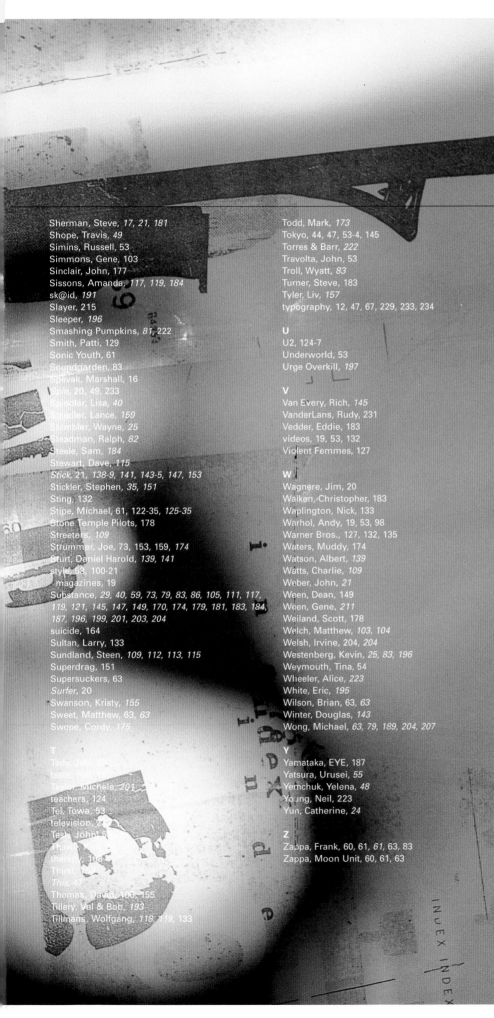

"I do have trouble finding the underground. I wanted to ask you about it, if perhaps you knew where it was. At this point, to the extent that there is an underground, it's lurking around on the Internet trying to find a form. But it's like a ghost trying to find a body." Laurie Anderson, huH #3, November '94

"It's all the wonderful world of entertainment, and to deny yourself access to any of it is rather stupid." John Lydon, Ray Gun #18, August '94

"Oh, brother, draw the line in the sand here and now! Seize the code and oust the boot-licking servants of the two dimensions! Multimedia will never go anywhere until the amateurs take over, until the primitives rule and the designers are driven back into their holes." David Thomas of Pere Ubu, Ray Gun #36, May '96

""To me, alternative rock was originally this egalitarian thing — Husker Du, R.E.M., the Replacements, the Minutemen, the Meat Puppets — There was no dogma among all those bands. What all those bands had in common, including Camper Van Beethoven, was that we were trying to invent a new kind of pop music. We weren't trying to play underground music, but to make a kind of pop music for us. We just figured, 'Well, fuck, I like this kind of music; there's got to be some other people out there who like this music, too.' The child of the original alternative bands was sort of indie rock. And that, in a lot of ways, was the opposite. That was about like, being obscure, only the cool people knew about your band, and not wanting to be popular. It's as if you had a disdain for everybody, a disdain for humanity. And as cynical as I am, I don't have that.' David Lowery of Cracker, Ray Gun #36, May '96

"I'm not technophobic. I was born in 1955, brought up in the white heat of technology, and led to believe that by now we'd all be in our hover-cars and wearing silver suits." Pete Shelley of the Buzzcocks, Ray Gun #36, May '96

"PAUL: I wish someone would pay me to not do my own music. It would be like the farming subsidies, the government paying farmers to not grow. If someone could do that to me, I'll fucking stop right now.
KING: I think parents would pay a lot more money for us to not make music than kids actually buy our music. Let's look into that. Get parents to all chip-in and make us not make music." The Butthole Surfers, Ray Gun #37, June/July '96

"What a DJ is doing is just act ally facing the obvious fact of the merger of human consciousness with electronic representation. This is only the beginning of what I call recombinant identity. You're always pulling bits and pieces from the media data cloud around you." DJ SPOOKY, that subliminal kid, Ray Gun #37, June/July '96

"We're all like the '90s mixed-up kid whose basically rootless and just living in the global village. But that doesn't mean we've left our culture; there's a mixture of culture. We are probably comfortable living anywhere. I do miss the quiet Japan of my childhood, which is gone now. (pause) Pre-war Japan. Strangely enough, the kind of feeling I had growing up in Tokyo exists more in Soho." Yoko Ono with Cibo Matto, Ray Gun #38, August '96

"I want to be the best at everything. If you're going to be the king of jungle, that's only because I'm going to let you be the king of jungle, because I don't make jungle music. But if you piss me off, I'll make jungle music and you won't be the king of it any more." — Tricky, Ray Gun #40, October '96

"I'm not scared of the word God. I believed in God when I got to jail. I just didn't like Him, and I didn't think that He had anything to do with junkies." Steve Earle, Ray Gun #40, October '96

"Don't be afraid of grief, or heartthrob; don't be intimidated by rock stars or presidents; be a slave to love and always remember twenty rejections in a row are wiped out by one acceptance." — Allen Ginsberg, Bikini #7, Dec/Jan '94

"To be a good actor or artist there has to be something inside you that is very clear and you have to be able to convey that...you can only be ambiguous if you know absolutely what you're saying and doing. — Christopher Walken, Bikini #10, June/July '95

"I have no responsibility to any thing other than my characters and being as true to them as I possibly can. I make movies for and everyone is just invited." — Quentin Tarantino, Bikini #13, Dec/Jan '95

"Acting is always about you. You're using you and it's exhausting...I come home, put my feet up, have twenty beers and watch Texas massacre...or you go into analysis." — Gary Oldman, Bikini #4, June/July '94

"So Elvis is an icon. And he was the first of the World Stars. But these things are the surface. The answer is below the surface where Elvis takes the moribund folk forms of hillbilly country-western and rural blues and brings to them the power and universality of Abstraction, in the process establishing a language for the hopes and dreams and fears of a culture, and sweeping away the flabby, alien art forms of the Novel, the Image and the Narrative forever. A powerful thing. He was the Voice. And in days such as these wherein all the words of the media and the artists and the wise men are nothing but lies and propaganda, why is it so surprising that folk culture coalesces around what seems to be the only incorruptible medium left to it? That which has no need for words! And why shouldn't they look instinctively to the Homer of the form? Elvis." David Thomas of Pere Ubu on Elvis, huH #8, April '95

"John Lee Hooker: I write songs that have meaning to them. (smiling big) Mostly about women.
Henry Rollins: Don't we all.
Hooker: (breaks out laughing.) You can't leave them out!
Rollins: Sometimes you wish you could though!
Hooker: Yeah! You can for a few hours and then they come right back. Boom!" — John Lee Hooker interviewed by Henry Rollins, huH Blues Special '95

"You get the urge to take a picture, and you do it. And the faster I travel, the more I travel, the more it seems like it's like that. It's literally a snapshot kind of mentality. You've got to capture something quickly because it's gone, it's fleeting...." — Michael Stipe, huH #14, Oct '95

"If you see E.T., you there's a poster of me on the bedroom wall." — Elvis Costello, Ray Gun #15, April '94

"I don't take any of my cues from the media. I'm not interested in any way, shape, or form what they think. I don't think that's got anything to do with the audience. I think the main problem is that if radio stations don't play your records, then people can't hear them. Loads of times, people would love what I'm doing, but will never get the chance to hear it because it doesn't fit into a format or because it's too controversial or whatever it may be. I think we're headed towards segregation, more polarization, everything being categorized to an incredible degree: format hell. I think it's just gonna get worse, but then there will be a major reaction against it. And you'll hear people playing the Partridge Family in protest, there will be a Donny Osmond revival...." — Boy George, huH #17, Jan '96

"Every relationship I've seen with everyone I've known in the last 15 years has kind of fallen apart with the exception of one. It's pretty disturbing. It's distressing seeing people around you that you think are really in love and you see everyone fall apart over a period of time. And then I'm wondering why it's never turned up in my life...and yet I have really seriously gone out of my way to produce insurmountable problems for everyone around me...." Robert Smith of the Cure, huH #21, May '96

"I don't act when I'm on stage. I don't get into character. Actors don't act. Robert DeNiro doesn't act. He gives a performance. Bad actors act. If you can do it, it's just a matter of giving it up. Literally, everything is totally exposed. It's like going out stark naked in Wall Street at lunch hour. 'Here I am!' It's a performance. It's all or nothing." Meat Loaf, huH #19, March '96

"Billie Joe: We live in Berkeley, so it's, like, the home of the politically correct people that can afford to be politically correct.
Jello Biafra: You're actually lucky. I grew up in a college town with a football school where there wasn't even a P.C. facade. People just showed up with their Porsches and parked them in the dorm lot with the New Jersey and California license plates and spilled their beer can up the wall to show how cool they were, went skiing all the time, and then daddy had a place in the company for 'em when they left. Or they could marry somebody who had a place in the company. And that was their idea of an education. Anyway, when you were growing up, what did you want to do?
Billie: Leave. (laughs) That was my only thing. When I was, like, a sixth grader I always wanted to just leave. I didn't really know why back then.
Biafra: Walk away, drive away, hop a train....?
Billie: On a motorcycle. The whole, like, James Dean Rebel Without A Cause kinda thing.
Tre Cool: Fonzie!" — Green Day interviewed by Jello Biafra, huH #17, Jan '96

"Jim Jarmusch: What about the shotgun? Has that ever